Folk horror on film

Manchester University Press

Folk horror on film

Return of the British repressed

Edited by

Louis Bayman and K. J. Donnelly

MANCHESTER UNIVERSITY PRESS

Copyright © Manchester University Press 2023

While copyright in the volume as a whole is vested in Manchester University Press, copyright in individual chapters belongs to their respective authors, and no chapter may be reproduced wholly or in part without the express permission in writing of both author and publisher.

Published by Manchester University Press
Oxford Road, Manchester M13 9PL

www.manchesteruniversitypress.co.uk

British Library Cataloguing-in-Publication Data
A catalogue record for this book is available from the British Library

ISBN 978 1 5261 6492 6 hardback
ISBN 978 1 5261 9120 5 paperback

First published 2023
Paperback published 2025

The publisher has no responsibility for the persistence or accuracy of URLs for any external or third-party internet websites referred to in this book, and does not guarantee that any content on such websites is, or will remain, accurate or appropriate.

EU authorised representative for GPSR:
Easy Access System Europe – Mustamäe tee 50,
10621 Tallinn, Estonia
gpsr.requests@easproject.com

Typeset by Newgen Publishing UK

Contents

List of figures	vii
Notes on contributors	viii
Foreword by John Das	xii

Introduction: what makes the folk horrific? – Louis Bayman and K. J. Donnelly 1

Part I: Debating *The Wicker Man*

1 The context of *The Wicker Man* – Ronald Hutton 25
2 A deeply religious people: *The Wicker Man*, contemporary Paganism and Dracula reversed – Laurel Zwissler 39
3 Folk horror: a discursive approach, with application to Robin Hardy's *The Wicker Man* and Neil Jordan's *The Company of Wolves* – Mikel J. Koven 57

Part II: Return of the British repressed

4 The folk of folk horror – Derek Johnston 75
5 *Doomwatch*: sacrifice zones and folk horror – Dawn Keetley 87
6 My ancestors died here: *Requiem for a Village* and the rural English horror of modernity and socio-cultural change – Paul Newland 104
7 Outsider history, or outside of history – K. J. Donnelly 117
8 Anglo creep and Celtic resistance in *Apostle* – Beth Carroll 131
9 Women's folk horror in Britain: history, industry, style – Amy Harris 146

Part III: Folk horror's cultural landscapes

10 Ritualistic rhythms: exploring the sensory affect of drums in British folk horror cinema – Lyndsay Townsend 163

11 'Nature came before man': human as subject and object within the folk horror anti-landscape – David Evans-Powell 178
12 Hieroglyphics: Arthur Machen on screen – Mark Goodall 194
13 Albion unearthed: social, political and cultural influences on British folk horror, urban wyrd and backwoods cinema – Andy Paciorek 209
14 'Isn't folk horror *all* horror?': a wyrd genre – Diane A. Rodgers 221

British folk horror filmography 233
Index 238

Figures

0.1	*The Wicker Man* (dir. Robin Hardy, 1973), image courtesy of STUDIOCANAL	6
0.2a–b	*Cry of the Banshee* (dir. Gordon Hessler, 1970)	10
0.3	*In the Earth* (dir. Ben Wheatley, 2021)	14
2.1	*The Witches* (dir. Cyril Frankel, 1966)	41
2.2	*The Wicker Man* (dir. Robin Hardy, 1973), image courtesy of STUDIOCANAL	42
2.3	*The Wicker Man* (dir. Robin Hardy, 1973), image courtesy of STUDIOCANAL	52
5.1	The 1972 poster for *Doomwatch* (dir. Peter Sasdy, 1972)	88
5.2	*Doomwatch* (dir. Peter Sasdy, 1972)	91
5.3	*Doomwatch* (dir. Peter Sasdy, 1972)	94
5.4	*Doomwatch* (dir. Peter Sasdy, 1972)	97
5.5	*Doomwatch* (dir. Peter Sasdy, 1972)	98
5.6	*Doomwatch* (dir. Peter Sasdy, 1972)	101
6.1	*Requiem for a Village* (dir. David Gladwell, 1975)	110
6.2	*Requiem for a Village* (dir. David Gladwell, 1975)	113
7.1	*A Field in England* (dir. Ben Wheatley, 2013)	125
8.1	*Apostle* (dir. Gareth Evans, 2018)	141
8.2	*Apostle* (dir. Gareth Evans, 2018)	143
11.1	*Blood on Satan's Claw* (dir. Piers Haggard, 1971)	182
11.2	*Dogged* (dir. Richard Rowntree, 2017)	188
12.1a–b	*Holy Terrors* (dir. Julian Butler and Mark Goodall, 2017)	205
14.1	Piers Haggard directing *Blood on Satan's Claw* (dir. Piers Haggard, 1971)	223
14.2	*Blood on Satan's Claw* (dir. Piers Haggard, 1971)	226
14.3	*In Fabric* (dir. Peter Strickland, 2018)	229

Contributors

Louis Bayman is an associate professor in film studies at the University of Southampton. He enjoys researching popular genres and is especially interested in melodrama and in horror cinema. He has written extensively on Italian cinema, including the monograph *The Operatic and the Everyday in Postwar Italian Film Melodrama*, as well as the co-edited collection *Journeys on Screen: Theory, Ethics and Aesthetics* with Natalia Pinazza. He is currently working on a project on the meanings of time in contemporary cinema.

Beth Carroll is a lecturer in film studies at the University of Southampton. Her research interests manifest around ideas of space and place, particularly the impact these have on issues of affect. Her monograph, *Feeling Film: A Spatial Approach*, explores how a methodological approach combining the two might be forged. Other research interests include sound and music.

John Das is a television producer and director. His credits include *A History of Horror with Mark Gatiss*, *Tomorrow's Worlds: The Unearthly History of Science Fiction* and *Mark Kermode's Secrets of Cinema*.

K. J. Donnelly is Professor of Film and Film Music at the University of Southampton. He is author of *The McGurk Universe* (2023), *The Shining* (2017), *Magical Musical Tour* (2015), *Occult Aesthetics* (2013), *British Film Music and Film Musicals* (2007), *The Spectre of Sound* (2005) and *Pop Music in British Cinema* (2001).

David Evans-Powell is a Ph.D. candidate at the University of Birmingham. He has published monographs on the 1971 film *Blood on Satan's Claw* (2021) and the 1984 *Doctor Who* serial *The Awakening* (2020), as well as numerous articles for Horrifiedmagazine.co.uk and Horrorhomeroom.com. He has articles to be published in upcoming collections, as well contributing to a forthcoming documentary series commemorating the fiftieth anniversary of Robin Hardy's *The Wicker Man*.

Mark Goodall is an associate professor in film at the University of Bradford. He has published books on the Beatles (*'The Beatles or 'The White Album'* (2018)), music and the occult (*Gathering of the Tribe: Music and Heavy Conscious Creation* (2013/2022)) and shock cinema of the 1960s (*Sweet and Savage: The World, through the Mondo Film Lens* (2018)). He co-edited *New Media Archaeology* (2018) and edited a special edition of *Film International* (2019). He has written for the *Guardian*, the *Independent*, the *New European* and *Shindig!*, and plays with the group Rudolf Rocker.

Amy Harris is a fully funded doctoral researcher at De Montfort University. Her thesis considers contemporary British horror films directed by self-identifying women. Amy has published chapters in *Bloody Women: Women Directors of Horror* and *Evil Women: Representations within Literature, Culture and Film*. In her spare time, she posts about her Ph.D. experience on Instagram under the handle @the_horrorhag.

Ronald Hutton is Senior Professor of History at the University of Bristol; the Gresham Professor of Divinity at London; and a Fellow of the Royal Historical Society, the Society of Antiquaries, the Learned Society of Wales and the British Academy. He has held a number of public posts and is currently a member of the Conservation Committee of Historic England. He has published eighteen books and ninety-four essays on a wide range of subjects, including British history between 1400 and 1700, ancient and modern paganism in Britain, the British ritual year, and Siberian shamanism.

Derek Johnston is Lecturer in Broadcast at Queen's University Belfast. His research encompasses horror, science fiction and representations of history, and he was one of the keynote speakers at the 'Fiend in the Furrows' conference on folk horror in Belfast in 2014. His first monograph, *Haunted Seasons: Television Ghost Stories for Christmas and Horror for Halloween*, was published in 2015 and explores horror seasonality. He has also written a number of articles and book chapters on horror and science fiction in television, film and culture, including the chapter on 'Gothic Television' for the *Cambridge History of the Gothic*, Vol. III (2021), and is editor of a collection on *Nigel Kneale and Horror* (due 2023).

Dawn Keetley is Professor of English, teaching horror/gothic literature, film and television at Lehigh University in Bethlehem, Pennsylvania. She has most recently published in *Journal of American Culture*, *Science Fiction Film and Television*, *Gothic Nature*, *Journal of Popular Culture*, *Horror Studies*, *Journal of the Fantastic in the Arts*, *Journal of Popular Television*, *Journal of Film and Video* and *Gothic Studies*. She is editor of *Jordan Peele's Get Out: Political Horror* (2020) and *We're All Infected: Essays on AMC's The Walking Dead and the Fate of the Human* (2014). She has co-edited (with Angela Tenga) *Plant Horror: Approaches to the Monstrous Vegetal in Fiction and Film* (2016) and (with Matthew Wynn Sivils) *The Ecogothic in Nineteenth-Century American Literature* (2017). Her book, *Making a Monster: Jesse Pomeroy, the Boy Murderer of 1870s Boston*, was published in 2017. Keetley is working on essays on horror and folk horror, and has recently co-edited a collection, *Folk Horror: New Global Pathways*, from University of Wales Press. She writes regularly for a horror website she co-created, HorrorHomeroom.com.

Mikel J. Koven is the author of *La Dolce Morte: Vernacular Cinema and the Italian 'Giallo' Film* (2006), *Film, Folklore and Urban Legends* (2008) and *Blaxploitation Cinema* (2010). He holds a Ph.D. in folklore studies and has written extensively on the relationship between folklore and popular cinema.

Paul Newland is currently Director of Research and Knowledge Exchange at the University of Worcester. He has also worked at Bath Spa University, Aberystwyth University, the University of Exeter and the University of Plymouth. He has published widely on representations of cities, landscapes, architecture and sound in film. Books include *The Cultural Construction of London's East End* (2008) and *British Films of the 1970s* (2013). Edited books include *Don't Look Now: British Cinema in the 1970s* (2010), *British Rural Landscapes on Film* (2016) and *British Art Cinema* (with Brian Hoyle, 2019).

Andy Paciorek is an artist, author, small press publisher and project creator, working mostly in the fields of folklore, Forteana, anomaly, weird fiction, nostalgia, hauntings, decadence and symbolism, occulture, and analysis of horror in film and literature. He is the founder of Folk Horror Revival, Urban Wyrd Project, Wyrd Harvest Press, drēmour press and Northumbria Ghost~Lore Society.

Diane A. Rodgers is Senior Lecturer in Media, Arts and Communications and co-founder member of the Centre for Contemporary Legend Research Group at Sheffield Hallam University. She specialises in teaching alternative media (including cult TV, films, music and comics) and storytelling in film and television, including textual analysis and folklore. Diane recently completed her Ph.D. on wyrd TV: folklore, folk horror and hauntology on television.

Lyndsay Townsend is a current Ph.D. student in film studies at the University of St Andrews. Her thesis is titled 'Feeling Folk Horror: Exploring the Sensory Affect of Folk Horror Screen Texts, from 1968–present'.

Laurel Zwissler is Professor of Religion at Central Michigan University. Her monograph, *Religious, Feminist, Activist: Cosmologies of Interconnection* (2018), focuses on global justice activists and investigates intersections among religion, gender and politics, relating these to debates about religion in the public sphere. Fieldwork with contemporary Witchcraft communities also inspired a series of articles about the shadows of women within classical scholarly theories of religion, exploring challenges to traditional notions of academic knowledge creation, disruptions grounded in imaginaries of female bodies and the moral values ascribed to them. She also co-edits the peer-reviewed journal, *Magic, Ritual, and Witchcraft*.

Foreword

There are many reasons to welcome this collection, not least the fact that it exists in the first place.

I certainly didn't anticipate the current fascination with folk horror back in the summer of 2010, when I was producing the BBC TV series *A History of Horror with Mark Gatiss* and wrestling with how to end the second episode, which focused on the British horror movie boom of the 1950s and 1960s.

The series presented horror cinema as a cyclical phenomenon, rising and falling. Just as the great age of black-and-white Hollywood horror ended as postwar audiences turned to science fiction films, the Technicolor gothic horrors of Hammer and their ilk also struggled in a more permissive, pop-culture era. As Mark explained in the programme, by the early 1970s there was 'a decline in British horror which proved pretty much irreversible'.

Reluctant to finish on such a downbeat note, we decided to conclude the episode with a sequence celebrating three films that ran counter to the general creative downturn – *Witchfinder General* (1968), *Blood on Satan's Claw* (1971) and *The Wicker Man* (1973). Mark described them as 'a loose collection of films which we might call "folk horror"', in which 'a new generation of British directors avoided the gothic clichés by stepping even further away from the modern world'.

The centrepiece of the sequence featured Mark interviewing *Satan's Claw* director Piers Haggard at one of his film's most evocative locations. Haggard was genial and reflective, and the episode's director, Rachel Jardine, imbued the sequence with an elegiac quality, matching our description of the three films as 'fascinating final flourishes'. Troubling, daring, idiosyncratic as these pictures were, they seemed unquestionably to belong to a bygone age.

Happily, those flourishes have proved not to be so final after all. In the years since *A History of Horror* aired, there has been a steady stream of striking British horror films, several with a distinctly folk flavour. A surge in critical interest, culminating in this collection, has identified folk as a defining force in British horror. *Witchfinder General*, *Blood on Satan's Claw* and *The Wicker Man* have gone from being outliers to landmarks.

The following pages offer plenty of explanations for the current fascination with folk. A key factor for me, at least, is folk horror's ambivalence about community and tradition, an antidote to the all too polarised mindset that seems to prevail today. For a genre that ostensibly steps back from the modern world, folk speaks with remarkable power to the present. That capacity to provoke and engage is reflected in the energy and range of these essays, which draw on everything from Julius Caesar's memoirs to the feminist writings of Hélène Cixous.

The collection's subtitle, 'Return of the British repressed', has its perfect visual metaphor in the demonic skull uncovered in the field at the start of *Blood on Satan's Claw*. Given how much the contributions here capture the genre's richness and appeal, I doubt folk horror will be disappearing back underground any time soon.

John Das

Introduction: what makes the folk horrific?

Louis Bayman and K. J. Donnelly

Can folk be fashionable? The quaint products of a once handicraft tradition are at the time of writing enjoying a rebirth as the latest trend in contemporary horror. Folk horror has become a global phenomenon spanning television, music, literature, fan circuits and social-media communities. Three famous films from 1960s and 1970s Britain – *Witchfinder General* (1968), *Blood on Satan's Claw* (1971) and *The Wicker Man* (1973) – sometimes called 'the Unholy Trinity' (Scovell 2017: 8), have achieved cult status and ongoing tributes, providing a template of a peculiar community of agricultural folk hostile to the ways of outsiders.

This revival of interest only accentuates a curious aspect of folk horror, which is that nobody seems willing to say what it actually is. The only critical book on the topic is Adam Scovell's *Folk Horror: Hours Dreadful and Things Strange* (2017). Dawn Keetley has edited a special issue of *Revenant* (2020), while blogs can be found at the *Folk Horror Revival* website and the Facebook group of the same name, founded by Andy Paciorek (both Keetley and Paciorek contribute chapters to this volume). This relative paucity of writings means that discussion remains dominated by very vague notions of folk horror, or by the particular aesthetic choices of a specific text. The eerie silence surrounding what the genre actually is contrasts to a wild overgrowth of things gathered together as examples of 'folk horror'. The three-hour documentary *Woodlands Dark and Days Bewitched: A History of Folk Horror* (2021) sets out a sprawling universe of texts either based on folk tales or set on the land, and so is the first time that US vampire chiller *Let's Scare Jessica to Death* (1971) has been placed alongside BBC children's animation *Bagpuss* (1974).

In this collection we choose to take a different path. We restrict ourselves to the particular importance British cinema has to the development of the genre,[1] not because British cinema offers a universal standard, but to seek a focus that too much discussion of folk horror lacks. We hope our discussion will be useful to scholars working in television, other media or beyond

Britain, and invite them to make their own minds up as to its applicability. We posit that this applicability lies in the fact that we think the significance of folk horror will be proven not by by increasing the size of the corpus but by understanding the cultural function it has. We therefore try to avoid what Mikel J. Koven calls 'motif spotting' (2008: 3), the practice of listing the recurrent features of a genre without identifying the underlying dynamics that give it coherence. Recognising that our opening propositions represent a minority position in horror studies, we have not insisted that the contributors to this book agree with them, as their subsequent chapters will show.

What is folk horror?

According to Marcus K. Harmes, folk horror began as a 'statement of difference from a small and newly (from 1966) established production company' (2013: 65). With funding from American International Pictures (AIP), the small Tigon British Productions tried to find a niche amid its better-known British studio rivals, Hammer Film Productions and Amicus. They did so with a trio of films that all feature witchcraft and an early modern historical setting, respectively the civil war of the 1640s for *Witchfinder General*, Elizabethan times for *Cry of the Banshee* (1970), and the eighteenth-century Jacobite rebellions for *Blood on Satan's Claw*. Leon Hunt (2001) identifies a new interest in the 'witchcraft and the occult' in three contemporary-set horrors of the same period, Hammer's *The Witches* (1966) and *The Devil Rides Out* (1968), and British Lion's *The Wicker Man*.

Like noir and melodrama, folk horror was not a term initially applied to the films that retrospectively constitute the first phase of the canon.[2] But unlike noir and melodrama, there is no debate over how it entered popular consciousness. In the 'Home Counties Horrors' section of the 2010 BBC documentary *A History of Horror*, Mark Gatiss, presenter and former star of *The League of Gentleman* (a TV comedy and spin-off film, *The League of Gentleman's Apocalypse* (2005), that amount to a loving spoof of the folk horror tradition), asks director Piers Haggard if he was trying to make 'a folk horror' with *Blood on Satan's Claw*. Haggard responds that 'I think that I was … in a way, because we were all interested in witchcraft and we were all interested in free love'. Derek Johnston discusses the pre-Gatiss origins of the term folk horror in his chapter in this book. But it was Gatiss's use that caught on, describing a 'loose collection of films' that sought to avoid 'the gothic clichés' of 1960s British horror through an 'obsession with the British landscape, its folklore and traditions'.

This looseness has dominated scholarship on folk horror ever since. Dawn Keetley identifies folk horror in 'communal stories of monsters, ghosts, violence, and sacrifice that occupy the threshold between history and fiction' (Keetley 2020: 4). Her wide-ranging study spans cinema, television and literature, according with a scholarly reluctance to set boundaries to the genre. For Adam Scovell, folk horror is only 'a prism of a term', because 'arguing for it to represent a single body of artistic work with strict parameters and definition is impossible' (2017: 5). Andy Paciorek warns that to try to define folk horror would be 'like building a box the exact shape of mist', since aspects of folk belief and practice pervade a variety of films (2015). Thus, when Paul Cowdell points out that 'clear generic definitions [of folk horror] are elusive' (2019: 296), he identifies what critics generally agree is an analytical strength.

One would surely mark oneself as the village idiot of the scholarly community to try to delimit the amorphousness of either 'folk' or 'horror', two immense terms that span diverse cultures across centuries and even millennia. Who would choose, like a petty parish patriarch, to impose categories on creative activity when one could contemplate instead the rural mist? An indefinable unease is after all characteristic of the genre, while a misty indeterminacy insures the critic against the continual expansion that makes the genre a living, changing organism. But would a meteorologist – or perhaps let's say a farmer – not benefit from being able to tell the difference between rain and mist; or the artist, from distinguishing its aesthetic character from near cousins such as fog or drizzle? What horror can't somehow trace its roots in the ritualistic communalism of tales around the campfire, or to atavistic fears of monsters, ghosts and sacrifice? Yet folk horror represents only a very small number of the hundreds of horror films produced annually worldwide. What might slip from sight when we adopt too expansive a view?

Throwing aside, like a medieval doctor, the possibility that our diagnosis will do more harm than good, we propose a working definition of folk horror and a sketch of what further knowledge this definition might enable. We do this in the knowledge that time, and the perspective of the beholder, mean that no genre can be fixed in place. What follows is therefore a proposal, if not the offering of our intellectual credentials for potential sacrifice. That proposal is that we summon the old gods of genre theory to work on the field of folk horror and see what fruits their work might reap.

First, we need to dispel the idea that genre is a simple grouping of films with little analytical potential. As Rick Altman pointed out, the identification of a genre by journalists and industry practitioners is only a starting point for critical analysis, which needs then to determine the given genre's cultural significance (1987: 13–4). As leading genre theorist Steve Neale states:

> genres are not simply bodies of work or groups of films, however classified, labeled, and defined. Genres do no consist only of films: they consist also, and equally, of specific systems of expectation and hypothesis ... [which] help render films, and the elements within them, intelligible and therefore explicable. They offer a way of working out the significance of what is happening on screen: why particular events and actions are taking place, why the characters are dressed the way they are, why they look, speak and behave the way they do, and so on. (Neale 2021: 58)

For folk horror to 'make sense', it needs established expectation in a systematised form.[3] Rather than just a broad 'tendency' we argue that folk horror thus makes sense as a genre, with particular recurrent images and narratives and an apparent supposition that audiences will recognise recurrent elements across different films. In fact, folk horror provides a particularly fertile example of what Thomas Schatz identified as the 'familiar *social community*' that binds an individual film to a wider genre: the insular collective at the centre of so many folk horrors seems ripe for reading in terms of what Schatz called that 'cultural milieu where [a genre's] inherent thematic conflicts are animated, intensified and resolved' (Schatz 2011: 455).

Adam Scovell proposes that we think of folk horror not as a genre but as a 'chain', one that connects 'disparate forms of media through their shared summoning of ... themes and ideas' (2017: 8). Scovell invokes some key theories to make this connection: psychogeography, hauntology, and topography – but his disparate, prismatic approach leaves them uninterrogated. For example, while psychogeography now appears to have moved some distance from Debord's original meaning, it is pertinent to folk horror's sense of an active landscape, which seems to uncover something of the psyche or even the unconscious. Folk horror exhibits a historical awareness of the abandoned or destroyed pasts that lie beneath the present; making it one more instance of what Derrida described as hauntology. We might say further, however, that British folk horror deals in hauntology not in the Derridean or even the Fisherian sense, but more like the insoluble parts in a mixed-up drink, the dregs of the past that stubbornly remain, like a faint stain on history that will not quietly go away.

Another problem with liberating ourselves from the bounds of generic categorisation is that discussion still requires some idea, examined or otherwise, of what folk horror actually is. Adam Scovell finds this in four key traits: isolation, a landscape with an alien quality, a skewed belief system or morality, and a happening or summoning (Scovell 2017: 17–18). But these are very general characteristics that can be found across horror as a whole. Such generality reduces their explanatory power with regard to the particularity of folk horror. Isolation is a component not just of horror but of fear itself, and consequently it is as important to the haunted house film as it is to folk horror; meanwhile, *Alien* (1979) is about as far from folk horror as it is possible to imagine, but reminds us that in space nobody can hear you scream. The landscape has an 'alien quality' in *The Evil Dead* (1981), whose trees are enchanted by evil spirits, but there are no folk present. In fact the ascription of threat to the very setting is an extension of the first point, that fear is increased by isolation. A 'skewed system of beliefs' might motivate the men of *Stepford Wives* (1975), the white community in *Get Out* (2017) or the serial killer in *Seven* (1995), none of which are folk horror. This is because a common requirement of horror is to show that human beings can be motivated to commit terrible deeds. Meanwhile a 'summoning' is a basic dramatic property of the monstrous of all kinds. So what makes the presence of any of these things in folk horror special?

To enact a summoning from a skewed belief system of our own, it is time for us to attempt a definition of what we think this genre actually is – of what provides the analysis Altman called for, the recurrent expectations Neale described and the social milieu Schatz detected. Our definition comes from the principle that any type of horror can be differentiated by what, specifically, it finds horrific. The common factor in the films most often cited as folk horror, sometimes noted but rarely examined by critics as the central distinguishing point, is therefore this: folk horror is a horror of the folk themselves, and of the wider conditions that sustain their existence. It is not the horror of what threatens that existence from outside, but of the very customs, land and lifestyle that keep the folk going. Folk horror is thus more immersed in and more estranged from rural life than related forms such as the gothic or rural horror. Its horror is less of monstrous others to the folk than of the beliefs that produce meaning, the rituals that provide festivity, and the land that brings forth nourishment. While remaining open to the ever-changing nature of the genre, this definition does not extend to peripheral films with tenuous links, nor to all films that are set rurally or feature folk tales. But it does put us in a position to identify the particular cultural function it performs, and the artistic innovations it makes.

Folk horror is a horror of the folk themselves

This definition immediately removes from folk horror the vampires, werewolves, goblins and other folk devils that make up the traditional gothic. These all emerge from folk superstition – which is precisely why we think it worth distinguishing them from folk horror. Peasants may mass with pitchforks to expel Frankenstein's monster or recoil at Dracula's looming castle. But these are fears of forces external to the community, that threaten it from outside, and whose eventual destruction returns it to some kind of normality. In folk horror, the horror is already inside that community (see Keetley 2020: 11–13). It is not witchcraft that causes mayhem in *Witchfinder General* but a witchhunt. It is not pagan gods but pagan rituals that threaten life in *The Wicker Man*. The folk-horror sci-fi *Quatermass and the Pit* (1967) hinges on an archaeological discovery that Martians landed in ancient Britain: not as a prelude to a *War of the Worlds*-style invasion, but as a realisation of the alien beginnings of an entire national heritage. In *Doomwatch* (1972), discussed by Dawn Keetley in Chapter 5, the very sea itself produces monstrous physical and mental defects in its Cornish island inhabitants. Even *Blood on Satan's Claw*, which features demonic possession, gives less narrative importance to supernatural forces than to the violent historic conflict between two belief systems: church religion and pagan heresy.

The supernatural may be present in folk horror. But unlike in the gothic, it appears in folk horror to help define the community and protect it from outsiders. In *The Lair of the White Worm* (1987), discussed by Kevin Donnelly in Chapter 7, an archaeological dig discovers the remnants of ancient pagan worship of a white worm, whose reappearance disrupts the

Figure 0.1 Fear of the folk in *The Wicker Man,* 1973

sexual repression of modern society. In *The Company of Wolves* (1984), which Mikel J. Koven discusses in Chapter 3, fairy tales help a girl subversively to navigate gender expectations. Amy Harris discusses in Chapter 9 how recent female-directed folk horrors *Following the Wicca Man* (2013) and *Maya* (2021) feature magical women as a way to challenge male dominance; the fantastic is also part of female empowerment in *She Will* (2021) and patriarchal power in *Men* (2022).

The horror in folk horror may be supernatural or real, actual or imagined. Unlike the slasher, which typically culminates with the reason for the killer's pathology, folk horror does not need to determine any ultimate explanation, preferring, as Diane Rodgers explains in Chapter 14, the eeriness of uncertainty. In two films discussed by Evans-Powell in Chapter 11, a soldier with PTSD takes repose in the countryside in *The Unkindness of Ravens* (2015), while the protagonist in *The Fallow Field* (2009) suffers strange blackouts. In *The Shout* (1978), a professional couple's retreat to the Devon countryside is undone by a mysterious stranger who summons a special shout learned from Aboriginal Australian tribesmen. Either demonic possession or magic mushrooms afflict the protagonists of two Ben Wheatley folk horrors, *A Field in England* (2013, also discussed by Donnelly) and *In the Earth* (2021). In *Enys Men* (2022) the fear comes either from a traumatic past, a threatening community, a psychic or a supernatural force, or all or none of these. Rather than explain, each example instead removes the epistemological bases of our accepted knowledge of reality.

Its setting may be historical or contemporary, its threats supernatural or real, but folk horror weakens any claim made by bourgeois modernity to universal truth. As *The Wicker Man* shows, Police Sergeant Howie's faith in a Christian God and Her Majesty's Constabulary is little more than a ritually observed fanaticism of its own, when removed from the community that gives it meaning. But nor is folk horror a straightforward celebration of the vitality of folk life. It is set in times of social disorder, such as *The Black Death* (2010) or the Jacobite rebellions in *Blood on Satan's Claw*. It exposes the political machinations behind religious fervour, whether in the Civil War setting of *Witchfinder General* or *A Field in England*, or in the art-horror *Anchoress* (1993), set in 1329, when a Machiavellian village religious authority accuses a woman of witchcraft to gain notoriety for the parish. In *Apostle* (2018), discussed by Beth Carroll in Chapter 8, an entire congregation is exiled to rural Wales for being 'traitors and enemies of the King', only for their commune to fall into murderous factional struggle internally.

As these conflicts show, folk horrors feature not only isolation but also travel and exogenous contact. Protagonists in *Blood on Satan's Claw* and *Witchfinder General* journey to other parts of England, *A Field in England* takes the form of a road trip, while *Psychomania* (1973) is about a suburban motorcycle gang. Folk horror is distinguished not by isolation alone but by the clash of incompatible but encroaching belief systems and their consequent forms of social organisation. This clash may be associated with more recent history: the witchcraft practised in a rural village in *The Witches* (1966) is repeatedly referred to as 'African', reminding us that folk horror emerges during the latter years of British decolonisation. Later folk horrors occur against the backdrop of deindustrialisation. In *Darklands* (1996) a journalist travels from London to Wales to encounter a murderous sect who practise amid the remnants of the steelworks. In *Outcast* (2010), a woman on an Edinburgh housing estate casts a spell against the social services.

Folk horror thus foregrounds the problems of progress but shows the alternatives to it to be violently insane. Horror is often discussed in terms of expelling threats to the social order in categories such as the monstrous feminine or the abject. Folk horrors instead deal less with monstrous threats to the social order than the removal of any normative order at all, showing community, both modern and traditional, to be based on repression and violence. It demonstrates that what is taboo for one society can be totemic for another, what is horrific to one the basis of worship and authority in another. Folk horror thus offers a historical, and an anthropological, take on horror. It provides the frightening realisation that cultural values, including those of life and death or good and evil, are relative. It recognises that our ways of life, our joys, the powers we implore to keep us safe, our very knowledge of the world and our place within it, are the products of the community we are born into rather than objective truth.

Folk horror is only one development of horror

In *A Heritage of Horror*, David Pirie (1973) argued that postwar British horror cinema formed the disreputable wing of the broader construction of a national heritage. Hammer had made its reputation with adaptations of the literary works *Dracula* and *Frankenstein*, which it combined with the sensational melodrama and special effects of traditions drawn from the popular theatre. But folk horror moves away from the mansions and castles of the gothic. Its heritage is that of the mud and earth where 'farming is an actual practice in folk horror, not a pretextual backdrop' (Cowdell 2019: 301), and of a village green where festivity, ritual and judicial violence intermingle. Peter Hutchings groups the films of folk horror within a minority tendency of a 'British anti-landscape', a land that is not green and pleasant but is instead abandoned, alien and pagan (Hutchings 2004: 29). For Leon Hunt, the early films of folk horror can be associated with the

1960s counterculture, the real-life black magician Alastair Crowley and the backlash represented by Mary Whitehouse's moral crusade for Christian values and the 1970–74 Conservative Government (Hunt 2001).

It remains open to debate whether folk horror aligns itself with the counterculture (see Andy Paciorek in this volume) or with conservative protest against it (Harmes 2013; Newland in this volume), or whether instead it displays a cynical ambivalence about both. Nevertheless, folk horror was made possible by changes in censorship and the liberalisation of society that fostered an array of new forms of horror from the late 1950s and into the 1970s, from Hammer in Britain to Roger Corman's AIP in America, the German *Krimi* and later the snuff movie, the Italian *giallo*, and the US slasher film and body horror, as a by no means exhaustive list of the revolution in horror filmmaking across this period. Yet, as Diane Rodgers considers in her discussion of the genre's aesthetic character in Chapter 14, folk horror is distinct from them all.

Folk horror does not exhibit the same libidinal explicitness of many of its contemporaries. Isobel Pinedo has discussed the 'Wet deaths' of the splatter and slasher as examples of 'postmodern horror' that make a spectacle of opened, ruined bodies (1997: 51–69). Folk horror generally avoids excessive viscera and gore. Its brutality is found instead in whippings, shackling, torture devices and ritual sacrifice, which are no less voyeuristically sadistic but whose focus is more on the frisson provided by the exercise of discipline than by explicitness per se. Yet while the slasher film is often thought of as punishing teenage promiscuity, folk horror seems to do something else. Punishment in folk horror culminates in ritual sacrifice, as part of a theatrical affirmation of group belonging that further underlines the importance of community to the horror. The eponymous *Witchfinder General* gets a clear erotic thrill from the bodily mortification of suspects of witchcraft, but he is also an embodiment of the exercise of justice. This personal embodiment is removed from the detached legal institutions of the State and exposes both the cruel arbitrariness of punishment and its role in ensuring the functioning of the community. Sometimes this is in keeping with backlash politics: *Psychomania* parallels the 'misbehaviour' of a youth biker gang with the pagan rituals its leader sees in visions. Even when the reason remains mysterious, some relation to punishment is made: *Kill List* (2011) repeatedly states that the victims of a pair of hitmen are guilty of child abuse. More generally, we can connect the focus on punishment to a wider concern over discipline present in both phases of folk horror, from the backlash against 1960s and 1970s countercultures to the development of the concept of 'antisocial behaviour' and fears of 'feral youth' in the 2000s.[4]

Figure 0.2a–b Punishment and heresy in *Cry of the Banshee*, 1970

Folk horror may be considered an example of rural horror, if that simply means all horror with a rural setting. But it is distinct from trends identified by Carol Clover (1992) as 'urbanoia', the fear held by the city-dweller of bestial rural savagery in the 'hillbilly' or 'backwoods' horror – ideas that Laurel Zwissler discusses at length in her analysis of *The Wicker Man* in Chapter 2. But the conflict animating folk horror is not between civilisation and savagery. It is not the absence of culture, religion, belief, justice, law and social organisation that causes terror in folk horror, so much as their presence. The harvest festival of *The Wicker Man* is so disturbing precisely because of the absence of animalistic rage from the participants when they burn Sergeant Howie; it is their organised, cheerful incorporation of an integrated system of belief and their relation to the land and the cosmos.

Killing serves to bind the community together and to demonstrate that folk horror's principal fear is not of criminal insanity or crazed individuals but of a community openly convinced of its collective righteousness. This open element produces a relative absence of the unclaimed point of view shot in folk horrors, a trait of the slasher movie where the camera seems to adopt the perspective of a hidden attacker (the most famous examples being the opening sequences of both *Peeping Tom* (1960), and *Halloween* (1979)). Killing in folk horror instead belongs to public ritual. Those few examples that it does have of an unclaimed point of view are interesting in themselves – two occur in *Blood on Satan's Claw*, one from the unearthed dirt and another from the tree-tops as if of a bird; in Ben Wheatley's folk horrors *A Field in England* and *In the Earth*, unclaimed point-of-view shots occur from vegetation. Each gives a perspective to nature itself, suggesting its uncanny animation, in a context where boundaries between death and new life are not clearly demarcated, nor those between harvest, justice and worship.

The generic traits of folk horror are then expressive of its central feature: that folk life is the source of its horror. There are no franchises in folk horror and the only sequel is Robin Hardy's rather unsuccessful *The Wicker Tree* (2011). Similarly, folk horror does not have the serial structure that Richard Dyer (2000) has discussed as an organising principle of both industrial modernity and of serial killer films, where the killer predictably 'kills and kills again'. Its narrative structure typically develops more gradually towards one grand finale. This structure has less in common with the meaningless seriality of (post)modern life and more in common with the rhythms of folk festival, or the fruition of a final harvest, as part of the creation of meaning in the protagonists' world. The culminating moment of ritual spectacle is a participatory, public intertwining of belief, nature and social structure.

Folk horror is an apt term

The films of folk horror have variously been grouped together in relation to 'anti-landscape' (Hutchings 2004), witchcraft (Harmes 2013), necromancy (Hunt 2001) and 'folksploitation' (Newland 2008). These categories overlap but are not coterminous. None has taken root in the popular imagination like folk horror; nor has 'Tigon' come to stand for a category of horror as Hammer does. So what does 'folk horror' encapsulate that these other terms do not?

The term 'folk horror' expresses a fundamental dynamic. This dynamic might provide what genre studies used to refer to as its 'core problematic': the idea that genre works as myth, resolving contradictions that are intractable in reality. 'Folk' refers to the 'people' of a particular area, the common or ordinary people who do not belong to aristocratic or courtly culture, the Church, high office or institutional roles. It suggests a way of life prior to electrification, mechanisation or urbanisation, and a culture that is oral and live. To pair it with horror is to disrupt its conventional associations with bucolic images of pastoral simplicity through the sensational dislocations of horror. Folk horror demonstrates that the obedience, hierarchy and harmony belonging to the ideal of rustic simplicity are achieved through fanaticism and violence. By positioning the folk not as pleasant but as horrific, folk horror undermines belief in a homogeneous, simple and happy people at the basis of the British people with the class struggle, dirt, ideological fanaticism and ethnic heterogeneity evidenced by history.

Folk horror is just one instance of a broad popular interest in folklore detailed previously by Mikel J. Koven (2007) and Cowdell (2019), and elaborated further by Koven and Ronald Hutton in Chapters 1 and 3 here. The term 'folk-lore' was coined by William Thoms in 1846, in distinction to classical antiquities. The institution of the Folk Lore Society in 1878, the publication of James Frazer's *The Golden Bough: A Study in Magic and Religion* (1922 [1890]) and Margaret Murray's proto-feminist *The Witch-Cult in Western Europe* (1962 [1921]) demonstrated the popular appeal of studies of a non-Christian, bygone national past, and were influential on the twentieth-century reinvention of pagan and Wiccan practice (even if their academic rigour has troubled scholars ever since; see Cowdell (2019)). The 'English popular art' catalogued by Enid Marx (1946) represents another contribution to this common heritage. But notions of a bygone folk culture were changing in the period preceding folk horror's appearance. Alan Lomax undertook to preserve the songs of the coal miners in the 1950s, the beginning of industrial heritage and the protection of another culture in the early phase of a long decline. E. P. Thompson's historical *The Making of the English Working Class* (1963) focused on the disappearance of popular forms of life in a work that might better have been titled 'The Unmaking of the English Rural Classes'. Meanwhile, Keith Thomas's *Religion and the Decline of Magic: Studies in Popular Beliefs in Sixteenth and Seventeenth Century England* (1971) details the erasure of older superstitious beliefs in early modernity. These works each place a greater focus on class struggle and religious diversity, relativising a present that itself was undergoing historical change. Folk horror is also the product of a postcolonial Britain left to contemplate the foreignness of its own domestic population. In *The Break Up of Britain* (1981 [1977]), Tom Nairn postulated the end of the union; the films of folk horror offer historical and heretical visions of the same sentiment. Its interest in unearthing forgotten pasts perhaps also implies the possibility that one day Britain might itself pass into history.

The demythologisation of Britain's rural past also determines how folk horror positions the folk in their landscape, a theme discussed by Adam Scovell (2017), James Thurgill (2020), David Evans-Powell (2021) and Paul Newland (2016), which David Evans-Powell reprises in Chapter 11 here. British folk horror films revel in landscape shots and the implication of an active landscape. The rural landscape can often manifest a 'distancing effect' ('far away and long ago ...', as folk tales can begin). These hidden-away places may evade placement on the map, in places where no one looks: the village hidden in the mist in *The Monster Club* (1981) or even *Brigadoon* (1954). Hutchings notes that these locations appear to wrestle with modernity (2004: 29), and Scovell elaborates that the landscape is 'far more than a backdrop' (2017: 33). A psychogeographical view might point to the fact that landscapes hold the past's secrets, which are evident for those who look and listen carefully. As Scovell (2017) and Keetley (2020) point out, even the most banal landscape can hold mysteries, and some, beneath the surface, can hold a wealth of shocking remnants from the past. In popular metaphor, the past is buried, perhaps ploughed under, and in recent years, archaeologists of all sorts can unearth what we thought was dead and buried. This matches recent approaches to history that understand the past as a repository of objects and ideas, a magic shop of things that can be brought back.

Peter Hutchings defines anti-landscape as nature made uncanny, but uncanniness can be achieved through varying aesthetic dispositions whose variances each express different relationships between nature and humanity. The sublime shows the indomitable power of nature, as if defying its eighteenth-century context of colonial and scientific domination. In *Wolf Creek* (2005), nature is made uncanny instead by the immensity of the Australian outback, indicating a desolate emptiness of human presence. Alternatively, the opening sequence of *Deliverance* (1972), where an industrial river project is referred to as a 'rape' of nature, creates uncanniness through the human bespoiling of nature. Disused landscapes such as that of *The Texas Chainsaw Massacre* (1974) show a disregard of its rural inhabitants' lives as unfeeling as that of any killer.

Folk horror conforms to none of these aesthetic types. Its earthen colours give a relatively realist depiction of the British countryside and its arable land, which is already parcelled and cultivated by the farming community. Paul Newland has likened this to landscape painting, arguing that *Blood on Satan's Claw* displays 'a distinctly painterly view of the rural landscape. The camera is at ground level, at a slightly canted angle, looking up a hilly field. The spectator is thus placed in the earth' (Newland 2016: 166). Yet this placement differs from traditional features of landscape painting. As John Berger famously pointed out in his 1972 television documentary *Ways of Seeing*, landscape painting developed during the ascendancy of the land-owning bourgeoisie and it typically gives a feeling of mastery, a mastery that it thereby ascribes to nature rather than to appropriation. Landscape painting was a major contributor to the common association of the folk with peace and serenity. Its image of rurality was emphasised by Raymond Williams, who pointed to the urban–rural divide as 'one of the major forms in which we become conscious of a central part of our experience and of the crises of our society' (Williams 1973: 289). This imaginary offers an ideal of country life that makes its dirt and brutality invisible.

Haggard's crew dug trenches in the ground for *Blood on Satan's Claw*, in whose opening scene an eyeball is found staring back at a labourer in the newly ploughed soil. This scene is exemplary of how folk horror destabilises the spectator's gaze but without recourse to either the grandeur of the sublime nor the pleasantness of landscape painting. The land typically dominates the frame, placing the spectator lower down and so creating a sense not of mastery but of servility. Its nature is that of twigs, moist grass and drizzle, not vertiginous mountains, ferocious animals or tempestuous storms. *Crow* (2016) features property developers who arrive at a farmstead in Wales planning to redevelop it; their arrival is intercut with close-ups of

Figure 0.3   The folk horror landscape in *In the Earth*, 2021

raindrops on leaves, millipedes and crows, small in stature but thus all the more pervasive because impossible to shut out. The view in folk horror is thus unbalanced by a nature that is neither immense nor controllable.

Newland notes that the farmland in *Blood on Satan's Claw* is surrounded by woods, and this setting indicates the proximity of settlement to wildness. Typically, folk horror features the woods as a common point of demarcation with the uncultivated, or if not the woods then the sealine. This setting indicates the power of nature but without recourse to the sublime of mountain gorges or river rapids such as the Carpathian Mountains of *Nosferatu*'s (1922) gothic expressionism. Folk horror thus offers a limited yet not fully tamed nature, and it is this tension that is played out in the final ritual performances that mark the climax of folk horror films.

The final ritual is the most recurrent of all the genre's special traits, as Lyndsay Townsend discusses in relation to the use of drums in Chapter 10. The final ritual typically takes place a short walk beyond the cultivated settlement, at the woods or shore, setting the stage for the close relationship of civilisation to nature. It occurs as night falls, thus drawing attention to the natural cycle of the day and allowing a creative use of fire – most grandiosely in *The Wicker Man*, but included in the proliferation in the genre of bonfires, torches and the like. Fire encapsulates the harnessing of natural energies crucial to the emergence of human settlement, but its potential is towards a consuming rage. Makeshift ritual objects indicate peasant handicraft rather than the institutionalised professionalism behind official iconography. Masks are a crucial generic element in the final ritual, always featuring natural material covering the heads and often the faces of the participants. In *Dogged* (2017) it is an outsized dog's head, in *Blood on Satan's Claw* a crown of twigs in blossom and in *Kill List* wicker masks, while *The Wicker Man* combines both animal heads and wicker. These masks subsume individuality and humanity itself within a oneness with nature, a oneness that is, in the context of sacrifice, horrific.[5]

Ritual performance brings folk horror to a climax that recalls the Britain that lies beneath the triumph of science and technology, work discipline and the modern State, the British reserve and rules of civility. This prior world is one of peasant ribaldry, ancient festival and shamanic religion, and the celebration of harvest and fertility, as they come into conflict with the religious wars; puritanical control of behaviour; private ownership of nature; and the dictates of wage-labour that kill off that prior way of life with discipline, regulation and self-denial. The historical consciousness of folk horror is thus one of the continual violent erasure of free-living forms of existence: of pagan Britain overcome by the Roman invasion, of a rich variety of Celtic cultures overcome by Anglicising powers; of peasant communality overcome by the lordly class's enclosures of the land; of female-centred power overcome by witch trials; of heresy by orthodoxy; of life-affirming festivity by puritanical discipline; of organic existence by the rational detachment of technology. The only officially permissible zealotry that then remains is the special national glee with which regulations are enforced. This is not the bestial savagery that belongs to other forms of rural horror. It theatricalises the institution of rules at the heart of a violent past of national historical development, while expressing a terror of strong ideals and unofficial forms of authority as objects of fear that can only mean irrationality and fanaticism.

The structure of the book and the individual chapters

In the analysis above we have tried to show that folk horror invokes not only a 'geographical' but also a prominent 'archaeological' sense. What was hidden underneath is brought to light. What is dead and buried returns renewed. Its generic concern is with elements of the past that have been forgotten, or psychologically repressed as too disturbing to envisage. Other concerns are filtered through these, including social class and order, the relationship to the land, old religions, the unwritten and hidden parts of British history. Indeed, folk horror films are a crucible from which disturbing repressions from Britain's past might be reborn, with the sedimented layers of pagan, premodern, superstitious, feudal and Celtic pasts coming to the surface.

Such repressed elements remind us that 'Old Religion' dominates British folk horror films both literally and figuratively. Modernity thought it had vanquished much, but some things survived in remote outposts while others can be revived from the dead. This offers a profound and potential alternative way of questioning modernity and the path to the present, as well as the implied future. This anti-modern aspect is hardly necessarily positive but more often an outburst of atavism and recidivism, a reversion to type to challenge the collapsing paradigms of modern Britain. Narratives can often be about 'testing the community', and while some might assume that communities such as the islanders in *The Wicker Man*, *Doomwatch*, *Black Death* or *Apostle* represent alternative, outsider communities, perhaps they represent more clearly the community of Britain itself, its drawbacks and potentialities, and questions about its coherence and unity.

Accordingly, the first part of the collection stages a debate over the most canonical of all folk horror films, *The Wicker Man*. Recounting 'The Context of *The Wicker Man*', Ronald Hutton accounts for the three main sources that gave the film its subject: Ancient Roman accounts of the barbarian practices of Celtic Britain, James Frazer's nineteenth-century reimagination of those accounts in *The Golden Bough*, and the subsequent history of neo-Paganism that the film's makers sought both to critique and to bring to life. Laurel Zwissler takes an alternative perspective and asks what makes the film a source of celebration for Pagan communities in 'A Deeply Religious People: *The Wicker Man*, Contemporary Paganism, and *Dracula* Reversed', in a chapter that considers the canonical film in relation to horror studies and wider categories of race, gender and the rural. Mikel J. Koven then proposes 'Folk Horror: A Discursive Approach, with Application to Robin Hardy's *The Wicker Man* (1973) and Neil Jordan's *The Company of Wolves* (1984)', demonstrating how folk horror participates in the negotiation of the meaning of three key ideas – the pagan, the rural and folklore.

This debate acts as a prompt then to understanding folk horror as a return of the British repressed, a theme that structures the second part of the book. Asking who exactly are 'The Folk of Folk Horror', Derek Johnston discusses this question in relation to the horrific vision of popular rural life established by the famous 'trilogy' of *Witchfinder General*; *Blood on Satan's Claw* and; once more, *The Wicker Man*. The other chapters in this section move on to less canonical films. Dawn Keetley discusses the importance of sacrifice to folk horror in '*Doomwatch*: Sacrifice Zones and Folk Horror', focusing on a folk horror/sci-fi filmed in 1971 that, Keetley argues, features the 'sacrifice' of an entire coastal community to the forces of globalisation. Paul Newland's chapter, 'My Ancestors Died Here: *Requiem for a Village* and the Rural English Horror of Modernity and Socio-Cultural Change', develops similar concerns in relation to the tension in folk horror between the conservation – or perhaps conservatism – of the 'old ways' and the threat of a growing suburban consumer culture: a tension he sees played out in the genre's aesthetic choices. Moving from contemporary tensions to the past, K. J. Donnelly then considers folk horror's fascination with history's marginal or unwritten subjects in 'Outsider History, or Outside of History', through analysis of *The Lair of the White Worm* and *A Field in England*. Moving then geographically, Beth Carroll considers the Welsh setting of *Apostle* in 'Anglo Creep and Celtic Resistance in *Apostle*', arguing that the recurrent Celtic settings of folk horror displace the hegemonic position of Englishness in British identity. Amy Harris then discusses gender in *Following the Wicca Man* and *Maya*, examples of the recent increase in female-directed horror, in her chapter, 'Women's Folk Horror in Britain: History, Industry, Style'.

In a process similar to Marshall McLuhan's notion of 'Rearview Mirrorism', this examination of the British repressed suggests that perhaps in order to move forward Britain needs to come to terms with some spectral aspects of its past. And looking into it, this is a dark glass. While some areas of British culture address aspects of the Empire and slavery, perhaps the British folk horror film addresses characteristics more clearly and immediately close to home – and rooted in the island of Britain rather than 'overseas adventures': the industrial revolution, Old Religion and the persecution of Catholicism, a nation permanently divided in a number of significant ways but with the thinnest of membranes unifying it in denial of its fragmentation. But where does British folk horror stand on this? Not in a conservative or progressive position but somewhere more ambiguous. It offers no celebration of modernity, but nor does it straightforwardly offer a call to go back, unless at the cost of violence.

The collection thus finishes with a part that discusses such ambivalences in folk horror's cultural landscapes. Lyndsay Townsend's 'Ritualistic Rhythms: Exploring the Sensory Affect of Drums in British Folk Horror Cinema' explores the recurrent use of drumming first in *Kill List* and then more generally in the folk horror soundtrack: a marker of folk culture, drumming invokes group belonging, affective engagement and ultimately panic. Returning to debates over the rural, agricultural setting of folk horror in ' "Nature came before man": Human as Subject and Object within the Folk Horror Anti-Landscape', David Evans-Powell compares the representation of the landscape in *Blood on Satan's Claw* and two later folk horrors, *The Fallow Field* and *The Unkindness of Ravens*. Mark Goodall's 'Hieroglyphics: Arthur Machen on Screen' establishes the importance of the writer in providing a template for the predominant mood and atmosphere of the genre, which he discusses in relation to his own experience in making a folk horror film. Closing this part are then two complementary panoramas of folk horror in its broader culture, the first social and the second aesthetic. Andy Paciorek provides an overview of the wider history to which British folk horror belongs, with 'Albion Unearthed: Social, Political and Cultural Influences on British Folk Horror, Urban Wyrd and Backwoods Cinema'. Finally, Diane Rodgers concludes the collection with the crucial question ' "Isn't folk horror *all* horror?": A Wyrd Genre'. Rodgers argues for a much wider conception than our deliberately restrictive one in this introduction, focusing on aesthetic effect. She thus provides a different perspective on a number of issues also raised here, seeing 'wyrd' as the genre and folk horror as a mode, distinguished from classic horror through its particular incorporation of the eerie and the weird, and by extension the folkloric and the hauntological.

What we hope these chapters collectively show is that to analyse British folk horror as a genre is not simply to find a new way of celebrating the films, but to understand how they generate ideas that have a social and political effect. Indeed, the folk horror genre is about rediscovering or imagining possibilities and potentials whose traces have not yet entirely been erased by contemporary neoliberal culture and late-capitalist consumerism. Folk horror is thus not history, but on some level it is always about history, or rather about the present's relationship to the past, to what has not been remembered, what might have happened and what still might be. Discussing hauntological aspects of music, Mark Fisher noted: 'When the present has given up on the future, we must listen for the relics of the future in the unactivated potentials of the past' (2013: 63). Similarly, Michael Löwy comments on Walter Benjamin's celebrated 'Theses on the Philosophy of History' (1940) about how Benjamin understood nostalgia as 'a revolutionary method for the critique of the present' (2005: 2).

We can close, then, by remarking that the idea that Britain maintains an eerie relationship to its own past is not new. The Romans thought of Britain as 'the Isle of Ghosts': Plutarch's essay 'The Cessation of Oracles' tells of Demetrius of Tarsus's visit to Britain and stories of places that were only inhabited by the spirits of the dead; Procopius claimed that Britain was where the Franks ferried across their ghosts every night; the Ancient Greeks and Celts believed that isles of the dead existed to its west; and the Roman invasion started at the Isle of Thanet, named after *Thanatos* (Death) (Burn 1955: 258–60). But Britain is perhaps now more than ever thinking about its own past, and the films discussed in this book are part of this process. Recent decades in Britain have seen radical developments: exponentially increased population that is more mobile and diverse, the fragmentation of established communities, the destruction (and marginalisation) of the countryside, and a fitful attempt to make Britain regain international cultural power, but greatly diminished from its status at the end of the Second World War with its worldwide empire. These issues form the backdrop for the films under discussion in this book, but not as any simple 'reflection'. Films can offer the realisation that the past is a bad place rather than some fantastic wonderland. It was a Paul Klee painting that prompted Walter Benjamin to discuss the 'Angel of History' (1940), a being shocked and horrified at the past as literally a pile-up of atrocities. Folk horror acknowledges this more than most culture, and amplifies certain cultural characteristics that are more commonly attenuated. Svetlana Boym notes: 'There is a deep-seated fear of reflection on history and its blank spots, on the irreversibility of time, that challenges the dream of eternal youth and possibility of eternal recreation' (Boym 2001: 38). British folk horror films certainly posit a disturbed relationship with Britain's past, sometimes suggesting it remains alive in the present but hidden or marginalised. It is this hidden presence, in all its horror and its allure, that this collection hopes to bring to light once more.

Acknowledgement

With thanks to Silvia Angeli for her helpful comments.

Notes

1. Despite many co-productions with Britain, we exclude Irish folk horror. Not only would it be insensitive to lump it in with British horror, it would open a different debate, as Irish horror films can often include elements that relate directly or indirectly to Ireland's relationship to Britain and its past of colonial repression. Indeed, Irish folk horror deserves a volume of its own.
2. Except in passing to describe *Blood on Satan's Claw*; see Derek Johnston, this volume.
3. Of course it might be also be approached as two historical cycles of film: the first before and after, but clustered around, the 'Unholy Trinity', and the second the later 'Revival', which has brought the earlier concerns into a more cohesive, self-conscious sense of folk horror and a more stable film genre.
4. Indeed, a consequence of New Labour's 'modernising' neoliberalism was the creation of an underclass of those left behind by what it deemed progress, at turns ignored, vilified and subject to continuous admonition and sanction. See Jones (2011) for one discussion of this phenomenon, and Embery (2021: 9–12) for a very different take.
5. Alexandra Heller-Nicholas's *Masks in Horror Cinema* (2019) covers this topic, although without mentioning folk horror.

References

Altman, Rick (1987), *The American Film Musical*. Bloomington: Indiana University Press.
Boym, Svetlana (2001), *The Future of Nostalgia*. New York: Basic Books.
Burn, A. R. (1955), 'Procopius and the Island of Ghosts', *English Historical Review* 70:275 (April), 258–261.
Clover, Carol (1992), *Men, Women and Chain Saws: Gender in the Modern Horror Film*. Princeton: Princeton University Press.
Cowdell, Paul (2019), '"Practicing Witchcraft Myself during the Filming": Folk Horror, Folklore, and the Folkloresque', *Western Folklore* 78:4, 295–326.
Dyer, Richard (2000), 'Kill and Kill Again', in José Arroyo (ed.), *Action/Spectacle Cinema*. London: BFI, pp. 145–150.
Embery, Paul (2021), *Despised: Why the Modern Left Loathes the Working Class*. Cambridge: Polity Press.
Evans-Powell, David (2021), *The Blood on Satan's Claw*. Liverpool: Liverpool University Press.
Fisher, Mark (2013), 'The Metaphysics of Crackle: Afrofuturism and Hauntology', *Dancecult: Journal of Electronic Dance Music Culture* 5:2, 42–55.
Frazer, James George (1922 [1890]), *The Golden Bough*. New York: Macmillan.
Harmes, Marcus K. (2013), 'The Seventeenth Century on Film: Patriarchy, Magistracy, and Witchcraft in British Horror Films 1968–1971', *Canadian Journal of Film Studies* 22:2 (Autumn), 64–80.

Heller-Nicholas, Alexandra (2019), *Masks in Horror Cinema: Eyes without Faces*. Cardiff: University of Wales Press.
Hunt, Leon (2001), 'Necromancy in the UK: Witchcraft and the Occult in British Horror', in Steve Chibnall and Julian Petley (eds), *British Horror Cinema*. London: Routledge, pp. 82–98.
Hutchings, Peter (2004), 'Uncanny Landscapes in British Film and Television', *Visual Culture in Britain* 5:2 (Winter), 27–40.
Jones, Owen (2011), *Chavs: The Demonisation of the Working Class*. London: Verso.
Keetley, Dawn (2020), 'Introduction: Defining Folk Horror', *Revenant* 5 (March), 1–32.
Koven, Mikel J. (2007), 'The Folklore Fallacy: A Folkloristic/Filmic Perspective on *The Wicker Man*', *Fabula* 48:3–4, 270–280.
Koven, Mikel J. (2008), *Film, Folklore and Urban Legends*. Lanham, MD: Scarecrow.
Löwy, Michael (2005), *Fire Alarm: Reading Walter Benjamin's 'On the Concept of History'*. London: Verso.
Marx, Enid (1946), *English Popular and Traditional Art*. London: Collins.
Murray, Margaret (1962 [1921]), *The Witch-Cult in Western Europe*. Oxford: Clarendon Press.
Nairn, Tom (1981 [1977]). *The Break-Up of Britain: Crisis and Neo-Nationalism*, 2nd edn. London: Verso.
Neale, Steve (2021), 'Questions of Genre', in Frank Krutnik and Richard Maltby (eds), *Film, Cinema, Genre: The Steve Neale Reader*. Exeter: University of Exeter Press, pp. 67–84.
Newland, Paul (2008), 'Folksploitation: Charting the Horrors of the British Folk Music Tradition in *The Wicker Man* (Robin Hardy, 1973)', in Robert Shail (ed.), *British Cinema in the 1970s*. London: British Film Institute, pp. 119–38.
Newland, Paul (2016), 'Folk Horror and the Contemporary Cult of British Rural Landscape: The Case of *Blood on Satan's Claw*', in Paul Newland (ed.), *British Rural Landscapes on Film*. Manchester: Manchester University Press, pp. 162–79.
Paciorek, Andy (2015). 'From the Forests, Fields and Furrows: An Introduction', *Spectral Times* 12, available at *Folk Horror Revival* website, folkhorrorrevival.com/about/from-the-forests-fields-and-furrows-an-introduction-by-andy-paciorek/ (accessed 22 April 2023).
Pinedo, Isobel (1997), *Recreational Terror: Women and the Pleasures of Horror Film Viewing*. Albany: State University of New York Press.
Pirie, David (1973), *A Heritage of Horror: The English Gothic Cinema 1946–1972*. London: Gordon Fraser.
Schatz, Thomas (2011). 'Film Genre and the Hollywood Film', from *Hollywood Genres*, in Timothy Corrigan, Patricia White and Meta Mazaj (eds), *Critical Visions in Film Theory: Classic and Contemporary Readings*. Boston, MA: Bedford/St. Martin's Press, pp. 453–465.
Scovell, Adam (2017), *Folk Horror: Hours Dreadful and Things Strange*. Leighton Buzzard: Auteur.
Thomas, Keith (1971), *Religion and the Decline of Magic: Studies in Popular Beliefs in Sixteenth and Seventeenth Century England*. London: Weidenfeld & Nicolson.
Thompson, E. P. (1963), *The Making of the English Working Class*. London: Victor Gollancz.
Thurgill, James (2020), 'A Fear of the Folk: On *Topophobia* and the Horror of Rural Landscapes', *Revenant* 5 (March), 33–56.
Williams, Raymond (1973), *The Country and the City*. London: Chatto and Windus.

Part I

Debating *The Wicker Man*

1

The context of *The Wicker Man*

Ronald Hutton

Introduction

Many people fond of the folk horror genre, if asked to name a single classic film that typifies it, would probably choose the one released by British Lion in 1973, directed by Robin Hardy, and entitled *The Wicker Man*. It has, indeed, been called Britain's best horror movie.[1] To date, it has been the subject of two remakes, a number of television documentaries, and a popular book on its making and its cinematic and critical fortunes.[2] There have been scholarly studies of it as a work of cinema, and of the folkloric and religious elements in it (Murray 2005; Franks *et al.* 2006; Jones 2012). There is therefore no doubt that by the present day it is a 'cult movie', and movies attract cults both because they come to represent special things to those who watch and enjoy them, and because they embody important cultural images, ideas and assumptions, which existed before them. The preoccupation of the present essay is with the pre-existing cultural context to the work, and it will be suggested that there are three aspects of this that really matter: an image, a book and a genre. These will be treated one after the other.

First, however, it may be necessary to provide a brief summary of the plot. This commences with a fervently and bigotedly Christian Scottish policeman, with absolute devotion to his duty as well as to his religion, being called to an isolated island to investigate a report of a missing girl there. The island concerned is privately owned, by its resident aristocrat, and is traditionally prosperous because of the produce of its orchards. Strangers are not permitted, and the interloper, having forced his way onto it by virtue of this office, is amazed and appalled to find that its inhabitants all practise a revived pagan fertility religion. This venerates ancient deities of the land, sea and sun, and embodies a joyous celebration of sexuality. The unfortunate officer spends an uncomfortable few days and nights there, in which the sympathies of the viewer are generally tilted towards the hedonistic inhabitants. The mood veers towards comedy, though with hints of darker undertones. These become suddenly and shockingly dominant at the end, when the villagers celebrate the festival of May Day and the policeman realises that he has been lured to the island to serve as a human sacrifice. The film closes with his burning alive (along with farm animals) in a huge wickerwork effigy of a human being.

The image

That giant figure is the image that dominates the climax to the film, and so the whole work, to which it gives its name; and it indeed predates the other factors identified for consideration – the book and the genre – by around 2,000 years. It first appears in a work mostly written by the most famous Roman of all time, Julius Caesar, in the 50s and 40s BCE. Caesar's greatest military accomplishment, as far as he and his fellow Romans were concerned, was to conquer Gaul, the region of Celtic-speaking peoples that today is occupied by France, Belgium and Germany west of the Rhine. The work concerned is his narrative of the wars in which he made that conquest, and is one of the most celebrated books to survive from the ancient world. The section that concerns us here is a standalone one that interrupts the accounts of campaigning to describe the social customs of the people of Gaul (Julius Caesar, *De bello gallico*, VI.13–18). Its best-known bit, for modern readers, is his description of the Gallic priesthood, the druids. It portrays these as powerful, learned, highly trained and grouped in a cohesive order that transcended tribal divisions, but also as leaders of a brutal religion that included human sacrifice. If this descriptive section really is by Caesar, then it is the only account of them left by somebody who would actually have encountered them at first hand, in the society to which they belonged. Note, however, the caveat – if it really is by Caesar – because for centuries scholars have commented that it is a rather odd insertion, bearing no relationship to what precedes and follows, and indeed in some respects seeming to make a bad match with it.[3] For example, the descriptive section emphasises the central importance of the druids to Gallic society and politics, and their dominant influence over those; and yet in the detailed descriptions of the fighting, which are certainly by Caesar, as they track his thoughts and actions stage by stage, they are completely invisible. This is startling, because the druids described in that section should, on the contrary, have been prominent in exactly the kind of emergency created for their peoples by the Roman invasion.

It may therefore have been added by somebody else, who thought that some kind of panoramic view of Gallic society before the Roman conquest was needed to complete the book. We have one such possible candidate in

Aulus Hirtius, another Roman politician who is known to have completed Caesar's book after the latter's assassination. If so, we have no idea how good the information was with which that unknown person was working. Moreover, even if the section concerned was by Caesar, he may well have misrepresented the druids for his own purposes, to make them more powerful, important, well organised, menacing and barbaric than they actually were. To do this would greatly enhance the significance of his conquest of their territory, and its moral justification: by this time human sacrifice had become a practice held in especial abhorrence by the Romans, and functioned for them as a litmus test for savagery. Caesar was an extraordinarily brilliant, ruthless and unscrupulous politician, and was regarded as untrustworthy at the time: a Roman historian, Gaius Asinius Pollio, commented that he 'was too quick to believe others' accounts of their actions and give a false account of his own actions, either on purpose or through forgetfulness'.[4] Modern historians have accordingly become wary of taking his representations of people and events on face value.[5] All this needs to be borne in mind when considering the precise passage in the section on the druids in his book that concerns us here. It described how, in times of great danger from disease or attack, they would offer mass human sacrifices, by packing victims into colossal figures made from woven twigs, and setting them on fire. He added that the people selected to die like this were supposed to be those convicted of serious crimes, but if not enough of those were available, innocent individuals were burned instead.

Some support was given to these statements by another writer, a Greek geographer called Strabo, who published between twenty and thirty years later, in the 20s BCE. For most of his life he seems to have been based in Asia Minor, never travelling any further west than Italy: so he would have had no first-hand experience of Gaul. When describing that region he declared that the druids put to death those convicted of heinous crimes as human sacrifices, and thought that the more of these that were offered, the better the harvest would be. He then listed a number of lurid methods used to kill the victims, one being to pack them into an enormous figure of straw and wood, with cattle and other animals, and set fire to it. He went on to say that such evil customs had been abolished under Roman rule (Strabo, *Geographia*, IV.4.4–5). Strabo was inclined to sneer at the inhabitants of Gaul in general, as simple and silly people. In general he was a thorough and scrupulous scholar, but for regions of which he had no personal knowledge he naturally relied completely on others for information. These sources were overwhelmingly Greek, the Roman authors whom he consulted being both few and sometimes in bad copies; one of these was Caesar's book. When dealing with Gaul he made some serious mistakes of geography.[6] He was fond of naming his literary sources, but conspicuously failed to do so in his passages concerning the customs of the druids, emphasising only 'as we understand that they existed in former times' (Strabo, *Geographia*, IV.4.2). It therefore looks as if his sources here were based on gossip, and when describing the alleged druidic methods of human sacrifice he indeed distanced himself from them by using the construction 'it is said'.

So, we are left with two brief ancient reports, neither of which can be either trusted or dismissed, for lack of any means of verification, and one of which might possibly be a garbled version of the other. A rational response might be to declare the accuracy of both of them unknown and unknowable. For most of the succeeding two millennia, however, it was generally convenient to writers to accept them as literally true. The Romans, as said, made a suppression of the cruel practices of the druids into a key justification of their conquest of north-western Europe. Subsequently, Christians cited the same practices as good evidence for the barbarism and savagery of paganism, so making laudable the imposition of their own, new and better, kind of religion. Nineteenth-century authors added to these traditional reasons for credulity an admiration for progress, which tended to regard human societies as becoming more primitive and bloodthirsty the further back in time they went, and an imperial mission to expand colonial empires across much of the rest of the world, which produced an identification with the Romans as forerunners in a conquering and civilising mission. Really only one key development has happened in the matter over those 2,000 years, and that came in 1676 when an English lawyer called Aylett Sammes published a history of ancient Britain. A major selling point of this was its dramatic illustrations, and one of the most sensational was a highly imaginative reconstruction of one of the colossal figures mentioned by Caesar and Strabo (Sammes 1676: 105). This huge woven wicker image, with a male face, filled with writhing human bodies and with the fire being prepared to ignite it – a folk horror creation in its own right – immediately became iconic. It has passed down the centuries since, frequently as if it were an objectively accurate historical record. As will be shown, it was directly to inspire the film.

The book

One iconic figure, however, did not itself supply the package of motifs and customs associated with paganism in the film. That came out of the book mentioned above, which was one of the most influential works of scholarship in the entire twentieth century.[7] It was produced by a shy Scottish academic, a classics don at Cambridge in the late Victorian and the Edwardian period, called Sir James Frazer (1922).[8] He gave it the catchy name of *The*

Golden Bough, taken from an episode in the ancient Roman epic the *Aeneid*, by Virgil, in which the hero makes his way through the underworld with the aid of a magical branch of shining gold. Frazer's own golden bough, to light and guide his progress, was the power of human reason, helping him and his readers through primeval chaos and darkness. His hidden purpose was to discredit religion in general and Christianity in particular. Having been brought up a strict Scottish Presbyterian, he had a particular loathing for religious rituals, robes, ornaments and priesthoods, whether embodied by Roman Catholicism or by paganism. The central argument of his book was that ancient peoples had all believed in a dying and reviving god, representing the spirit of vegetation. Those peoples had accordingly shared a religious system intended to re-enact his death and resurrection, and so renew the fertility of crops. This god, Frazer went on to argue, was represented on earth by sacred kings, who were killed ceremonially when they had reigned for a set term or when their powers began to fail. His intention was to suggest that the figure of Christ had been an outgrowth from this body of mistaken and unnecessary religious belief; though when he did so, even with some hedging, in the second edition of the book, the outcry was such that he withdrew the explicit argument from the third edition. His own religion was science, and the spirit of rational enquiry. He wanted both religion and a belief in magic to wither away across the modern world, to be replaced by that spirit.

If he disliked Christianity, he was disgusted by ancient paganism, which he associated with ignorance and backwardness. He made his reconstructed universal archetype of it a medley of bloodshed, sex and sensual self-indulgence. That reconstruction was made by mixing together evidence from three different source groups. The first were the accounts of actual ancient pagan practices made by authors at the time, or soon after: above all Greek or Roman. The second consisted of those recorded among tribal peoples in the modern world, by European travellers, missionaries and conquerors. He believed that these so-called primitives had retained customs that had been universal in ancient times. His third source comprised accounts of folk rites and beliefs recorded in modern Europe among the common people, especially rural people. With the disdain of an urban intellectual, Frazer regarded these as exemplars of backwardness comparable to the tribes of Africa, South Asia and the Pacific. He expressed the view that the European working classes, including the British, remained barbarians and savages at heart, even if their social superiors had given them an appearance of civilisation. In the process, he provided readers with a huge catalogue of rituals and customs that were frequently colourful to the point of being lurid. They included human sacrifice, sacred prostitution, ritual nudity and festive orgies. The joke in all this, unappreciated by almost all of his readers, and probably not realised by Sir James himself, was that Frazer was personally one of the most chaste, retiring and innocent of men: a classic introvert, recluse and bookworm. The knock-on irony is that whereas he expected his readers to be appalled and repelled by the paganism he portrayed as a religion of sex and violence, many were entertained, titillated and excited. Some found in his descriptions, in varying proportions, a prurient, a sensuous and a romantic pleasure.

Frazer became the most heavily decorated anthropologist of all time, and his book the world's most famous work of anthropology. This was because he was the leading scholar to apply to the history of religion two of the great new intellectual resources of the nineteenth century: the theory of evolution, and the unprecedented amount of detailed information about beliefs and customs among the European populace and among peoples in other parts of the world made available by the new movement of folklore collection and the expansion of European trade and colonies. Nobody before him had ever studied religion, as he did, by comparing data from all over the world, and from all of history, on such a scale.[9] Even before his death, however, classicists, historians and anthropologists were starting to reject his ideas, and after it he became one of the most reviled and discredited of scholars among his fellow academics. This was because they had discarded two of the foundations of his methodology. The first was his assumption that human beliefs evolved in the same way all over the world, without the need for cultural contacts. The second was his belief that rural Europeans mindlessly acted out the same ancient customs century after century. More recent scholarship also values three tactics that he almost completely disregarded: to check the reliability of sources, to avoid wildly speculative interpretations and to put material in its own proper context. By contrast, Frazer accepted at face value the most outrageous of travellers' tales, myths and legends, and accusations made by ancient and tribal peoples against their enemies. He interpreted innocent folk and indigenous customs as relics of brutal and lascivious ancient rites, and he contemptuously dismissed explanations put forward by people for their own beliefs and customs if they did not accord with his theories.[10] As a result, he made out primeval religion to be a great deal more brutal and lascivious, and preoccupied with fertility, than it actually was.

In that sense, and in some other respects, *The Golden Bough* is a work of creative literature as well as of scholarship, and as such has been immensely influential. In the early twentieth century explicitly creative writers who were notably affected by its ideas included William Butler Yeats, D. H. Lawrence, T. S. Eliot, Ezra Pound, Edith Sitwell, E. M. Forster, James Joyce, John Synge, John Buchan, Joseph Conrad and Wyndham Lewis.[11] In the late twentieth century it made its impact on Dan Brown's best-selling novel *The Da Vinci Code*, and it was long a major source for authors of works of popular history that have themselves shaped the popular imagination. These included Robert Graves in his own imaginative reconstruction of ancient religion, *The White Goddess*, and Margaret Murray in her creation of the argument that the people executed as witches in early modern Europe were practitioners of a surviving Frazerian fertility religion.[12] Murray may in fact be awarded the prize for the most extraordinary non-fiction book ever directly inspired by Frazer, *The Divine King in England*, published in 1954, which argued that a whole string of English kings and politicians, from William Rufus to the Elizabethan Earl of Essex, had been human sacrifices according to Frazer's model of sacred monarchy. In view of all this it is not surprising that when the script-writer of *The Wicker Man* wanted to find out about paganism he simply went to *The Golden Bough*, and took from it practically the whole portrait of paganism that the film provides.[13]

The genre

So now we have the motif and the source-base that underpin the screenplay. These could, however, only have been used to fill in a particular storyline because a genre of that kind of story was already around, and popular. By 1973 it had in fact been around for over seventy years. It was one spin-off from increasing anxiety about the progressive loss of power by Christianity in the modern world, as more and more people embraced atheism or agnosticism, or alternative forms of religion and spirituality, including paganism. Interest in a revival of paganism had been growing in the nineteenth century, especially among avant-garde writers and artists, who saw in the religions of the admired classical civilisations of ancient Greece and Rome a love of nature and beauty, and an affirmation of life, pleasure and self-expression, that they missed in Christianity. Not only Christians, however, but many of their opponents among rationalists and atheists, could be uneasy about such a project. To the latter sort of person, Christianity, though erroneous, was still familiar and embedded in the parent society, and inculcated a responsible social and moral ethics, whereas paganism (especially as represented by writers such as Frazer) could be associated with superstition, savagery and immorality. It was in the 1890s that the term 'neo-Pagan' was coined for people who proposed a revival of selected aspects of ancient paganism, and a new genre of storytelling swiftly developed to discredit them. It did not depend on an argument that Christianity was literally true or wholly good, but on one that it acted as a bulwark to defend society against things that were even worse.[14]

These were portrayed as the two belief systems against which Christianity had traditionally defined itself: Satanism and paganism. The theme of concealed groups of Satanists operating secretly within modern society, doing atrocious and disgusting things and thriving on the ignorance and disbelief of most people, was one aspect of the new genre. It featured in novels and films in English all through the twentieth century, the most celebrated of the former being those of Dennis Wheatley, and the most commercially successful of the latter being *Rosemary's Baby* (1968) and *The Omen* (1976). Paganism was made to play a similar role. The classic plotline in which it did (and does) so always took (and takes) two alternative forms. One is that of an outsider visiting or coming to live in a rural community, only to discover that its inhabitants are secretly pagans. Either they have always remained that way, through the centuries of Christian dominance of their nations, or else they have revived paganism in the modern period. The other form is that of somebody who discovers an ancient pagan shrine or ritual and decides to reactivate it, either because of romantic personal inclination or because it takes them over and possesses them. The basic point behind both plotlines is that, whichever one is preferred, things almost always end in tears. Paganism usually turns out to be a malign force that makes the people who embrace it do dreadful things, or destroys them, or both.

The first notable appearance of the theme of the concealed pagan community seems to have been in 1895, with a short story by the Anglican Christian Arthur Machen, entitled 'The Novel of the Black Seal'.[15] This featured the Little People, the degenerate descendants of pre-Celtic races, who dwell underground in remote countryside and creep forth in search of virgins to sacrifice in their pagan rituals. Thereafter the storyline was more usually that of somebody who settles in a contemporary, outwardly normal, rural community, only to realise that the ancient paganism is still persisting there in secret. A trickle of such works over the succeeding seven decades produced two literary best-sellers. The first of these was *Witch Wood*, published in 1927 by the celebrated novelist and politician John Buchan, who remained a lifelong devout Scottish Presbyterian.[16] It features a heroic young minister of that faith, who comes to serve a parish in Scotland's Southern Uplands in the 1640s, only to realise that most of its inhabitants still secretly adhere to a depraved and disgusting native religion centred on a Romano-British altar. He is unable to convince the authorities of its existence – which is a standard feature of the genre – or to win over most of his parishioners, but does manage to destroy the high priest of the cult, aided by what could plausibly, in the context, be interpreted as a benevolent divine power accessed through his identity as a Christian.

The second of the best-selling novels was Norah Lofts's *The Devil's Own* (1960), set in a modern Essex village where the 'old ways' are secretly still carried on by most of the inhabitants. These turn out to centre on a religion celebrating ancient festivals with sexual orgies, naked dancing and gluttonous feasts, led by a high priestess; and it seems, moreover, to equip its devotees with genuine and malevolent magical powers. It is detected and opposed by a newcomer, an obsessive celibate spinster who, though once again given no support by official authority and no effectual help within the village, manages to wreck it and bring about the death of the priestess.[17] Seven years after Lofts's success, a minor author called David Pinner published a proportionately minor contribution to the genre, a novel entitled *Ritual*, concerning a London policeman sent to investigate the mysterious death in a Cornish village of a teenage girl, who (of course) uncovers a secret pagan sect surviving there.[18] So far, so usual, except that this book eventually came into the hands of a successful playwright and screenwriter called Anthony Shaffer, who decided to convert it into a film. In 1971 he recruited two friends for the project, the actor Christopher Lee, who wanted to break out of his standard role as Dracula in the Hammer horror movies, and Peter Snell, a Canadian who was about to become the managing director of British Lion Productions. When Shaffer started the job, however, he realised that Pinner's story was not good enough and resolved to write one of his own. He was looking for ideas when he leafed through a book on ancient paganism and came across Aylett Sammes's famous picture of the druid sacrifice in a wicker image. At that moment his plotline suddenly fell into place, and only *The Golden Bough* was needed to flesh out (so to speak) the details of the revived pagan religion that it concerned.[19]

Conclusion

If this, then, is the context of the film, it is worth considering in conclusion what it has done to augment that context, and the genre to which it belongs, and how that in turn explains its subsequent (eventual) success and transformation into a classic. Shaffer's script in fact made a number of key innovations in the long-established theme of the concealed pagan community in modern Britain that gave it a new freshness and power. First, it eliminated the supernatural element. Most of the previous treatments of the theme had suggested a genuine spiritual power, malevolent and sometimes overtly demonic, to lie behind the pagan activities. This story was purely a human one. Second, although the island that is the setting is a secret pagan community in the sense that it exists in a private domain closed to visitors, and so is not known to the outside world, it is also a fully functioning society. Instead of the pagans operating hidden within an outwardly normal village or valley, they comprise the entire population of islanders. Their paganism is public, overt and official, and informs every aspect of communal life and identity. Third, and most important, the usual sympathies of the genre of the discovery of paganism by an outsider in a modern British rural community are reversed for most of the story. Not only is there no taint of Satanism to the beliefs and customs of the pagans, but there is none of witchcraft either. Instead they embody a life-affirming, nature-loving, sex-celebrating counterculture that has constructed a harmonious, cohesive, efficient and successful community. In many ways their values are those of the hippies of the period in which the film was made, and the intrusive stranger who discovers the local paganism is not, for most of the film, a sympathetic character. He is, on the contrary, a bigoted, authoritarian, repressed and repressive figure with poor personal skills and an utter lack of charm. There are, however, enough hints that all is not well beneath the surface of island life to prevent a total rejection of him and his viewpoint; and this is of course dramatically confirmed in the final plot twist – his burning alive as a sacrifice – which comes as a genuine shock to most first-time viewers.

This radically reverses the sympathies of the audience, by seeming to show that even the relatively wholesome and benign paganism on display hitherto has the potential to turn superstitious, violent and bloodthirsty. The occasion for the luring of the policeman to the island turns out to be the sudden and unprecedented failure of the place's famous fertility, placing its whole economy, and so its future as a community, in jeopardy. In the storyline, the fertility-related pagan religion concerned had been reintroduced to the island by the present lord's Victorian ancestor, a rationalist, as a way of getting the populace to accept farming methods that would revolutionise traditional practices and maximise yield. Two generations on, however, the religion concerned has won the complete adherence of the community at all levels, and precludes a rational solution to a natural problem, propelling the inhabitants into ritual murder instead. The film therefore ultimately reverts to the norms of its genre, by representing paganism as dangerous in a way that either Christianity or modern scientific scepticism are not. Nonetheless, it retains popularity among very different audiences, and its initial ascent to celebrity was the result of its success in America, equally and simultaneously, with both irreverent college students and devout Christians from the Bible Belt. To the former the hedonistic islanders seemed very attractive for most of the story, and some remained too alienated by the policeman to be greatly upset by his dreadful end. To the latter, it was a moving tale of Christian fidelity, piety and martyrdom, and a further reminder of the essential iniquity of the older religion.

It is hard, indeed, to escape a sense that the film's ultimate message is a wholly conventional and traditional one for mainstream western culture since the Victorian period, and one inimical to a multi-faith, multicultural society. To most viewers, Christian, post-Christian or rationalist, it does seem to carry a warning that paganism cannot be tolerated or trusted: however nice it may seem, once revived, it has a lethal potential. To those still personally Christian or emerging from Christian backgrounds, this warning is a reassurance that the religion of Christ is a superior one, and has rendered a service to humanity in general by suppressing that which had preceded it. To agnostics and atheists, the message of the film could be read as being that all religions are social constructs, with no objective reality behind any of them, but that some are socially and morally healthier than others. Moreover, the work even has a notable following among modern Pagans, who – even more than the American college students – relish the general affirmation that most of the film seems to provide of their values, and treat the ending either as a joke or as a price worth paying for the rest of the message.[20] The finished result therefore plays with equal success to a considerable range of audiences. One of the marks of a great story is that it can carry different messages for different people, and that is clearly the case with this one. To a large extent, it allows viewers to think for themselves.

In closure, it may be worth asking who benefited from the film, of those who originally created it. Its long progress to popularity, which spanned about a decade, meant that it gave virtually no uplift to the careers of any of the cast or people involved in its production. Both the screenwriter, Anthony Shaffer, and the director, Robin Hardy, tried hard to cash in on its subsequent fame, Hardy more ardently because his work in directing had completely failed thereafter. The main effect of this, however, was to produce a lasting quarrel between them as each tried to take more credit.[21] Instead, the real beneficiaries, in the long term, have been the people of the region of south-west Scotland, Galloway, in which the filming took place in late 1972, and especially those of the tiny seaport of Creetown. This is a place so obscure that even in the long and exciting history of the region in general nothing else ever seems to have happened there. As a result, nothing much has changed since 1972 either, and it has become the centre of a lively and lucrative tourist trade based on fans of the film. In particular the Ellangowan Hotel, which supplied the interior scenes supposed to be in the island's Green Man Inn, is a focus for them. This seems appropriate. So much of the genre of the secret and sinister pagan cult discovered by a sophisticated newcomer among modern rural people has been based on an urban and bourgeois fear and contempt for country folk. It is arguably a good thing, therefore, that the genre has at last given something back to at least some of them.

Notes

1. By the critic in *Empire* magazine.
2. The remakes were an American version with the same title and similar plot starring Nicolas Cage, which seems generally to be regarded as a comparative failure, and a transplantation of the theme into a different setting and story, entitled *The Wicker Tree*, which seems generally to be regarded as a brave try but still inferior to the original. There seem to have been three documentaries by different companies, in one of which I took part myself. The book is Allan Brown, *Inside* The Wicker Man: *How Not to Make a Cult Classic* (2013).
3. This was first pointed out by Fustel de Coulanges (1891: 3).
4. Quoted by the later Roman historian Suetonius, in his *Julius Caesar*, LVI.4.
5. For one analysis of his stylistic tricks see Braund (1995: 41–66). It is summed up in the sentence (on p. 49) that 'any understanding of Caesar's campaigns in Gaul and Britain requires not so much an appreciation of his military strategies as an awareness of his literary strategies'.
6. For example, he places Aquitane in the centre of the country.
7. Strictly speaking it was four different books, because Frazer constantly brought out new versions with more research and slightly different ideas in them. First came a two-volume edition in 1890, then a three-volume one in 1900, and then a twelve-volume one between 1911 and 1915. Finally, in 1922, he published a condensed version of the third edition, in one volume, with Macmillan; this is the one that the general public has known ever since and is still in print.
8. There is a splendid biography of him by Robert Ackerman, *J. G. Frazer* (1987), which also charts the changing scholarly context and reception of his work. For this see also Leach (1961); Downie (1970); Fontenrose (1971); Fraser (1990a); and Beard (1992).
9. He did get some things right: his comparative method, more carefully enacted, still has merit, and his classification of magic, worldwide, into sympathetic and contagious kinds also stands up. His book remains a useful compendium of human belief and custom, much of which is accurately recorded.
10. For example, he explained the two-headed image of the Roman god Janus by imposing on it an explanation given by former black slaves in Surinam for their own two-headed god, dismissing that provided by the Romans themselves as 'tedious and unsatisfactory' without even citing it (Frazer 1922: 166–167).
11. For this see Block (1952); Vickery (1973); and Fraser (1990b).
12. *The White Goddess* was published in London by Faber (Graves, 1948). Murray's books on witchcraft were *The Witch-Cult in Western Europe* (Oxford: Oxford University Press, 1921); *The God of the Witches* (London: Sampson Low, 1933); and *The Divine King in England* (London: Faber, 1954).
13. This was a conclusion of three of the essays in the collection edited by Benjamin Franks *et al.* (2006), *The Quest for 'The Wicker Man'*: Richard Sermon (2006), '*The Wicker Man*, May Day and the Invention of Beltane' (pp.26–43); Luc Ricaut (2006), 'Sacrifice, Society and Religion in *The Wicker Man*' (pp. 56–69); and Mickel J. Koven (2006), 'The Folklore Fallacy' (pp. 83–97).

14 For the development of these opposed modes of thought in the nineteenth century see Hutton (2019: 5–53).
15 Published by John Lane in a collection called *The Three Imposters* (Machen 1895).
16 It was issued in London by Hodder and Stoughton (Buchan, 1927).
17 Lofts published the book under the pseudonym of Peter Curtis, with Macdonald. It was then republished by Pan in 1966 as *The Witches*, and subsequently filmed under that title (Lofts 1960). Of the lesser works in the genre that appeared between these two stand-out examples, perhaps the most striking was L. T. C. Rolt's short story 'Cwm Garon' (1947), published in his collection *Sleep No More*. It involves the discovery by its earnest English hero of a remote Welsh valley where the inhabitants have forsaken Christianity to worship a pagan horned god who is actually a demonic force of evil, with nude rites. Conversely, in 1927 (and in London, with Putname), Lord Dunsany brought out a novel entitled *The Blessing of Pan* (Dunsany 1927), which very cleverly sent up the whole genre of a pagan revival in a modern rural British community. It has the Greek god leave his pipes on the edge of a very dull and conventional Cotswold village, where they are picked up and played by one of its children. At once the magic and allure of the pagan past begins to return, slowly seducing the villagers and returning them to the old religion. The vicar is finally left abandoned in the parish church, from which he senses that all power has departed, and decides to bear solitary witness for his faith by interrupting and denouncing the restored pagan rites now being carried out at some standing stones in the locality. He is prepared to die a martyr at the hands of the worshippers, and the reader is prepared for tragedy according to the traditions of the trope. Instead the music seizes him too, and he becomes the priest leading the rites. The community subsequently settles down happily and self-sufficiently in its revived religion. Dunsany, alas, had no imitators.
18 It was republished in London by FindersKeepers (Pinner 2011 [1967]); I have yet to locate an original edition.
19 This sequence of events is assembled in Brown (2013: 3–17). I have confirmed the details in conversations with Peter Snell.
20 It is certainly a popular feature at Pagan conferences and a topic of talks given there.
21 This is one of the themes of Brown (2013).

References

Ackerman, Robert (1987), *J. G. Frazer*. Cambridge: Cambridge University Press.
Beard, Mary (1992), 'Frazer, Leach and Virgil', *Comparative Studies in Society and History* 34, 203–224.
Block, Haskell M. (1952), 'Cultural Anthropology and Contemporary Literary Criticism', *Journal of Aesthetics and Art Criticism* 11, 46–54.
Braund, David (1995), *Ruling Roman Britain*. London: Routledge.
Brown, Allan (2013), *Inside 'The Wicker Man': How Not to Make a Cult Classic*. Edinburgh: Polygon.

Buchan, John (1927), *Witch Wood*. London: Hodder and Stoughton.
De Coulanges, Fustel (1891), *La Gaule romaine*, Paris.
Downie, R. Angus (1970), *Frazer and 'The Golden Bough'*. London: Gollancz.
Dunsany, Lord (1927), *The Blessing of Pan*. London: Putname.
Fontenrose, Joseph (1971), *The Ritual Theory of Myth*. Berkeley: University of California Press.
Franks, Benjamin, Stephen Harper, Jonathan Murray and Lesley Stevenson (eds) (2006), *The Quest for 'The Wicker Man': History, Folklore and Pagan Perspectives*. Edinburgh: Luam.
Fraser, Robert (1990a), *The Making of 'The Golden Bough'*. Basingstoke: Macmillan.
Fraser, Robert (ed.) (1990b), *Sir James Frazer and the Literary Imagination*. Basingstoke: Macmillan.
Frazer, James (1922), *The Golden Bough*. New York: Macmillan.
Graves, Robert (1948), *The White Goddess*. London: Faber.
Hutton, Ronald (2019), *The Triumph of the Moon: A History of Modern Pagan Witchcraft*. Oxford: Oxford University Press.
Jones, Leslie Ellen (2012), 'The Folklore of *The Wicker Man*', *The Pomegranate* 13, 38–47.
Koven, Mickel J. (2006), 'The Folklore Fallacy', in Benjamin Franks, Stephen Harper, Jonathan Murray and Lesley Stevenson (eds), *The Quest for 'The Wicker Man': History, Folklore and Pagan Perspectives*. Edinburgh: Luam, pp. 83–97.
Leach, Edmund R. (1961), 'Golden Bough or Gilded Twig?', *Daedalus* (Spring), 371–389.
Lofts, Norah (1960), *The Devil's Own*. London: MacDonald.
Machen, Arthur (1895), 'The Novel of the Black Seal', in *The Three Impostors; or, The Transmutations*. London: The Bodley Head.
Murray, Jonathan (ed.) (2005), *Constructing 'The Wicker Man': Film and Cultural Studies Perspectives*. Glasgow: University of Glasgow Press.
Murray, Margaret (1921), *The Witch-Cult in Western Europe*. Oxford: Oxford University Press.
Murray, Margaret (1933), *The God of the Witches*. London: Sampson Low.
Murray, Margaret (1954), *The Divine King in England*. London: Faber.
Pinner, David (2011 [1967]), *Ritual*. London: FindersKeepers.
Ricaut, Luc (2006), 'Sacrifice, Society and Religion in *The Wicker Man*', in Benjamin Franks, Stephen Harper, Jonathan Murray and Lesley Stevenson (eds), *The Quest for 'The Wicker Man': History, Folklore and Pagan Perspectives*. Edinburgh: Luam, pp. 56–69.
Rolt, L. T. C. (1947), 'Cwm Garon', in *Sleep No More*. London: Constable.
Sammes, Aylett (1676), *Britannia antique illustrata*. London.
Sermon, Richard (2006), '*The Wicker Man*, May Day and the Invention of Beltane', in Benjamin Franks, Stephen Harper, Jonathan Murray and Lesley Stevenson (eds), *The Quest for 'The Wicker Man': History, Folklore and Pagan Perspectives*. Edinburgh: Luam, pp. 26–43.
Vickery, John B. (1973), *The Literary Impact of 'The Golden Bough'*. Princeton: Princeton University Press.

2

A deeply religious people: *The Wicker Man*, contemporary Paganism and Dracula reversed

Laurel Zwissler

Introduction

The Wicker Man (2001 [1973]), while hailed as a third of the 'unholy trinity' of folk horror, nonetheless fits uneasily within the horror genre more broadly.[1] The film is also embraced by contemporary Pagans, despite the ethic of non-violence clearly promoted by their religious communities. These two mysteries of the film's reception are linked. The differences between *The Wicker Man* and other folk horror films, before and after it, mark it as participating in a different moral cosmology, one in which it stands nearly alone, and one that reflects uniquely contemporary Pagan sensibilities.[2]

What is it about *The Wicker Man* that affirms Pagan practitioners in contrast to other folk horror films? For example, no one Ren-Faires the coven from *Blood on Satan's Claw* (1971) or cosplays *Kill List* (2011) lawn parties. I argue that in reflecting actual Pagan practice – the crucial exception of human sacrifice aside – *The Wicker Man* is open to Pagan reclamation in ways that other folk horror films are not, specifically because it is the only one that does not depict Pagan folk practices as ultimately satanic.

This discussion charts two angles. One is the continuity that folk horror generally has with a millennia-old tradition of associating non-Christian religions, and pre-Christian religions especially, with Satanism. This tradition coincides with anti-cult scares of the 1970s, which morph into the satanic panics of the 1980s and 1990s in Great Britain and North America. The other is how *The Wicker Man*, despite the intentions of its creators to continue in this tradition, instead follows a different trajectory, driven in part by a desire to distinguish the project from Hammer gothics. This difference also helps explain why, despite its status as a folk horror classic, *The Wicker Man* is not easily summarised as a horror film.

Defining folk horror: Bad religions

The work of Victorian anthropologist James Frazer, *The Golden Bough* (1947 [1922]), which inspired *The Wicker Man*, is a quintessential example of the colonially inflected process of eliding multiple diversities into a singular difference, specifically through ideas of comparative religion. For Frazer there was continuity between the religious practices of ancient peoples, colonised societies abroad and contemporary rural Britain. His universality contextualised Christianity as just one religion among many, seemingly gesturing beyond xenophobia towards a comparative-religion worldview in which past and 'foreign' religions are also valuable expressions of human potential. However, his approach also devalues all religions as developmentally behind a Protestant-influenced secularity, described by Frazer as a scientific outlook, and suggests that rural British peasants are as backward as foreign 'savages'. Thus there is a racialisation of rural people in Frazer's thought that easily feeds prejudice both against people of colour abroad and against working-class people within the homeland. This discourse is clearly expressed through folk horror when rural people are depicted as driven to savage violence by their misguided religions.

While critics have been quick to categorise wide-ranging backwoods horror films as folk horror (e.g. Scovell 2017: 115–116), there are logical and significant distinctions between them. We can distinguish particular embodiments of paranoia based on the nature of the specific 'horror'. Is there a supernatural monster in the woods (e.g. *Wolfman* (1941))? Is there a human monster in the woods (e.g. *Friday the Thirteenth* (1980))? Is there a subgroup of humans in the woods with a monstrous social system (e.g. *Deliverance* (1972); *The Hills Have Eyes* (1977))? Does that monstrous social system involve alternative religious ideas and practices (*Blood on Satan's Claw*; *The Wicker Man*)? I argue for reserving the latter category for 'folk horror' proper.

The horror of the folk is not simply that they are acting against outsiders, but that they are doing so based on an alternative religious system, one that is oriented away from mainstream culture and towards other moral cosmologies. Both *The Texas Chainsaw Massacre* (1974) Sawyers and the eponymous *Witchfinder General* (1968) torturously murder people, both the assailants in *I Spit on Your Grave* (1978) and in *Blood on Satan's Claw* brutally rape, but in each case they are motivated by significantly divergent worldviews. Folk horror invokes specifically religious horror; the other films express 'sociophobics' (Cowan 2008: 58–59) without the distinctly religious component.

The distinction between legitimate religions and 'cults' has always been an exercise in power and woven into the project of dehumanising cultural opponents. The very idea of human sacrifice within immolated wicker figures is a product of this process, recorded by Roman generals about their opponents, the Gauls, and supposedly committed in honour of their 'foreign' gods (Koven 2008; Hutton, this volume). It carries through to medieval Church-consolidation projects of accusing opponents of 'heresy' and then attributing satanic worship and antinomianism to those so accused (Zwissler 2018b). If people do not follow the rules determined by institutional hierarchy, then they must have no rules, and therefore they must be capable of any atrocities imaginable (Cohn 1975). This is how accused 'witches' within Europe and 'savages' abroad could be conceived as practising the same horrible religion: that is, satanism (Silverblatt 2006).

This historical thread continues to be woven into depictions of 'folk' traditions as antinomian and explicitly satanic. *The Witches* (1966) provides an especially clear example of universalising multiple forms of difference into inextricably commingled otherness. Rural folk practices, learned ritual magic and 'African' religious practices are all the same satanic 'witchcraft'. Thus the white English witches are racialised, even to the point of 'African'-inspired drumming during their off-putting sabbath frenzy.

Figure 2.1 Promotional Poster for *The Witches*, depicting British folk religion as racialised witchcraft, 1966

Tracing this history of representations helps highlight how ultimately different *The Wicker Man* is from most folk horror, in that it does not collapse the alterity of Summerisle's Paganism into Satanism. Summerisle's culture is different, it is other, but it is not ultimately devil-worship, in contrast to the paganism of other films, such as *Night of the Demon* (1957), *The Witches* and *Blood on Satan's Claw*. In making a horror film about religion versus secularity, rather than about folk religion versus Christianity in which folk religion must default to satanic, *The Wicker Man*'s creators inadvertently legitimise Paganism as a contemporary religious option (Krzywinska 2000: 109–111; Sutcliffe 2005). Against Howie's disciplining Christianity, Paganism appears functional and joyous.

Religion is bad

Indeed, Howie's religiosity, which Melanie J. Wright describes as 'the film's somewhat inconsistent construction of Christianity' (Wright 2007: 84), is quite literally created in contrast to Summerisle's religion. The representation of Paganism is a Frazerian pastiche of real and imagined folk practices across time and cultures (Sutcliffe 2005: 48; Koven 2008). In parallel, Howie's Christianity is 'a composite Christian stereotype' of denominational contradictions, catalogued by Steven J. Sutcliffe as including the High Church service, which places Howie within an Episcopal or Catholic context, but one in which his role as lay reader at the altar would be impossible. Though he receives a wafer at the altar, Howie's 'stern moralism' enacts

Figure 2.2 Howie at Eucharistic altar receiving chalice in *The Wicker Man*, 1973

a caricature of Presbyterianism, in which that ritual practice is explicitly rejected (Sutcliffe 2005: 39n7). Confirming the filmmakers' priorities, director Robin Hardy owns, 'Although much effort had gone into recreating a Pagan faith for our times, we had spent a lot less time on Howie's Christian faith' (Hardy 2006: 21). Rather than a satanic foil for normative Christianity, Summerisle's Paganism and Howie's constructed Christianity join as traditions set in contrast to secularising modernity (Sutcliffe 2005).

High Church ritual, such as the Episcopalian Eucharist at the beginning of the film, is a crucial aspect of the filmmakers' vision for Howie's Christianity (Hardy 2006: 21). The importance of complex ritual to the intended critique of both Christianity and Paganism illuminates a further facet of the religion/secularisation dichotomy proposed by the filmmakers. Hardy attributes the importance to creating parallel sacrifices to bookend the film (21). Both sacrifices invoke competing visions of British heritage: Howie is focused on the narrative of triumphant missionary bringing the discipline of Christianity to godless heathens; the islanders see his missionary bet and raise him martyrdom at the hands of the unconverted.

From an etic perspective the emphasis on ritual as dangerous places the filmmakers' critique of religion in the long, historical context of Protestant and Protestant-influenced secular anti-Catholicism (Asad 2003; Orsi 2016). Adapting venerable crusade templates, English anti-Catholicism portrayed practitioners as slavish agents of a foreign power, the Pope, but now potentially disguised enemies within the nation (Tumbleson 1998). The Protestant/Catholic dichotomy maps easily onto white/Black, self/other, racialising Catholics. However, with help from theorists such as Frazer, Protestant anti-Catholicism also ultimately develops to denigrate religion itself in the context of secularising modernity (Zwissler 2018c: 128–132). In this vein, then, *The Wicker Man* troubles religion in general through its manifestations in both Howie's Christianity and the Summerislanders' Paganism, but in doing so also implicitly presents them as equally possible religious options.

'Cults' as white people problems

Despite its singular treatment of religious alterity as non-satanic, *The Wicker Man* does align with folk horror's broader concerns with race. Urban elites have historically projected fears onto rural areas, an aversion Carol Clover (2015 [1992]: 124) terms 'urbanoia'. Clover argues that underlying urbanoia is a thinly veiled white-settler narrative inherited from Westerns, that civilisation is a precarious project threatened by colonised 'savages' (162–165). In the backwoods horror movies she analyses, class now stands in for race, but the films nonetheless process the same historical traumas: dominant outsiders fear the justified resentment with which they are met by 'indigenous' people when those outsiders stray into their territory. Her argument easily extends beyond her American focus to help make sense of British folk horror.[3] Here, a wider-ranging set of colonised oppressed can be represented by the 'folk' encountered at the edges of civilisation, demarcated by the fields and furrows of the rural countryside.

As scholars such as Geraldine Heng (2018) and Cord J. Whitaker (2019) demonstrate, English concern with difference began to take on racialised dimensions long before the early modern era, drawing on religious crusade models to construct self-identity over and against foreign others, reductively coded as 'black'. For literate elites, this category could include not only the people of colour expected from today's racial discourses; not only the non-English others within the Atlantic Archipelago, such as the Irish (Ignatiev 2009); but also rural English peasants, made 'black' from their physical labour in the sun (Whitaker 2019: 101, following Campbell 2006: 50). The early modern period further weaponised racial thinking to justify colonialism and chattel slavery.

Victorians at the height of British Empire, such as Frazer, continued to engage with foreign/racial othering tropes to justify their place-claim of dominance at the centre of the world. To be clear, this project is not exclusively a racial project, but one that concomitantly draws on interconnecting hierarchies of class, geography, culture and religion to create mutually reinforcing signifiers of dangerous others. Difference in one category is simultaneously understood as both cause and symptom of difference in the others. Thus religious difference, in and of itself, can serve as both sign of and cipher for racial difference, while also obfuscating racial anxieties under the cover of theological disagreement or cultural critique (Smith 1998; Nye 2019; Whitaker 2019).

White-dominant culture perpetuates itself by coding whiteness as non-race, as neutral (Frankenberg 2001; Yukich and Edgell 2020). The importance of whiteness in *The Wicker Man* (and to all British folk horror and western cinema in general) can be demonstrated through the technique of switching the races of characters and observing how the narrative diverts into alternative genres. The exercise disrupts habits of seeing in which whiteness 'in the Eurocentric West more broadly is *invisible*, the unmarked norm' (Whitaker 2019: 3, emphasis in original). Switching in more systemically 'visible' or 'marked' racial codes throws into relief the importance of whiteness as already raced, though unacknowledged. This process can be applied to any film or genre to yield insights into ways that, even within – and often especially within – white-dominant contexts, racial concerns are nonetheless operating.

If Edward Woodward's Sergeant Howie is a person of colour, then the story becomes a simpler, and arguably more horrific, one of a premeditated lynching.[4] If Christopher Lee's Lord Summerisle is a person of colour, then the character falls into the racist trope of the foreign magician (Hutton 2017: 109–110). If the people of Summerisle are a community predominantly of colour, then the story becomes an iteration of Joseph Conrad's *Heart of Darkness* (1899), in which a colonial representative of civilisation must journey to the edge of the world to confront murderous savagery. This alternative spin is highlighted by Hardy (2006: 20) through the example of *Apocalypse Now* (1979), in which Marlon Brando's Kurtz has Frazer's *Golden Bough* by his side, the same source material as *The Wicker Man*, but used symbolically to distinctly different ends. Lest one argue that the islanders *must* be white, because they are an isolated Scottish community, consider how Ingrid Pitt's eastern European, Jewish librarian came to join them.

The fact that race (other than whiteness) cannot be introduced into the narrative without significantly changing its meaning is important: what is being processed in the film is a distinctly white set of concerns. More specifically, those concerns revolve around the perceived threat of religious diversity and the decline of white Christian cultural hegemony brought on by the changes of the 1960s and 1970s (Sutcliffe 2005; Frankfurter 2006). Clover argues that rural horror films are driven by sublimated racism, coded as class conflict; I argue that, in continuity with long-standing British concerns about the ineluctability of religious difference and essentialised otherness, moral panics around 'cults' are also coded anxiety about challenges to white supremacy, especially in the form of ideas of cultural purity. The fact that Britain as a nation was at the time of filming – and remains – overwhelmingly white-dominated underscores the well-established racial component to traditional national self-identify, especially as constructed in contrast to 'less civilised' former/colonies, immigrant communities and 'foreign' religions (see Nye 2019). Folk horror is just one of the many places such anxieties over difference play out.

Lord Summerisle is Dracula reversed

In developing the Summerisle cult, director Robin Hardy has been very clear that he and writer Anthony Shaffer were inspired by Hammer Film Productions' gothic horror films, in that they wanted to produce something that was markedly *not* in their vein. Hardy uses terms such as 'camp' to describe the type of Hammer aesthetics they wanted to avoid (Hardy 2006: 19). Christopher Lee also sought to distance himself from that studio's Dracula series, for which he was most famous. Moreover, Hardy describes the producer, Peter Snell, realising that the film could be 'a kind of antithesis of the Hammer Horror film' (21). Differentiating the project from Hammer was, however, more than just a matter of personal artistic vision, but also a crucial way to stake identity for the studio (Cowdell 2019: 300). Together these orientations illuminate a trajectory that starts with gothic Dracula and ends with Pagan Summerisle. Resistance to Hammer can help explain why *The Wicker Man* is such an odd duck in the canons of horror more generally, but it can also help explain why it is the odd one out among the folk horror genre it helped create.

The Wicker Man remains difficult to categorise as a film, blurring genre markers across horror, mystery, exploitation, comedy and musical. The key is to read it as a reaction to Hammer. Like an inverted tarot card, it is not exactly a Manichaean opposite to the original from which it varies, but is instead askew. Using Lee as fulcrum, we can invert out from gothic horror and trace several important elements within *The Wicker Man*.

Hammer remains well known for a particular brand of gothic horror in the 1960s and 1970s (Pirie, 2008). These films often centre on vampires and their victims, all explicitly sexualised and trussed up in period costumes, and the – inevitably male – vampire hunters who would stave off evil at the last moment. Lee made a franchise out of his Count Dracula, an exotic nobleman who uses sly charm to wear down resistance in people who ought to know better, until his full demonic powers become more useful. In keeping with the vampire complex, at least since Bram Stoker's *Dracula* (1897), a major theme in the films is the elision between vampirism and seduction, the collapsing of dual penetrations of bite and sex. More specifically, they are morality tales about the vulnerability of women's sexual continence, especially when targeted by seductive outsiders (Brown 2000: 64; Mendes 2016).

The action in Hammer vampire films takes place almost entirely at night, often in tapestry-draped chambers or midnight gardens and cellars, and their colour palette is dark and sumptuous. In contrast, *The Wicker Man* is sun-soaked, the outdoor landscape features prominently and the colour palette tends towards nature. Dracula is a creature of the night and the moon. Lord Summerisle literally worships Nuada, god of the sun. Dracula lives on blood. Summerisle's life's blood is apples.

If the sexuality in Hammer's vampire films is dangerous and repressed until it boils over, though unspeakable, then the sexuality in Summerisle is frank and unashamed. Rather than sex being linked with death, it is Howie's denial of sex that causes his death. If women are in constant danger in vampire films, it turns out Howie is instead. If Dracula slinks around in silk-and-velvet shadows, Lord Summerisle strides about in kilt-kit, drag, and, as he's pronouncing Howie's execution, tweed.

A deeply religious people 47

The trick of *The Wicker Man* is that Howie believes he is the protagonist of a different kind of story. In fact, the send-up comes from the way he acts as if he is a Van Helsing, come to town to save a young woman from predation. He is too obtuse to imagine that the narrative could be inverted: that he, an abstinent, adult man, may be in danger. As a viewer comments to Brigid Cherry (2006: 113), 'the hero dies in the end'.

The horror of the traditional Stoker *Dracula* is the threat of Dracula's predatory pansexuality. Jonathan Harker, like Sergeant Howie, goes off on business to a distant place with another culture, encounters a strange nobleman and begins to suspect that he is being subjected to mind games. Both characters leave behind chaste sweethearts to whom they plan to return.

However, isolated in Dracula's castle, Harker becomes increasingly manipulated. Essentially, he is being treated as trapped women are treated in gothic narratives; Dracula's supernatural powers serve as explanation for Harker's increasing subjection. *Dracula* is easily read as a homophobic nightmare based in Victorian misogyny: women are sexually endangered because that is the proper feminine role; men are sexually predacious because that is the proper masculine role; Dracula is an androcentric nightmare because he is a sexual threat not only to women, but also to men, putting them in a feminised victim position. The danger that Dracula poses, both homophobic and homoerotic, is made blatant in his relationship with Van Helsing. Both men pursue each other in an attempt to be the first to penetrate: Dracula with his fangs and Van Helsing with his stake.[5]

Treating *The Wicker Man* as an inverted gothic tale also helps explain the total lack of homoeroticism within the film. The explicit coupling is exclusively heterosexual. Even when Howie bursts in on Lord Summerisle at night, he is already with Miss Rose, her robe and goblet signalling established physical intimacy. If Lee's Summerisle is the inverted tarot card of Lee's Dracula, it makes significant sense that he is not interested in Howie sexually. If *The Wicker Man* is the inverted tarot card of Hammer's Dracula films, it also follows that the sex in the film is explicitly consensual and joyful, often initiated by women.

This last point is crucial in disambiguating *The Wicker Man* from other British folk horror. It is one of the few canonical entries that does not include sexual assault.[6] The threat of assault is implicit, though one could hardly claim subtle, in Hammer's gothics, but in folk horror it is generic practice to include explicit rape as a sign of the savagery of the 'folk'. The trope of sexual assault can be traced through folk horror and the broader category of urbanoia of which it is a part, but one need look no further than the other two films of the 'unholy trinity' to see how starkly *The Wicker Man* differs on this point. Both *Witchfinder General* and *Blood on Satan's Claw* explicitly depict vicious sexual assaults on major female characters. In the context of folk horror, the lack of rape in *The Wicker Man* is idiosyncratic and important.

Is *The Wicker Man* a feminist film?

Given all the ways that *The Wicker Man* deviates from the gendered power dynamics of horror more generally, and folk horror in particular, it is worth considering whether or not it can be categorised as feminist. On one hand, this question is quaint, in that it must ignore all the structural ways that the film, like most studio films, is a product of men's creativity. The script writer, director, producer, protagonist and championing star are all men. Diegetically, the film remains solidly androcentric.

Yet in its celebration of 1970s Paganism, *The Wicker Man* draws on the proto-feminist religious cosmology of Gerald Gardner and his vision of Wicca, publicised in the 1950s. As an alternative to the patriarchal monotheism of the Christian God, Gardnerian theology offers a gynocentric duotheism, based on the Goddess and her consort (Hutton 1999). The mythology of their relationship is expressed through seasonal cycles.

As critical as Gardner was of misogyny within Christianity, his alternative system is difficult to categorise as truly feminist from current perspective (Zwissler 2018b). Through encounters with second-wave feminist spirituality in America during the 1970s, Wicca took on more feminist forms, familiar to many Pagans today (Clifton 2006; Zwissler 2018a; Feraro 2020). However, in Gardner's original formulation, Wicca is based in dualistic gender complementarity, fundamentally tied to biological essentialism. This is the basis for *The Wicker Man*'s gender politics.

Nonetheless, androcentric art may still be feminist if it exposes contradictory constructions of masculinity, which *The Wicker Man* certainly does. In fact, the title can be read not only as the name of the monstrous method of execution, but as a description of Howie himself (Murray and Rolston 2002: 18), perhaps also of Lord Summerisle, and the very notion of performative gender (Ashurst 2005: 103). Howie's sense of self is inextricably tied to his role as a policeman playing the hero, rescuing a young girl. His hegemonic masculinity, both rooted in and hindered by his strict Christianity, turns out to be a sham. In a masculinist game of wits, Lord Summerisle roundly defeats him. The victory is so clear that Summerisle can be magnanimous in giving Howie the consolation prize of folding his defeat into a cosmology that preserves a version of Christian manhood: martyrdom.

However, there is more to the film than this reductionist *mano a mano* narrative. Summerisle is not operating alone. He is playing a necessary role in the community project of snaring Howie. As representative of the patriarchal institutions of Church and State, Howie needs a male authority figure against whom to react. Summerisle presents himself as such a figure. His conspicuous male headship is important in a serious game that the whole village is playing. Others have their own roles, so Summerisle's is only most important in that Howie, given his investment in class and gender, believes it to be.

The game is only being played at all because Summerisle's role as male leader of the island community is in jeopardy. The exchange with Howie during the big reveal makes clear that if Howie were found to be an inappropriate sacrifice, Summerisle would be on the line, just as Howie assumed Rowan was. Even if Rowan were sacrificed that year, Howie's curse would still hang over Summerisle's head. If fertility does not return, next year's sacrifice will have to be the 'king'; no substitute will do. Summerisle's headship is only real as long as it suits the community. Like every king in Frazer's sacred grove, he can be replaced.

The community that sets Summerisle up as Howie's foil is, in contrast, not androcentric. Howie runs into influential and independent women throughout his investigation. The three that stand together as Howie emerges from the cave – Britt Ekland's Willow, Diane Cilento's Miss Rose and Ingrid Pitt's librarian – form a familiar Wiccan tryptic of the Goddess.

To push Lord Summerisle's precarity further, consider the social structures of the film beyond diegesis. Summerisle is leader of a tightly knit island community whose resourcefulness and organisational skills have already been proven by the successful ensnarement of Howie. Summerisle's narrative is that, when his Victorian grandfather bought the island, he 'allowed' the islanders to return to their old gods as a condescending incentive to renew enthusiasm for agricultural labour. However, as Belle Doyle (2005: 87) points out, the scenario can also be read as the islanders persuading their new lord to support their Old Ways, freeing them from imposed priests. It is easy to imagine the villagers pulling off another set of performances aimed at getting Grandfather Summerisle to think he had come up with the whole thing himself, happily letting the islanders get back to, or continue, a matriarchal culture with a disposable male figurehead, necessary, or at least convenient, for interfacing with the outside world.

That brings us to the current state of the Summerisle line. If Howie's curse comes true, Lord Summerisle burns next May with no heir (Doyle 2005: 88). Perhaps Miss Rose, as his consort, is already on the case? Whether or not she is, we then have an island community, essentially already run by women in practice, without a laird who thinks he is in charge. After all, the emphasis on sacred kingship within the film is a result of Howie's perspective, which is explicitly blinkered in several ways, and implicitly we can add androcentric to that list (Cherry 2006).

The sacred king comes through Frazer, an androcentric Victorian, to Lord Summerisle and then on to Howie. When all of these straws of circumstantial evidence are bound together, they shape a plausible etic reading of the film in which it is the very notion of sacred kingship itself that is consciously constructed and easily burned down. It becomes a story of wicker men, created, sustained and ultimately turned back under to fertilise the future by a gynocentric culture.[7]

Returning to the question as to whether *The Wicker Man* is a feminist film, there are many answers, depending on the manner of measure. It is solidly androcentric, but not misogynist. It portrays a ritual community built on gender complementarity reliant on biological essentialism, but that structure includes power for women. Finally, *The Wicker Man* also stands out starkly in contrast to most other folk horror films in its lack of sexual violence.

The Wicker Man as a Pagan film

The Wicker Man is celebrated by contemporary practitioners as a Pagan film (Higgenbotham 2006; Jones 2000). Through *The Golden Bough* the film shares Victorian source material with contemporary Paganism as a new religious movement (Hutton 1999, this volume). Although Koven (2008) has criticised the film for participating in 'folklore fallacy' by taking Frazer at face value, one film scholar's hodgepodge is another religion scholar's 'ritual creativity', 'bricolage spirituality' or 'religious reflexivity' (Magliocco 2004; Fedele 2013; Schaap and Aupers 2017). The film depicts a community unironically celebrating real Pagan values: reverence for nature and human integration in the ecosystem; polytheism as a common articulation of pantheism; cooperative community; and an emphasis on joy and pleasure, rather than shame, expressed through sexual liberation, especially women's.

John Lyden (2019: 83) has analysed the act of watching a film as a religious experience, not exclusively but especially when viewed with others, triggering experiences of transcendence and Victor Turner's *communitas*: the very category of 'cult film' developed to explain the love that dedicated audiences have for odd, imperfect and financially unsuccessful films that nonetheless become popular through shared screening experiences (Havis 2008). Devoted fans become literal devotees of subgenres and specific films. *The Wicker Man* is a core example of such a movie, its troubled distribution history only enhancing its value.

For Pagans practising an alternative religion in the Christian-dominant West, gathering together with fellow fans to watch the film can give a sense of community. However, the replication of actual religious experience goes much further. The action culminates in a carnival, world-upside-down rite; therefore, the film itself can also serve as a carnivalesque experience for viewers, both Pagan and otherwise.

World-inversion narratives often serve a social function of reinforcing the hierarchies of the status quo, by offering a vision of a world without them as chaotic and dangerous (Clark 1999). *The Wicker Man* can certainly be read this way, and such a reading is most loyal to its creators' intentions (Bartholomew 1977: 12). For non-Pagans, Howie's fate is a warning about wandering beyond civilisation and secular rationality into spaces where barbarous transgressions against normative values are possible (Sutcliffe 2005). This is surely the way those 'Bible-belt' Christians were reading the film when they invited Hardy and Lee to prayer breakfasts during their shoestring American screening tour (Hardy 2005: vi). For both these American Christians and the religion-suspicious creators, Summerisle's counterculture threatens the proper order of the world.

However, for non-dominant subcultures, world-inversion narratives may hit differently. When disempowered by the status quo, a narrative in which dominant structures are overturned may be inspiring, rather than threatening. We see this across many subcultures in which identification with and cosplay of villains and outsiders are celebrated (Stanley 2002; Frankfurter 2006; Spracklen and Spracklen 2012). With *The Wicker Man* referential identification is further looped, because the existence of contemporary Paganism inspired the film (Hardy 2006: 19, 21) and the film has further affected Pagan communities (Jones 2000). All a practising Pagan has to do to act the role of a Summerislander is to be themselves.

The Wicker Man's carnival is received differently for Pagans because the film reverses their own lived experience within Christian-dominant culture. Judith Higgenbotham's Pagan informants appreciated *The Wicker Man* as 'the only film they know of in which the action takes place in a Pagan context, where Paganism is the norm, rather than a transgressive, exotic practice, and where the validity of Pagan belief is accepted' (2006: 130–131). In a switch, Howie's Christian beliefs are shrugged off, even mocked by others, as when Lord Summerisle identifies Jesus as the son of a ghost. The contrast of Howie's repressive Christianity paints the Paganism of the Summerisle community in a very positive light. While Howie's sacrifice at the end of the film was intended by the filmmakers to undo that positive portrayal entirely, they do not fully succeed, at least not with all audiences.

Moreover, Jones (2000) notes that Howie's ultimate fate is a reversal of the popular 'Burning Times' myth that Christians burned Pagan forebears as witches (Zwissler 2016). Contrast this once-in-three-generations execution of a domineering male representative of the State to the hundreds of years of executions of marginalised women that took place during the

Figure 2.3   Paganism is a party! *The Wicker Man*, 1973

early modern witch trials, or even to contemporary police violence against marginalised groups. Originally underwritten by police aggression against countercultural movements of the 1960s (Sutcliffe 2005: 40), this reading continues to resonate with contemporary police brutality and lack of justice for victims of structurally conditioned violence, critiques elevated by movements such as Black Lives Matter and #MeToo. Beside historical discourses that lump multiple differences into a single alterity, Paganism can come to represent identification with diversity and tolerance (Zwissler 2018b) and signal a resistance to contemporary mainstream structures that anthropologist Sabina Magliocco (2004) calls 'oppositional culture'. If shoving Howie into the wicker man is the extent of the violence that a community commits, then Summerisle looks pretty good when contrasted with the apparatus of the patriarchal, Christian-dominant State. Instead of sacrificing the marginalised, Sumerislanders are literally burning The Man.

It is also not difficult for a religious community that often finds itself egregiously misrepresented in popular culture to celebrate a somewhat realistic portrayal, even if the cost of that portrayal is supposed to be demonisation. Chas Clifton, a founder of Pagan studies as an academic field and author of *Her Hidden Children* (2006) reminiscences: 'I was introduced to *The Wicker Man* by a Wiccan friend and he insisted that we watch it on VHS. "Ignore the last few minutes", he advised. I was yet another contemporary Pagan who cared less about the plot and more about Summerisle as an ideal of what a small-scale Pagan society might look like' (personal communication).[8] For Pagan communities, seeing themselves positively reflected on screen at all remains a pleasant surprise.

Conclusion

The reclaimability of *The Wicker Man* for Pagans has everything to do with its contrast to other folk horror. It is unusual for portrayals of religious alterity not to default to satanic. Yet the 'folk' religion presented in *The Wicker Man* incorporates many elements that are familiar to actual Pagan practitioners.

The filmmakers' deliberate choice not to centre Christianity as the social norm, but instead to problematise both Christianity and Paganism, positions the two religions together in contrast to rational, secular modernity. Assuming that both the islanders' Paganism and Howie's Christianity will be equally off-putting to viewers, leading to the morality-tale conclusion that religion is dangerous, the creators leave open alternative readings. One of these alternative readings is that Paganism is morally superior to – and much more fun than – either Christianity or secularity, an interpretation that Pagan audiences have continued to embrace for the film's past fifty years.

Acknowledgements

Thanks to David Ferris for supporting my folk horror binge of the last few years, fast-forwarding rape scenes, and talking through All The Things. Thanks also to Sylvia Zwissler for sitting through *The Wicker Man* with us at all, despite her better judgement.

Notes

1. This chapter focuses on the 2001 extended version of the film. For an overview of the different versions and the circumstances behind their creation, see Brown (2000).
2. Following standard anthropological practice, I capitalise 'Pagan' when referring to religious self-identity and use lower-case, 'pagan,' when describing a label imposed by others to identify pre- or non-Christian practices. I follow the same distinction between 'Satanist' and 'satanic'.
3. Using this model, a film such as *Welcome II the Terrordome* (1993) can be read as reversed urbanoia, which goes some way towards explaining the backlash against it (see Jones 2020): it upends the conventions of the genre by portraying the perspective of the colonised, whose carceral 'reservation' is violated by racist outsiders.
4. On lynchings of Black men in Britain see Sherwood (1993).
5. The recent BBC version (2020) elevates the homoerotic subtext into text with Harker, but then gender-switches Van Helsing in order to romanticise that relationship.

6 Not only do its triune partners contain graphic sexual violence, but the trope is far from underrepresented in the genre more broadly. To put this another way, it is not unexpected to encounter a rape scene within British folk horror, and, for its scholars, it is a predictable professional hazard. While the following list is not meant to be exhaustive, it should suffice for the larger point: *Witchfinder General*; *Blood on Satan's Claw*; *Cry of the Banshee* (1970); *Straw Dogs* (1971); *Requiem for a Village* (1975); *The Red Shift* (1978). In *Kill List* sexual torture is off-screen, but is heard as Jay and Gal play the pornographer's films. Explicitly *sexual* violence is over and above the ubiquitous, if varied, threats to women, in for example *The Witches*, *The Owl Service* (1969) and *The Stone Tape* (1972) – an expectation that *The Wicker Man* gleefully subverts, as does *Robin Redbreast* (1970) before it: 'What good would a woman's blood be for the land?'.

7 Perhaps Summerisle is even somewhat aware of this? His role as 'teaser' aligns him with the women of the community (as noted by Cherry (2006): 122–123).

8 Chas Clifton, personal email communication with the author, 26 January 2022.

References

Asad, Talal (2003), *Formations of the Secular: Christianity, Islam, Modernity*. Stanford: Stanford University Press.

Ashurst, Gail (2005), ' "The Game's Over." Breaking the Spell of Summerisle: Feminist Discourse and *The Wicker Man*', in Jonathan Murray, Lesley Stevenson, Stephen Harper, and Benjamin Franks (eds), *Constructing 'The Wicker Man': Film and Cultural Studies Perspectives*. Glasgow: Crichton Publications, pp. 91–106.

Bartholomew, David (1977), '*The Wicker Man*: III. Research and Background', *Cinefantastique* 6:3, 10–14.

Brown, Allan (2000), *Inside 'The Wicker Man': How Not to Make a Cult Classic*. Edinburgh: Polygon.

Campbell, Kofi (2006), *Literature in the Black Atlantic: From Pre- to Postcolonial*. New York: Palgrave Macmillan.

Cherry, Brigid (2006), 'The Wicca Woman: Gender, Sexuality and Religion in *The Wicker Man*', in Benjamin Franks, Stephen Harper, Jonathan Murray and Lesley Stevenson (eds), *The Quest for 'The Wicker Man': History, Folklore, and Pagan Perspectives*. Edinburgh: Luath Press, pp. 111–125.

Clark, Stuart (1999), *Thinking with Demons: The Idea of Witchcraft in Early Modern Europe*. Oxford: Oxford University Press.

Clifton, Chas (2006), *Her Hidden Children: The Rise of Wicca and Paganism in America*. Lanham, MD: Alta Mira.

Clover, Carol J. (2015 [1992]), *Men, Women and Chainsaws: Gender in the Modern Horror Film*. Princeton: Princeton University Press.

Cohn, Norman (1975), *Europe's Inner Demons: The Demonization of Christians in Medieval Christendom*. St Alban's: Paladin.

Conrad, Joseph (1899), *Heart of Darkness*. Edinburgh: Blackwood's Magazine.

Cowan, Douglas E. (2008), *Sacred Terror: Religion on the Silver Screen*. Waco, TX: Baylor University Press.

Cowdell, Paul (2019), ' "Practicing Witchcraft Myself during the Filming": Folk Horror, Folklore, and the Folkloresque', *Western Folklore* 78:4, 295–326.

Doyle, Belle (2005), ' "Here on Official Business": Production, Patriarchy, and the Hazards of Policing a Pre-Industrial Utopia', in Jonathan Murray, Lesley Stevenson,

Stephen Harper, and Benjamin Franks (eds), *Constructing 'The Wicker Man': Film and Cultural Studies Perspectives*. Glasgow: Crichton Publications, pp. 75–90.
Fedele, Anna (2013), *Looking for Mary Magdalene: Alternative Pilgrimage and Ritual Creativity at Catholic Shrines in France*. Oxford: Oxford University Press.
Feraro, Shai (2020), *Women and Gender Issues in British Paganism, 1945–1990*. Basingstoke: Palgrave Macmillan.
Frankenberg, Ruth (2001), 'The Mirage of Unmarked Whiteness', in Birgit Brander Rasmussen, Eric Klinenberg, Irene J. Nexica and Matt Wray (eds), *The Making and Unmaking of Whiteness*. Durham, NC: Duke University Press, pp. 72–96.
Frankfurter, David (2006), *Evil Incarnate: Rumors of Demonic Conspiracy and Ritual Abuse in History*. Princeton: Princeton University.
Frazer, James (1947 [1922]), *The Golden Bough: A Study in Magic and Religion*, abridged edn. New York: Macmillan.
Hardy, Robin (2005), 'Foreword', in Jonathan Murray, Lesley Stevenson, Stephen Harper and Benjamin Franks (eds) *Constructing 'The Wicker Man': Film and Cultural Studies Perspectives*. Glasgow: Crichton Publications, v–vii.
Hardy, Robin (2006), 'The Genesis of the Wicker Man', in Benjamin Franks, Stephen Harper, Jonathan Murray and Lesley Stevenson (eds), *The Quest for 'The Wicker Man': History, Folklore, and Pagan Perspectives*. Edinburgh: Luath Press, pp. 17–25.
Havis, Allan (2008), *Cult Films: Taboo and Transgression*. Lanham, MD: University Press of America.
Heng, Geraldine (2018), *The Invention of Race in the European Middle Ages*. Cambridge: Cambridge University Press.
Higgenbotham, Judith (2006), ' "Do as Thou Wilt": Contemporary Paganism and *The Wicker Man*', in Benjamin Franks, Stephen Harper, Jonathan Murray and Lesley Stevenson (eds), *The Quest for 'The Wicker Man': History, Folklore, and Pagan Perspectives*. Edinburgh: Luath Press, pp. 126–136.
Hutton, Ronald (1999), *Triumph of the Moon: A History of Modern Pagan Witchcraft*. Oxford: Oxford University Press.
Hutton, Ronald (2017), *The Witch: A History of Fear from Ancient Times to the Present*. New Haven: Yale University Press.
Ignatiev, Noel (2009), *How the Irish Became White*. London: Routledge.
Jones, Ellen E. (2020), 'Has Terrordome's Time Come? How a Black British Film Found Its Moment', *Guardian*, 23 July, www.theguardian.com/film/2020/jul/23/has-terrordomes-time-come-how-a-black-british-film-found-its-moment (accessed 22 April 2023).
Jones, Leslie Ellen (2000), 'The Folklore of *The Wicker Man*', *The Pomegranate: The International Journal of Pagan Studies* 14, 38–47.
Koven, Mikel J. (2008), *Film, Folklore and Urban Legends*. Lanham, MD: Scarecrow Press.
Krzywinska, Tanya (2000), *A Skin for Dancing In: Possession, Witchcraft and Voodoo in Film*. Trowbridge: Flicks Books.
Lyden, John (2019), *Film as Religion: Myths, Morals and Rituals*, 2nd edn. New York: New York University Press.
Magliocco, Sabina (2004), *Witching Culture: Folklore and Neo-Paganism in America*. Philadelphia: University of Pennsylvania Press.
Mendes, Maria do Carmo (2016), 'Who's Afraid of Don Juan? Vampirism and Seduction', in Isabel Ermida (ed.), *Dracula and the Gothic in Literature, Pop Culture and the Arts*. Leiden: Brill, pp. 271–292.
Murray, Andy and Lorrane Rolston (2002), *Studying the Wicker Man*. Leighton Buzzard: Auteur.

Nye, Malory (2019), 'Race and Religion: Postcolonial Formations of Power and Whiteness', *Method & Theory in the Study of Religion* 6:3, 210–237.

Orsi, Robert (2016), *History and Presence*. Cambridge: Cambridge University Press.

Pirie, David (2008), *A New Heritage of Horror: The English Gothic Cinema*. London: I.B. Tauris.

Schaap, Julian and Stef Aupers (2017), ' "Gods in World of Warcraft Exist": Religious Reflexivity and the Quest for Meaning in Online Computer Games', *New Media & Society* 19:11, 1744–1760.

Sherwood, Marika (1993), 'Lynchings in Britain', *History Today* 49:3, 21–23.

Scovell, Adam (2017), *Folk Horror: Hours Dreadful and Things Strange*. Leighton Buzzard: Auteur.

Silverblatt, Irene (2006), 'Colonial Conspiracies', *Ethnohistory* 53:2, 259–280.

Smith, Jonathan Z. (1998), 'Religion, Religions, Religious', in Mark C. Taylor (ed.), *Critical Terms in Religious Studies*. Chicago: University of Chicago Press, pp. 269–284.

Spracklen, Karl and Beverley Spracklen (2012), 'Pagans and Satan and Goths, Oh My: Dark Leisure as Communicative Agency and Communal Identity on the Fringes of the Modern Goth Scene', *World Leisure Journal* 54:4, 350–362.

Stanley, Richard (2002), 'Dying Light: An Obituary for the Great British Horror Movie', in Steve Chibnall and Julian Petey (eds), *British Horror Cinema*. London: Routledge, pp. 183–195.

Stoker, Bram (1897), *Dracula*. London: Archibald Constable.

Sutcliffe, Steven J. (2005), 'Religion in *The Wicker Man*: Context and Representation', in Jonathan Murray, Lesley Stevenson, Stephen Harper and Benjamin Franks (eds), *Constructing 'The Wicker Man': Film and Cultural Studies Perspectives*. Glasgow: Crichton Publications, pp. 37–56.

Tumbleson, Raymond D. (1998), *Catholicism in the English Protestant Imagination: Nationalism, Religion, and Literature, 1660–1745*. Cambridge: Cambridge University Press.

Whitaker, Cord J. (2019), *Black Metaphors: How Modern Racism Emerged from Medieval Race Thinking*. Philadelphia: University of Pennsylvania Press.

Wright, Melanie J. (2007), *Religion and Film: An Introduction*. London: I.B. Tauris.

Yukich, Grace and Penny Edgell (2020), 'Introduction: Recognizing Raced Religion', in Grace Yukich and Penny Edgell (eds), *Religion Is Raced: Recognizing American Religion in the Twenty-First Century*. New York: New York University Press, pp. 1–18.

Zwissler, Laurel (2016). 'Witches' Tears: Spiritual Feminism, Epistemology, and Witch Hunt Horror Stories', *The Pomegranate: International Journal of Pagan Studies* 18:2, 176–204.

Zwissler, Laurel (2018a), ' "I am That Very Witch": On *The Witch*, Feminism, and Not Surviving Patriarchy', *The Journal of Religion and Film* 22:3, Article 6, https://digitalcommons.unomaha.edu/jrf/vol22/iss3/6.

Zwissler, Laurel (2018b), 'In the Study of the Witch: Women, Shadows, and the Academic Study of Religions', in *Feminism and the Study of 'Religions*, special issue of *Religions* 9:4 (105), 1–18, DOI:10.3390/rel9040105.

Zwissler, Laurel (2018c), *Religious, Feminist, Activist: Cosmologies of Interconnection*. Lincoln: University of Nebraska Press.

3

Folk horror: a discursive approach, with application to Robin Hardy's *The Wicker Man* and Neil Jordan's *The Company of Wolves*

Mikel J. Koven

Across the past ten years, folk horror has emerged as perhaps the most fashionable topic in horror scholarship, amid what Paul Newland (2016: 163) calls 'a contemporary "cultification"' of the subgenre. However, as amateur groups online who likewise engage with folk horror have illustrated, pretty much anything old and vaguely weird can get thus labelled, and uncritically too. Rather than offer a concrete definition of what folk horror is, I would like to suggest a discursive methodology to see what signification befalls a text when labelled 'folk horror'.

Folk horror exists at the convergence of three discourses – the Pagan, the Rural, and the Folklore. By discourse, I refer to those ideas initially suggested by Michel Foucault in *The Archaeology of Knowledge* (1972), wherein discourse analysis is a means of qualitative study that explores not only what a text says, but more significantly power relations, and how it shapes what the text cannot say. We cannot think beyond the limits of our society, despite any alternative possibilities, since such cannot be uttered because language, as a social construct, does not permit it. Any discourse, when manifested through analysis, must be viewed as a product, or limitation, of those who control it.

To illustrate this, I will first define these three discourses within a kind of discursive methodology. Second, I will apply this methodology to one of the key films in the folk horror canon, Robin Hardy's *The Wicker Man* (1973), an uncontested member of the folk horror subgenre. Third, I will apply this discursive approach to a different film, one whose folk horror credentials might be contested: *The Company of Wolves* (1984). While the discussions developed are obviously going to differ between these films, taken together, they allow us to reflect on the range of possible discourse(s) in folk horror.

Pagan/rural/folk(lore)

The concept of the Pagan, is, in its etymology, defined by the Christian. All Others to the Christian are Pagan, unless the epistemology extends somehow to inculcate that Other into the Christian grand-narrative. Judaism, for example, is not Pagan, because Christianity has included it in its own, self-serving, chronicle – the Judeo-Christian tradition. Pagan consists of those Christianity cannot consume into its own story. Or, more damningly, the Pagan is Other because it refuses to recognise Christianity's 'truth' and join said hegemonic order. One might also say, recognising the psychoanalytic concept of the 'return of the repressed', that Paganism is that which Christianity murdered and then denied murdering – the Pagan becomes abject for the Christian – and Paganism's revival appears like Banquo's ghost, reminding the Church of its atrocities in the name of its God. Such a discursive dynamic may also partially explain why contemporary paganism is so popular with those who, likewise, not only do not wish to join the Christian hegemony, but also seek to be as wholly Other to that hegemony as possible.

This still puts Christianity at the heart of the discourse; the ancient Celts, to use a crude characterisation within popular culture, as in *The Wicker Man*, only subscribe to a *pre*-Christian belief system insofar as it was ultimately displaced *by* Christianity. Christianity is the victor; what existed prior is ultimately secondary. Such thinking denies the Pagan any agency in their own existence; they can only be seen through Christian eyes.

Alan Cameron's *The Last Pagans of Rome* (2011) traces the original Latin word, *paganus*, through to our modern conception of what the word 'Pagan' means, in a discursive analysis that is not as straightforward as it might appear. The Latin *paganus* initially simply meant rural (Cameron 2011: 14). This association of the word with rurality persists, for example, in many folk horror films. However, inspired by socio-linguist Christine Mohrmann, Cameron notes that the word is further applied to designate between dichotomies of civilian/military and Christian/non-Christian. What Cameron illustrates is not so much ever-evolving cultural dichotomous sets, but, in discursive form, the power imbalances between these two terms – one hegemonic and the other not – ultimately equating Christian and pagan with insider and outsider (Cameron 2011: 22).

The significant leap Cameron makes, by way of Mohrmann, is that the term 'Pagan' is always used as an opposite, and is, likewise, antonymically applied: this is how *we* define *you*. The Other is never allowed to identify itself. Herein lies the beginnings of how we can see the word 'Pagan' discursively: even to be in opposition to Christianity, to be anti- or non-Christian, is still to recognise the centrality of Christianity to the viewing position *by* its opposition. For the Pagan, to identify as Pagan is nonsensical because to do so would be to recognise the hegemonic power of the Church. As Cameron notes (2011: 27), 'Fourth-century pagans naturally never referred to themselves as pagans, less because the term was insulting than because the category had no meaning for them.' The term only has meaning for a Christian.

Within the folk horror discussions currently in vogue, Paganism slips synonymously towards Witchcraft and even Satanism; one becomes the other, despite these three being quite different things. What all three terms have in common is their discursive relationship to Christian hegemony, the default viewer position. It is less an issue of Paganism=Witchcraft=Satanism than it is a dichotomy between those who recognise Christian hegemony, and those for whom Christianity is irrelevant to their existence. This is the first discourse.

The governmental bodies the American Federal Office of Rural Health Policy (HRSA 2021) and the British Department for Environment, Food and Rural Affairs (Defra 2009) both likewise define the Rural antonymically, as 'not-urban': based primarily on population density. Such definitions exclude rural self-definition. The power imbalance between amounts of budgeting allocated to rural populations is tilted in favour of those classified as urban. Rural, as discourse, much like Pagan, suggests an antonymic relationship whereby it is defined by what it is not (not-urban).

While Adam Scovell's 'folk horror chain' (2017: 8) gives some recognition to the discourse of Pagan as the presence of 'skewed belief systems and morality', the centrality of the landscape in his theory roots folk horror within the discourse of the Rural, but without interrogating the Rural as discourse, as a negotiated space of ideological division. Thurgill (2020: 33) notes 'it [the Rural in folk horror] derives from a deliberate attempt to exploit the *othering* process manifest in the presentation of pastoral communities as something outside of the normative' (original emphasis). The Rural, therefore, is the second discourse.

The key discourse least developed from almost all discussions of folk horror is that which seemingly gives the genre its name: Folklore. Folklore exists in the folk horror discussions in a popular 'common-sense' guise, and nobody I have encountered who writes on folk horror to date bothers to define what *Folklore* is. The word, *Folk-Lore*, was coined by William John Thoms in 1846 to describe 'the manners, customs, observances, superstitions, ballads, proverbs, etc., of the olden time' (quoted in Bauman 1992: 29). Thoms's own definition was designed to replace the previously used term, 'popular antiquities', which covers the material Thoms lists. 'Weird old shit', by any other name. As Bauman notes (1992: 31), 'To view an item of folklore as traditional is to see it as having temporal continuity, rooted in the past but persisting into the present in the manner of a natural object.' It is very much in this sense that folk horror scholars understand the Folklore in folk horror: those items from the past that have persisted to the contemporary. However, the discursive aspects of Folklore need interrogation. And that discourse rests on the relationship Folklore has with Tradition.

Barre Toelken refers to the 'twin laws' of Folklore: that in any given time and place, an item of Folklore will embody elements of both continuity to the past and readaptation in the present (Toelken 1996: 39). Whether the Folklore is presented as romantic and authentic, or as constructed and artificial, determines the power inequity inherent by the discourse. Late twentieth-century historians, and other cultural theorists, began to challenge not only ideas regarding 'authentic' national identity (Anderson 2006), but also to investigate the (relatively recent) construction of Tradition (Hobsbawm 1983). Folklore was likewise re-evaluated, particularly in its relation to Tradition, with Bauman stating that 'Tradition ... [must be] seen as a selective, interpretive construction, the social and symbolic creation of a connection between aspects of the present and an interpretation of the past' (Bauman 1992: 31–32).

Folklore does not simply lie in the furrows awaiting discovery; it is a continuous process of signification. This is also noted by Scovell, who further defines folk horror as 'a work that presents a clash between such arcana [items of folklore, 'popular antiquities'] and its presence within close proximity to some form of modernity' (2017: 7). The haunting by Tradition, in this regard, is particularly apt for the discussion of folk horror. Folklore as discourse surely therefore must be at the centre of any consideration of folk horror; and it is conspicuously absent from most of the discussions. Folklore is the third discourse.

Folk horror then, is the convergence of these three discourses: Pagan, Rural and Folklore. While each can be considered in isolation, folk horror is only meaningful, or can only be said to be meaningful, when the three discourses come together.

The Wicker Man

Robin Hardy's *The Wicker Man* (1973) is probably the most written-about film within the folk horror canon. I do not wish to add to the pages produced on this film, except as an application of what I proposed in terms of a reading protocol of the intersection of the three above-noted discourses: Pagan, Rural and Folklore.

The representation of Paganism in *The Wicker Man* is an obvious topic for scholars (see Koven 2007; or Hutton, and Zwissler, in this current volume).

The juxtaposition between the Christian Howie and the Pagans of Summerisle creates the key dramatic tension in the film. If the Summerislanders were Jews, Muslims or Buddhists, Howie might appear less antagonistic, since such belief systems are at least recognised by Christianity. Within the theological backstory to the film, Lord Summerisle's grandfather, who originally bought the island and introduced the 'Old Gods' back into active worship, effectively reversed 2,000 years of British-based theological genocide; while Christianity wiped Britain of all remnants of its earlier belief systems, the Lords Summerisle, for at least three generations, have wiped the island of Christianity. This is what Howie cannot comprehend: for him, Christianity is the 'true faith'; Christ is the 'true God'.

What is upsetting for Howie is his realisation that, on Summerisle, *his* God is not at the centre of creation or worship. If, as Robin Wood asserted, the basis of horror is that 'normality is threatened by the monster' (2018: 83), then Howie is *The Wicker Man*'s monster, as he is a threat to the stability of the 'normality' of the island. And that monstrousness emerges from his Christianity. Howie experiences what non-Christians do on a day-to-day basis when they live in a country that might 'tolerate' their existence but excludes them in more subtle ways. Howie's initial response is to view the people of Summerisle as delusional and completely misinformed. The horror of *The Wicker Man* is supposing Christianity's failure. Might a Pagan victory in this culture war leave only relics of churches marring the landscape in the future? We already see evidence of that on Summerisle, even while Howie tries feebly to resanctify the island's dilapidated church with two pieces of a broken Summerisle Apples crate. As Pagan is an antonym to Christian, Howie is forced to realise that antonyms are two-way streets; his Christianity is antonymic to the people of Summerisle. He is the monster to them. The evil on Summerisle is thus a moribund Christianity.

Beyond simply noting that the people of Summerisle are, in fact, Pagan, and that their Paganism is a resurrected reconstruction courtesy of Victorian anthropology and theories of cultural evolution, Pagan as discourse opens the film to larger discussions regarding the theological power relations inherent in the word 'Pagan'. The dominance of Christian hegemony in contemporary Britain is experienced without question, and as such, it silences, if not outright *denies*, alternatives to the western ubiquity of the Christian worldview. Could *The Wicker Man* be made without *any* recourse or reference to Christianity? Could the people of Summerisle be subject, rather than object, of the cinematic gaze? Such reconstruction of the cinematic discourse of Paganism is impossible when the Church, as institution, is so woven into every part of the national British fabric. But we only see this impossibility, and the extent of the Church's impact on our thinking, if we can see Paganism discursively.

The discourse of the Rural returns us to Scovell and his 'folk horror chain'. To see the Rural as discourse is to recognise the centrality of the Rural/Urban split in our culture. First, as we explore the ideas of this chain and its relation to the discourse of the Rural, the phrase Scovell uses to characterise the belief system within these communities ('skewed belief[s] ... and morality') is deeply imbued with the kind of self-righteous prejudice that Sergeant Howie uses to characterise the Paganism on Summerisle. What are the beliefs of the isolated community 'skewed' against, if not, implicitly, Christianity? Paul Newland notes the following (2008: 120): 'Summerisle is a territory in which Howie encounters the type of degenerate practices that he believes should have no place in what he sees as a modern, Christian Britain.' This 'skewing' also affects the 'morality' of the residents of Summerisle, as their morality is at odds with Christian hegemony. The imposition of Christian morality onto the 'immorality' of the Summerisle sex rituals is, within the folk horror chain, a direct result of their isolation. And here is where the Rural becomes discursive: the very idea that country folk are running Pagan sex cults reveals strong urban biases against the Rural. Or, as Paul Newland put it (2008: 126), a 'backwards, rural folk-type of British communities in which evil stirs'. Implicit in this criticism is that because of their isolation and the difficulties of their terrain (in the case of Summerisle, being on a privately owned island off the Highlands of Scotland – in other words, about as remote as possible in the United Kingdom), such is the perfect soil for 'skewed beliefs and morality' to flourish.

The discursive biases the Urban have towards the Rural suggest that, in a 'civilised' area, one which is not so isolated by the landscape, Pagan sex practices would not be able to survive because of the civilising environment of the city. The relative safety of the city in marked opposition to the 'Wild West' associations of the country is not borne out by the statistics on 'abhorrent sex practices', such as child sexual abuse, in Rural versus Urban areas. Population density, and the available resources, do not determine the 'skewed beliefs and morality' of a community. But how much rural horror implies murderous sexual deviancy in isolated rural environments? In a similar way that the discourse of the Pagan in *The Wicker Man* operates from a Christian hegemony, so too does the film's discourse of the Rural reveal its urban bias: a point also raised by Thurgill (2020). As *Blood on Satan's Claw* (1971) illustrates, a director who grew up in the countryside would understand a different expression of the discourse on the Rural from that which Hardy gives us in *The Wicker Man*.

The final discourse to be applied in *The Wicker Man* is Folklore, or, specifically, Folklore's relationship with Tradition. There are two key points to make, both of which I made (albeit poorly) in my 2007 article on *The Wicker Man*, what I called 'the folklore fallacy' (Koven 2007). The first point is that the film's director, Robin Hardy, and its screenwriter, Anthony Shaffer, did minimal research for the film. There is an irony that the rituals of May Day, which play so central to the film and occur across its final half hour, are fully explained to Howie in a few short hours of library reading in the Summerisle library. He appears to have consulted only a single book: probably James George Frazer's *The Golden Bough*, the same singular book that Hardy and Shaffer appear to have read. So, what they know about ancient 'folklore' is no more than what Howie discovers in his short library visit. Their superficial research grabs hold of all (highly visual) 'popular antiquities' used to fill up their *mise-en-scène*, regardless of their context or function within the traditional societies the authors of the film pilfered from. *The Wicker Man* is like a museum room filled with poorly labelled arcana collected via the Colonialist project over several centuries of theft, exploitation and genocide. Particularly during the May Day celebrations leading up to Howie's 'appointment with the Wicker Man', we are presented with a huge list of Folklore items – John Barleycorn, the Salmon of Knowledge, Punch, the Hobbyhorse, the Hand of Glory, the Sword-Dance and the May Day procession itself. All of these items, while legitimate pieces of traditional folk culture, are decontextualised simply as 'tradition'.

As noted above, the Pagan culture of Summerisle was a nineteenth-century construction by the grandfather of the current Lord Summerisle. So, contrary to what I wrote in 2007, the authenticity of *The Wicker Man* is the authenticity of a nineteenth-century folklore reconstruction, not of ancient Celtic rites, which Shaffer and Hardy claimed. In this way, as Bauman noted (1992: 31), Summerisle is very much in keeping with those Victorian folklore romantic ideals in opposition to the horrors of modernity. Grandfather Summerisle sought to recreate a prelapsarian (pre-Christian) Celtic community based on the nineteenth-century ideas he was familiar with. The Folklore then is presented, by Hardy, in this sense of colourful and exciting romanticism. So, Folklore, as discourse, by way of Tradition and its connection to nineteenth-century romanticism, attempts to recreate a Celtic paradise.

But there is another side to the discourse of Tradition, one that addresses the position of Tradition within the diegesis, as well as for the film's audience(s): there is an assumed reality to the constructed society of Summerisle, one that Shaffer, Hardy and actor Christopher Lee spoke to whenever asked about the film. In the documentary *Burnt Offering: The Cult of the Wicker Man* (Andrew Abbott and Russell Leven, 2001), and included on the 2013 Blu-ray edition of the 'Final Cut', Robin Hardy makes the point that, when the gigantic bonfire was constructed with which the film concludes, its like had not been seen in Britain for 2,000 years. Implicit in Hardy's comment is that he fully recognised that the wicker man constructed and burnt for the film was a modern build, but that by orchestrating this ritual (as the film's director), he was engaging in a very old, but very real, ancient rite. What Hardy, Lee and Shaffer fail to realise is that 'no they didn't', or rather that the evidence for ancient Celts engaging in this kind of blood sacrifice ritual is highly dubious. Ronald Hutton, in this current volume, discusses extensively how constructed the stories about ancient Celtic barbarity were, including recognising the unlikeliness that the ancient Celts burned human sacrifices in wicker effigies; the Celts were, for late classical writers such as Julius Caesar, 'a litmus test for savagery' (p. 27), and this is a perception that *The Wicker Man* is all too willing to exploit. Howie makes this explicit when he refers to 'pagan barbarity which [he] can scarcely believe as taking place in the twentieth century'.

Therefore, to see Folklore itself as discourse is to interrogate the film's use of Tradition: whether as a romantic connection to an unproblematic, or uncontested, past, or as a modern construct attempting to give meaning to our present by connecting it to the past. But in order to access Folklore's discourse we need to do the research into the traditions represented, and interrogate their connection to, in this case, Britain's bloody past of colonial exploitation and murder.

The Company of Wolves

The Company of Wolves (Neil Jordan, 1984) is rarely written about in the context of folk horror; Scovell mentions it in passing (2017: 95), and a separate essay on the film by Monique Lacoste is included in Howard David Ingham's *We Don't Go Back* (Lacoste 2018). Although significantly, neither writer discusses the film *as* folk horror: Scovell's comment is about rural horror, and Lacoste presents a feminist critique of the film informed by Jungian analysis. Elsewhere, the film generated debates in feminist literary circles, as well as by folklorists discussing the film's relationship to the fairy-tale film (see Snowden 2010; Zipes 2011; Jowett 2012; Hughes 2020). However, by applying the discursive approach suggested in this current chapter, the place of *The Company of Wolves* as a folk horror film is as relevant as any of the 'unholy trinity'.

Based on three short stories by Angela Carter – 'The Werewolf', 'The Company of Wolves' and 'Wolf-Alice', all of which appear in her collection *The Bloody Chamber* (2011 [1979]) – *The Company of Wolves* is a 'Chinese box' (Lacoste 2018: 134) of storytelling, each story echoing variations on the 'Little Red Riding Hood' fairy tale. A framing narrative sees a contemporary young teenage girl, Rosaleen, asleep in her room in the middle of the afternoon. Her parents arrive home at their large country house, and her elder teenage sister, Alice, cannot wait to 'grass' on Rosaleen's bad behaviour. The main narrative of this film are Rosaleen's dreams: the first one sees Alice chased and then killed by a pack of wolves and the monstrous-sized toys we have just seen in Rosaleen's room. Rosaleen's second dream is an extended narrative following the 'Red Riding Hood' story: her sister is killed by wolves (echoing the previous dream), and Rosaleen goes off to stay at Granny's for the night. She returns to her village and home and is witness to the men-folk going out to hunt the wolf that killed Alice. Meanwhile, Rosaleen is flirting with a local boy her own age, listed only as 'Amorous Boy', before she is sent to Granny's with a basket of goodies. While en route, she meets a mysterious and handsome Huntsman, who seduces her, and they playfully wager on who will get to Granny's first – Rosaleen or the Huntsman. The Huntsman wins the bet, kills Granny and lies waiting for Rosaleen to show up. Cue the 'What big teeth you have' exchange between Rosaleen and the Huntsman, before he transforms into a wolf. But rather than being consumed by him, the girl takes pity on the wolf/man, and instead chooses to join him as a wolf/woman. At key points in the main Rosaleen narrative, first Granny, and then Rosaleen herself, tell a combined total of four stories, each of which is dramatised.

While *The Company of Wolves* includes no explicit reference to paganism or witchcraft, Granny does tell one story about a young boy who makes a deal with the devil to speed up his maturation and is transformed into a wolf, perhaps suggestive of an origin story to the werewolves of the forest. Reference is also made throughout the film to these werewolves being 'people of the forest' (it is how the Huntsman introduces himself to Rosaleen), and suggestive of a tribe of shapeshifters inhabiting the liminal spaces surrounding the village (forest, wells). But these explicit references to Otherness and contra-Christian/demonic forces are but surface details. Let us consider instead the geography in Rosaleen's dream, and in this regard, the Pagan overlaps tremendously with the Rural. There are at least three spaces in the dream: the village, Granny's house and the forest. While all three spaces are distinctly 'Rural', some are more isolated than others. The village, for example, where Rosaleen lives with her parents, is centred around a communal well. In a small community like this, everyone's safety is mutually reassured by close proximity to their neighbour. The village is also 'protected' by the church, and its attendant priest. Granny's house is outside the village, seemingly by several miles, and whilst safe(ish), is less safe because of its relative isolation. Granny herself plays with Paganism, not in the sense of witchcraft, but in her verbal antagonism towards the Old Priest. As Granny tells Rosaleen in the churchyard – with the Old Priest overhearing – a story about priests impregnating young parishioners: 'Well you can't trust anyone, least of all a priest. He's not called "Father" for nothing.' Despite Granny's apparent irreverence towards Christianity, in the one scene inside the church, Granny is an active parishioner. While the entire world of Rosaleen's dream is Rural, and there is no mention of any kind of larger settlement or city, there are degrees of rurality. The village is certainly Rural, but Granny's house is *more Rural*.

In between these two states of relative safety lies the danger of the forest. The association of the forest with danger runs all the way back to the first versions of 'Red Riding Hood'. The path through the forest, while recognised as dangerous, demarcates some degree of safety through all the danger. It is safer than the woods, but less safe than the village. A shot of Granny and Rosaleen walking along the path through the forest is an echo of an earlier shot, during the opening credits of the film and taking place in the contemporary framing story, where we see a car (diegetically, driven by Rosaleen's and Alice's parents returning home) driving through another/the same(?) forest, suggesting that we have always relied on the existence of paths to help us navigate our way through danger. The Church may be one such 'path' (metaphorically speaking), while Granny's wisdom is another: as she famously states to Rosaleen: 'You've got a lot to learn child. Never stray from the path, never eat a windfall apple [an apple that has fallen to the ground], and never trust a man whose eyebrows meet.' Granny's wisdom is a perversion of Christian doctrine (a 'skewing', if you will). Later that evening, as Granny and Rosaleen are sitting by the hearth, Granny tells her granddaughter that 'A wolf may be more than he seems ... The wolf that ate your sister was hairy on the outside, but when she died, she went straight to Heaven. The worst kind of wolves are hairy on the inside, and when they bite you, they drag you with them to Hell.' Granny's isolation outside the safety of the village encourages her warping of Christian virtue: here again we can see Scovell's 'skewed belief systems and morality' as both the consequence of her isolation, and hinting towards a counter-Christian paganism. And yet, given her references to heaven and hell, the Christian worldview is still present, but 'skewed'. It is a homespun Christian virtue, not official Church doctrine; a kind of folk religion, if you will. The Rural is the site for non-doctrinal Christianity to develop, a motif seen in many rural horror movies.

In *The Company of Wolves*, the Pagan is present explicitly in its single evocation of the devil and the hinted-at tribe of werewolf-people, but is further suggested by the antagonism between Granny and the Old Priest, and Granny's own 'skewed belief system', despite its grounding in vague Christian doctrine. The Rural is likewise evoked through the film's regional geography – of village, forest and fringe – and such geography feeds into the discourses of Paganism the film suggests.

But it is the discourse of Folklore, and specifically Folklore's relation to Tradition, whereby *The Company of Wolves* grounds itself in the folk horror genre. As is all too obvious, as *The Company of Wolves* is based on the fairy tale of 'Red Riding Hood', and fairy tales are a major narrative genre of Folklore, then the film's Folklore is worn on its shredded sleeve; and that connection is mostly from the source material, Angela Carter's short stories. Director Jordan takes the Folklore discourse further. In the film's opening credit sequence, establishing the frame narrative, a large German Shepherd dog is sniffing around an abandoned well. The dog unearths an old-fashioned abandoned doll with a porcelain head. Leaving the doll where s/he found it, the dog runs through the forest. It is in this sequence where the shot, noted above, with the sisters' parents returning home in a car, is included. The well will play a much more significant role later in the film. It is the centre of the dreamt village, a centre for the community to revolve around; and its inclusion in the opening credits suggests that the village may have once stood where the family's Georgian-style country manor now stands. The well is also the means of ingress and egress, into and out of the village, for the wolf-woman in the story Rosaleen tells the Huntsman/Wolf towards the film's conclusion. As Lacoste notes (2018: 135), 'Wells have long held spiritual significance, positioned in different mythic systems as sources of life, as representations of the womb, and as passageways between the material and the spiritual.' The porcelain-headed doll too is later echoed in how Granny's head explodes when it is flung against the wall by the Huntsman/Wolf. But it is the action of the dog unearthing the long-abandoned doll that speaks to the film's problematising of Tradition. Much like the finding of the 'fiend in the furrows' that opens *Blood on Satan's Claw*, the dog's discovery brings to the present that which had been buried. Jordan evokes several key themes of the film's use of Folklore in this moment: the rediscovery of things from childhood we have lost – abandoned dolls, fairy tales, innocence; the German Shepherd running through the forest reminding us that our modern and much-loved pets are barely removed from the wildness of wolves; and that the past and Tradition are never too far from our modernity and contemporaneity. Folklore, the film suggests, is just under the skin, under the surface, in the underbrush, abandoned and left behind, but never hidden for very long. We even travel along the same routes of safety through the woods that our ancestors traversed so many generations past.

    Linked with this discussion of Tradition and Folklore is the sense of cultural inheritance. In these opening sequences of the framing narrative, a pan around Rosaleen's room shows many antique-looking toys (incongruous for a young girl in 1984), including the teddy bear and little sailor doll that grow to enormous proportions and will attack Alice in Rosaleen's first dream. It is the hand-me-down suggestion of the antiquated toys in Rosaleen's room that makes them function as signifiers of inheritance. Nothing feels 'new' in Rosaleen's room, as if everything she has was first somebody else's. In her dream, Rosaleen receives a silver cross from her mother that was once her sister's, and at the end of the film, it is this cross hanging around the she-wolf's neck that enables Rosaleen's mother to recognise what happened to her daughter. Ironically, the silver crucifix, given 'for protection' to Rosaleen, saves the girl not from the wolf, but from being murdered by her own father (who does not recognise her as anything other than a wolf). Folklore, like the toys in Rosaleen's room, or the silver crucifix, is a connection to the past – much like the abandoned well and the suggestion of continuity from the dream village to the contemporary country house.

The key inheritance the film presents is, of course, storytelling, a point made explicit by Kim Snowden (2010: 167): 'The film ... refer[s] to oral storytelling traditions, particularly passing down stories through generations of women.' Rosaleen is the recipient of two of Granny's stories, the aforementioned boy who meets the devil in the woods, but also a complicated narrative that needs some unpacking. In Granny's first story, she tells of a young village woman who marries 'a travelling man' (Irish Traveller), but her husband disappears on their wedding night, seemingly taken by the wolves when he went outside to urinate. The young widow marries a second time, and in a few short years has several children from her second husband, when her first reappears on her doorstep. Angered that she had not kept her vows while he was gone, he attacks her, she defends herself, and in a tremendous rage the Traveller transforms into a wolf. The second husband returns, beheads the wolf, and slaps her hard across her face seemingly for allowing a strange man into the home, if not for the emasculating reminder that he was not her first man. Granny's narration is light and superficial – 'but she was a young thing. And cheerful of temperament. And she soon found another husband' – but the images Jordan includes of the young woman's life with the second husband are grim and difficult: cooking, cleaning and raising several screaming children. We do not know the occupation of the second husband, but we can clearly see that he is away and is not helping with the family life. However, in another sense, the return of the first husband suggests the psychoanalytic concept of the return of the repressed, where that which is repressed comes back in monstrous form until it is properly 'dealt with'. Here, the first husband's return is literally monstrous in that he is a werewolf, and his transformation into the monster is marvellously gory using the practical effects technology of the day. This monster is 'properly dealt with' in that he is beheaded by the second husband. But the second husband also turns out to be monstrous as an abusive wife-beater, slapping the young woman across the face. This second monster is *not* dealt with, however. An abusive husband is simply a woman's lot in life. Some monsters are acceptable in tradition, like abusers; some monsters need to be killed, like werewolves. But this double standard is there for us watching the film to problematise the concept of Tradition; as it may also be for Rosaleen listening to Granny. For Granny, this is just the way the world is. Folk horror embodies the return of the repressed graphically. Folklore, when ignored, when denied, remains just below the surface; it takes very little for it to be unearthed: it only takes a dog rummaging around an abandoned well, or a young farmer ploughing his field, for it to be discovered.

Rosaleen becomes a storyteller too, first to her mother, then to her beloved, the Huntsman/Wolf, keeping the inheritance of storytelling alive. But more important than the stories themselves is what the stories reflect, the kind of folk wisdom they are passing on. And in this regard, Granny and Rosaleen are on opposite sides of the Tradition/Modernity divide. Jack Zipes notes (2011: 149):

> the film ... could be viewed as a storytelling duel between a grandmother, who spreads idle superstitious lies to scare her granddaughter so that she will distrust men and sex, and her granddaughter who creates tales about outcasts who need more love and trust in the world, otherwise they will continue to be marginalized.

Granny's (skewed) morality is 'old-fashioned' to Rosaleen, while Granny thinks Rosaleen's ideas are 'foolishness'. Consider the following dialogue early on in the film:

Granny: Your only sister, all alone in the wood, and nobody there to save her.
Rosaleen: Why couldn't she save herself?
Granny: You don't know anything. You're only a child.

The dialogue may be heavy-handed, but it speaks to the changes in generational attitude regarding gender. Granny expects someone to come to a young girl's rescue, Rosaleen thinks young girls should learn how to save themselves. Even Rosaleen's mother thinks Granny's ideas are outdated: Granny may think all men are beasts, but Rosaleen's mother tells her daughter that women can be beasts too. As Snowden notes (2010: 171):

> Rosaleen rejects these traditional roles and stories. The narrative that she hears from Granny but retells to her mother and the werewolf invokes women who stray from the path and are comfortable in the forest, who are kin to the wolves, recognizing themselves in these animals' otherness.

Folklore, particularly those transcribed tales in archives, rather than the literary refashioning by nineteenth-century men (i.e. the Grimms, Joseph Jacobs, Andrew Lang, and of course Charles Perrault two centuries earlier), bears witness to the centrality of women storytellers in the passing on of traditional folktales (cf. Darnton 1999; Warner 1994). Rosaleen may very well keep up the tradition of women storytellers in her family, but she will update and modernise the gender politics in them, reflecting the 'twin laws of Folklore' I noted above.

Conclusions

Seeing the key discourses of the Pagan, the Rural and Folklore converging opens the film text to additional discussions beyond the now trite representation of the rural and spooky old stuff that dominates folk horror. Foucauldian discourse analysis offers a reading protocol that suggests investigating how power inequity shapes and controls the processes of signification, illustrating larger ideological issues that any appreciation of these films must contend with. Of course, understanding any aspect of cultural hegemony is *de rigueur* for film scholarship, but examining key aspects of folk horror, in particular through the lens of discourse analysis, enables us to engage discussions larger than the film can present on its surface. Of course, the ambivalent discourses of Folklore and Tradition further complicate such explorations in that we can neither completely abandon our cultural pasts, nor always face the repercussions from those pasts. Any discussion must take into account the power relations inherent *in* that discussion.

I have applied discourse analysis in two ways here. *The Wicker Man*, a film that literally defines the folk horror film phenomenon, illustrates that a discursive methodology works. To apply the methodology to a film not always recognised as a folk horror film, *The Company of Wolves*, shows what new discussions are possible when we try to read the film with a folk horror discourse. Of course, we can play spot-the-motif and annotate either film's use of decontextualised Folklore. We can critique the film's prejudiced depiction of Celtic pagan excesses or challenge the authenticity of the storytelling. But unless we can problematise the centrality of Christianity in *de facto* discussions about paganism, recognise the urban bias in the creation of rural horror stories, and question the relative purpose of Tradition and Folklore in one's connections to the past, we risk simply duplicating what the film text already tells us. Huge layers of meaning lie undisturbed beneath the surface of these films. But, if the concept of the 'return of the repressed' in horror cinema has taught us nothing, those things we try to bury, our cultural abject, have a nasty habit of catching up with us, usually in unpleasant ways.

References

Anderson, Benedict (2006), *Imagined Communities: Reflections on the Origin and Spread of Nationalism*, rev. edn. London: Verso.

Bauman, Richard (1992), 'Folklore', in Richard Bauman (ed.), *Folklore, Cultural Performances, and Popular Entertainments: A Communications-Centered Handbook*. Oxford: Oxford University Press, pp. 29–40.

Cameron, Alan (2011), *The Last Pagans of Rome*. Oxford: Oxford University Press.

Carter, Angela (2011 [1979]), *The Bloody Chamber*. London: Penguin Books.

Darnton, Robert (1999), 'Peasants Tell Tales: The Meaning of Mother Goose', in *The Great Cat Massacre, and Other Episodes in French Cultural History*. New York: Basic Books, pp. 9–74.

Defra [Department for Environment, Food and Rural Affairs] (2009), 'Defra Classification of Local Authority Districts and Unitary Authorities in England', assets.publishing.service.gov.uk/government/uploads/system/uploads/attachment_data/file/137661/la-class-updated-technical.pdf (accessed 2 March 2022).

Foucault, Michel (1972), *The Archaeology of Knowledge and the Discourse of Language*, trans. A. M. Sheridan Smith. New York: Pantheon Books.

HRSA [Health Resources & Services Administration] (2021), 'Defining Rural Population', www.hrsa.gov/rural-health/about-us/what-is-rural (accessed 2 March 2022).

Hobsbawm, Eric (1983), 'Introduction: Inventing Traditions', in Eric Hobsbawm and Terence Ranger (eds), *The Invention of Tradition*. Cambridge: Cambridge University Press, pp. 1–14.

Hughes, Bill (2020), '"The price of flesh is love": Commodification, Corporeality and Paranormal Romance in Angela Carter's Beast Tales', in Sam George and Bill Hughes (eds), *In the Company of Wolves: Werewolves, Wolves and Wild Children*. Manchester: Manchester University Press, pp. 147–162.

Ingham, Howard David (2018), *We Don't Go Back: A Watcher's Guide to Folk Horror*. Swansea: Room 207 Press.

Jowett, Lorna (2012), 'Between the Paws of the Tender Wolf: Authorship, Adaptation and Audience', in Sonya Andermahr and Lawrence Phillips (eds), *Angela Carter: New Critical Readings*. London: Continuum, pp. 58–73.

Koven, Mikel J. (2007), 'The Folklore Fallacy: A Folkloristic/Filmic Perspective on *The Wicker Man*', *Fabula* 48:3–4, 270–280.

Lacoste, Monique (2018), '*The Company of Wolves* (1984)', in Howard David Ingham (ed.), *We Don't Go Back: A Watcher's Guide to Folk Horror*. Swansea: Room 207 Press, pp. 133–141.

Newland, Paul (2008), 'Folksploitation: Charting the Horrors of the British Folk Music Tradition in *The Wicker Man*', in Robert Shail (ed), *Seventies British Cinema*. London: Bloomsbury, pp. 119–128.

Newland, Paul (2016), 'Folk Horror and the Contemporary Cult of British Rural Landscape: The Case of *Blood on Satan's Claw*', in Paul Newland (ed.), *British Rural Landscapes on Film*. Manchester: Manchester University Press, pp. 162–179.

Scovell, Adam (2017), *Folk Horror: Hours Dreadful and Things Strange*. Leighton Buzzard: Auteur.

Snowden, Kim (2010), 'Fairy Tale Film in the Classroom: Feminist Cultural Pedagogy, Angela Carter, and Neil Jordan's *The Company of Wolves*', in Pauline Greenhill and Sidney Eve Matrix (eds), *Fairy Tale Films: Visions of Ambiguity*. Logan: Utah State University Press, pp. 157–177.

Thurgill, James (2020), 'A Fear of the Folk: On *Topophobia* and the Horror of Rural Landscapes', *Revenant* 5 (March), 33–56.

Toelken, Barre (1996), *The Dynamics of Folklore*, rev. and expanded edn. Logan: Utah State University Press.

Warner, Marina (1994), *From the Beast to the Blonde: On Fairy Tales and Their Tellers*. New York: Farrar, Straus and Giroux.

Wood, Robin (2018), 'An Introduction to the American Horror Film', in *Robin Wood on the Horror Film: Collected Essays and Reviews*, ed. Barry Keith Grant. Detroit: Wayne State University Press, pp. 73–110.

Zipes, Jack (2011), *The Enchanted Screen: The Unknown History of Fairy-Tale Films*. London: Routledge.

Part II

Return of the British repressed

4

The folk of folk horror

Derek Johnston

This chapter considers the importance of 'the folk' in folk horror, focusing on the people of the communities portrayed. Through this examination of these representations of communities of 'common people', it considers the ways that folk horror texts engage with ideas of power and identity. This in turn may suggest some of the reasons that folk horror has faced something of a resurgence in the second decade of the twenty-first century, as well as why it was relevant to its original contexts primarily in the 1970s in the UK. Folk horror texts are frequently concerned with tensions between the people and their leaders, between the local and the national or international, and even between different interpretations of reality. They can appeal to romanticised notions of close-knit rural communities of certainty, where everyone had a place, while at the same time showing the horrific costs of those communities. None of this is to suggest that 'the folk' should be considered to be the defining feature of folk horror. Rather, the chapter picks at part of the term used to describe the genre, and some of the ideas that are associated with it, in order to consider what they might mean for the genre, and for how people engage with it, and the meanings they may derive from it.

The chapter will first outline some of the key ideas around this exploration of the folk of folk horror, considering constructions of the notion of 'the folk' that have been frequently linked to notions of national identity and questions of authenticity. The implications of these ideas will be drawn out through consideration of three case studies in the form of the original 'unholy trinity' of folk horror. The notion of community is developed in relation to *Witchfinder General* (1968), which shows how notions of the folk and horrors arising from folk beliefs need not be connected to individual, isolated communities but can infect a wider area, potentially connecting to ideas of nation. *Blood on Satan's Claw* (1971) is explored as the original usage of the term 'folk horror', which put the focus on ordinary people and their experience of the supernatural as a response to the dominant gothic strain of British horror at the time. This raises notions of authority and power, which are explored further in relation to *The Wicker Man* (1973) alongside questions of authenticity, centred around the figure of the sage who leads the community in their rituals. These three films thus demonstrate how folk horror can be interpreted through a consistent recurring concern with notions of belonging, and tensions in its presentation of supposed ancient beliefs and practices and their connections to identity.

The conception of 'folk' culture carries connotations of tradition, arising particularly from notions of a rural 'common people' who preserve older ways of life, frequently opposed to the populations of urban centres who were considered to represent modernity through their consumption of industrially produced popular culture. Paul Cowdell points to a preindustrial beginning to these concerns when he states that 'The upheaval of the British Civil Wars of the seventeenth century drove antiquaries to an ever greater interest in the oral traditions and culture they perceived as "lost" in the rapid and drastic political changes', leading to the development of the discipline of folklore (2019: 298). This suggests one of the reasons that the seventeenth century has become important to folk horror, not just as a time of national and cultural upheaval but also as a shift to recording the everyday and the stories of the folk.

Such ideas developed further in the eighteenth century with figures such as Johann-Gottfried von Herder and his collecting of *Volkslieder*, or the Brothers Grimm and their collections of folk tales. In preserving these songs and stories the folk carried ideas of authenticity, particularly authenticity in relation to the national past. This national past was in turn connected to the landscape and nature of the country through the folk and their habitation of rural areas and their agricultural practices, working in and with nature rather than in the artificial environments of the cities and factories. Returning to folk culture through the collection of folk tales, folk songs and folk practices such as dance was a way of returning to the roots of a culture, particularly a national culture, as an act of purification in which 'the soul of the nation could be made to rise above the contamination and corruption of a mechanical and material civilization' (Storey 2003: 3). The collectors of this folk culture often saw what they collected as the remnants of a larger, lost culture, and so as things that needed to be gathered and preserved by the educated middle classes as a way of protecting and reinvigorating the national culture. This counts just as well for the eighteenth-century antiquarians and collectors of folk tales at the birth of modern nationhood as it does with the folk-tale-, dance- and song-collectors of the early twentieth century. Led by figures such as Cecil Sharp, these collectors were again concerned with ideas of the national heritage and identity at a time of shifting global power, particularly in terms of the growth of mass media and accompanying fears of the loss of national identity.

Writing about this twentieth-century British Folk Revival, Georgina Boyes pointed out that this idea that folk song and dance were actual unchanged survivals of earlier, long-standing traditions was necessarily based on 'a definition of the Folk as manifesting a comprehensive absence of creativity' if they were not tempted to update and adapt this old material (Boyes 2010: 12). Not only that, but these ideas in the context of the British Folk Revival ignore just how much nineteenth- and early-twentieth-century England was already a well-connected, well-educated, literate society. While remoteness may certainly help to sustain traditions and locally specific knowledge and practices, the romantic conception of 'the folk' put forward by Sharp and his ilk was less a reflection of reality and more an idea of what they thought 'the folk' should be. It essentialised a view of who the 'true English' were, while simultaneously providing apparent support for claims about the 'purity' of the folk songs and traditions recorded as lines of contact with the otherwise lost past.

Paul Cowdell links folk horror to this collecting and interpreting of folk culture, claiming that 'folk horror as a subgenre essentially owes its structure and character to thinking around the historical emergence and development of folklore as a discipline in Britain' (2019: 296). He draws upon the conception of the 'folkloresque', material that attempts to represent the feeling of folklore, as theorised by Michael Dylan Foster, while also highlighting the debt that folk horror owes to antiquarianism, and to the antiquarian ghost story, such as those of M. R. James (Cowdell 2019: 297). As Cowdell points out, 'The impact of German Romanticism's later attention to survivals (pagan or otherwise) as a national cultural peasant heritage, which led directly to the identification of folklore as a separate field of study, also plays out through the films' (2019: 298). So we can connect the tensions around national identity and heritage that have played out through various folk revivals from the late eighteenth century onwards to the depiction of the folk in folk horror films. Yet it is important to remember the 'horror' element of 'folk horror', and so to consider what the genre or the individual texts may be suggesting about these relationships. As with other genres, while a concern over the folk and their relationship to the land and to identity may be common in many folk horror texts, what individual texts can be understood to do with that concern will depend on that individual text, not to mention the individual responses of audience members to that text and those ideas.

So we have a series of issues around the folk, identity and power. The folk are seen in these romantic conceptions to be the keepers of true national identity, tied to the land and old knowledge. However, they are also seen as remnants, hidden away in remote parts of the country and so detached from modernity and the reality of everyday life in the modern world. This very detachment and strangeness makes these communities and their ways unfamiliar and unsettling, as James Thurgill has argued:

> The positioning of folk horror as an inherently rural rendering of the eerie is not pure happenstance; rather, it derives from a deliberate attempt to exploit the *othering* process manifest in the presentation of pastoral communities as something outside of the normative. To this end, folk horror presents us with a spatial politics that works to further alienate rural communities from the contemporary 'mainstream', placing the pastoral within a context of both spiritual and physical threat. (2020: 33–34)

The modern world is seen as expanding and encroaching, meaning that the old ways need to be collected and protected by the educated middle classes, who would also take on the responsibility of disseminating this collected material. In this way, the voice of the folk and their control over this material is taken over by the educated middle classes, as part of a conscious programme of regenerating ideas of national identity and heritage against the homogenising forces of the globalising, interconnected modern world.

The remoteness of the communities in folk horror is thus part of explaining any survival of 'the old ways'. It also can represent a voluntary removal of the community, or at least key members of the community, from the modern world, as seen particularly in *The Village* (2004) or *Apostle* (2018). In particular, it signals not just a separation from the norms of modern life, but also a removal from the easy reach of the State. The people of these communities are thus able to continue or reproduce ideas of more traditional and more localised power structures, and enforcement of laws and cultural norms.

One of the founders of the Folk-Lore Society, Sir Edward Burnet Tylor, projected the view that the survival of folklore represented the survival of a more primitive stage of human social evolution:

> civilization had marched on, leaving behind, in the beliefs and practices of 'peasants' and 'savages,' the fragmented remains of a once shared antiquity – a reminder to the 'educated' (i.e. the dominant classes) of what they had once been and what still remained in both the colonies and the threatening darkness of the new industrial towns and cities of Europe and the USA. (Storey 2003: 6)

This suggests one of thrills of folk practice for some: a sense of accessing 'savagery' without the restraints of 'civilisation' and behavioural norms – 'savagery' here suggesting a sense of lack of emotional and legal and social control, an ability to enact fantasies of sexual and emotional freedom. It also suggests some of the horror of folk horror: that these 'savage' practices can still exist not in some distant, foreign land, waiting to be stamped out by the 'civilising' imperialist, but at the heart of the home nation. And if these survivals were also part of the original, 'true' national identity, then that meant that there was savagery at the heart of the nation. Of course, folk horror communities tend not to be outwardly 'savage', but instead typically offer a pleasant outward appearance and a focus on the local social structure rather than being part of wider governance, while retaining the appeal of greater emotional and sexual freedom, including a greater freedom to act violently in the service of the community.

In many folk horror texts this is emphasised by the presence of a recognised leader in these isolated communities, separated from the ordinary folk by education and/or social status: Lord Summerisle in *The Wicker Man*, Stephanie Bax in *The Witches* (1966), Arthur the vet in *Wake Wood* (2009), Fisher in the *Play for Today* episode 'Robin Redbreast' (1970). This figure of the sage is often responsible for continuing or introducing the ritual behaviours to the community, and can be understood either as a priest-protector of old beliefs, or as someone with greater formal and educational capital exploiting the folk, depending on how the individual text treats them. This reproduction of a form of class system can further reinforce the potential in reading folk horror communities as microcosms of the wider nation. With this idea of the individual text and the interpretation of the text in mind, this chapter now turns to three case studies to examine some of the themes and ideas around the folk of folk horror in particular practice.

Witchfinder General: Folk and nation

James Thurgill states that the 'unholy trinity' of folk horror depict the folk in the same way: 'unmodern, superstitious and, above all, capable of enacting extreme violence to conserve the rural idyll' (2020: 33). This is clearly seen in *Witchfinder General*, the earliest of these three films. It also has the earliest setting, being set during the English Civil War in 1645, establishing this as a time of chaos in the country. As the opening narration states, 'The structure of law and order has collapsed', and this provides opportunities for some of the people to assert power over others. This power connects to wider power structures and is exploited by those who see a way to profit by it, such as the Witchfinder General himself, Matthew Hopkins: as the film's opening narration states, 'In a time where the superstitions of country folk are still a powerful factor, Hopkins plays upon them, torturing and killing in a supposed drive to eliminate witchcraft from the country, and doing so with the full blessing of what law there is.' The film thus presents the folk as superstitious, and their superstitions as having power, in the same way that the rituals and beliefs of the people of Summerisle have power, in both cases focused through a leader of higher social and educational status: in this case Hopkins, a lawyer.

Yet Hopkins and his colleague, Stearne, are only exploiting the situation, and in doing so are being used by the ordinary people. It is the folk who are responsible for the witch panic: Hopkins is summoned to Brandeston by the people to try those they perceive as not belonging, such as the Catholic priest, John Lowes. Hopkins's host in Lavenham states that he (the host) is 'representing the town' in accusing the women that Hopkins has come to test. A gaggle of villagers surround Hopkins and Stearne on their arrival in Brandeston, giving their reasons for believing Lowes to be a witch, and they take part in the initial questioning. Villagers watch approvingly as Stearne interrogates people, villagers drag people to dunking or execution and participate in both, children in Lavenham poke the accused witches with sticks and cook potatoes in the ashes of the execution fire. One man even watches and laughs as Stearne rapes Sarah, using this witnessing to manipulate Hopkins. Frequently, the folk watch without much sign of either pleasure or disgust.

The summoning of Hopkins highlights a key aspect of this film: it is not about one isolated community but about a nation, with a high degree of mobility between places. There is the mobility of the army, and so of the hero Richard Marshall; there is the mobility of Hopkins and Stearne, who arrive in Brandeston from elsewhere, and move on to Oxney, Cambridge and Lavenham. There is also the mobility of the fleeing King, who escapes to France, and the mobility of the country folk who can send for Hopkins, or who themselves move about as part of their trade and lives: note the presence of Wilfrid Brambell as an Irish-accented horse trader in East Anglia, and of the boatman who seems not to know that there is a war in England, but who readily took the King to France and knows about the witch trials in Lavenham. This is not a single isolated community, but a connected network of communities that draws on structures of law and belief in order to create a society fitting their desires.

There is little real indication of what that society would look like. There is the sectarianism of the attack on Lowes. Hopkins does remark drily, on being informed that the suspected witches of Lavenham are all women, 'Strange, isn't it, how much iniquity the Lord vested in the female?'. However, there are no specifics as to why these individuals were targeted. It is also notable that witchfinding is not opposed by Marshall, in general, although he is clearly opposed to the persecution of Lowes and is generally portrayed as open-minded, non-sectarian and interested in expanding his horizons. Ian Cooper argues that:

> This depiction of the populace not as an amorphous, essentially decent, group of people but rather a baleful ignorant mass, is a disturbing one because it subverts a fundamental convention of the horror film. For Reeves, the 'monster' is not an abberation [sic] in an otherwise-ordered world; it is the world itself which is monstrous. (2011: 77–78)

This seems an unusual statement to make in the face of the beauty of the natural world presented in the film, so perhaps the argument should rather be that it is people, and particularly the ordinary, uneducated folk, who are monstrous.

The folk horror of *Witchfinder General* is the horror of the folk, and of what they are capable of when given the ability to choose, to manipulate power structures, to satisfy their own desires. *Blood on Satan's Claw* takes a more supernatural approach to this, presenting what happens when these possibilities are provided not by civil war, but when spurred on by supernatural power. It also moves 'the folk' from being largely nameless, part of a mob, to being individuals involved centrally with the narrative.

The original folk horror: *Blood on Satan's Claw*

Blood on Satan's Claw has a strong claim on being the original 'folk horror' text, as it appears to be the first film to which the label was attached. An article on the production of the film in the April 1970 *Kine Weekly* was entitled 'Folk Horror Study from Hemdale and Chilton', and director Piers Haggard later stated in a 2003 interview for *Fangoria* magazine that 'I was trying to make a folk-horror film, I suppose' (Evans-Powell 2021: 9–10). What Haggard meant by this is made slightly clearer by his preceding comments: 'As this was a story about people subject to superstitions about living in the woods, the dark poetry of that appealed to me' (quoted in Evans-Powell 2021: 10), suggesting a particular focus on the 'ordinary' people. Paul Cowdell has drawn a contrast between folk horror and the previously dominant gothic paradigm, to argue that:

> The superstitious peasantry, in all their muddy reality, move from background to centerstage in folk horror. They become less plot adjuncts than the defining milieu. Folk horror films are predicated on more complete visions of socio-economic worlds within a time and space [than Gothic horror]. Farming is an actual practice in folk horror, rather than a pretextual backdrop. (2019: 301)

This emphasises the focus on the folk, the 'people subject to superstitions', the 'peasantry', rather than the conflict between aristocracy and middle classes so common to the gothic paradigm. In doing so, the film can be seen as emphasising a different agency, making this a story of ordinary, working people rather than of those of higher social and educational status.

As with *Witchfinder General*, this film depicts folk beliefs not as revivals, but rather as current. Its early-eighteenth-century setting places it in relation to the disruptions of the Civil War, while other disruptions to English authority are suggested by the judge's toast to 'King James III', identifying him as a Jacobite and so 'also a rebel[;] his toast to the exiled King considerably complicates his status within the film' (Harmes 2013: 70). With order disrupted in this way, the land itself seems to respond by producing the demonic skull that appears to cause the following horrors. As Leon Hunt has pointed out, this suggests that 'This Green and Pleasant Land forever resists the onset of an Age of Reason' (2002: 87). In other words, there is something in the identity of the nation that is essentially non-rational, or that presents a different kind of rationalism, one based on the power of magical thinking and supported by an alternative moral structure.

Blood on Satan's Claw is also unusual in that the cult leader is one of the common people, not someone with book learning. Angel Blake appears supernaturally empowered to lead her youth cult, which is ultimately opposed by a group of older villagers led by the traditional, formally educated and officially empowered figure of the judge. Angel is killed by an unnamed peasant, while the judge squares off against the real, demonic leader. In this way, peasant faces peasant, while supernatural power is faced by temporal power and education, as the judge's actions against the cult are informed by his researches conducted away from the rural setting. Harmes considers the film to be ultimately reactionary, positioning the horror as female-led youth, which must be defeated by masculine age (2013: 71). Evans-Powell also connects this masculine authority to the urban, as the judge has to travel to London to consult formal book learning in order to gather the knowledge to defeat the female power of the cult, where the knowledge seems to be (super)natural and direct from the source, rather than transmitted and translated through the intermediary of books (2021: 92).

Blood on Satan's Claw therefore presents us with some key ideas about folk horror. Like *Witchfinder General*, it gives importance to ordinary people, the folk themselves. The folk are shown to challenge rationalist, established authority through their connection to ancient supernatural forces. These beliefs are themselves attached to ideas of the land and of identity, positioning the rural against the urban. However, through the judge's position as a Jacobite, the film also shows that authority is itself flawed and prone to emotional attachment to the past. As youth cult and demonic force are suppressed, it appears that the forces of rationalism and advancement have triumphed, but they have only done so through accepting superstition and drawing on past magic themselves, and they do so not as forces of progress but rather as forces of conservatism. This conflict between conservatism and progress lies at the heart of the next case study, which is particularly important in presentation of the idea of revival and in its presentation of a clash between authorities: *The Wicker Man*.

The Wicker Man: Authority and power

As Paul Newland has argued, *The Wicker Man* is primarily about:

> a clash that occurs between diametrically opposed belief systems and ideologies of governance. On the one hand, we have Howie's rigidly held Presbyterian Christian beliefs; on the other, what he sees as the degenerate practices of an island community that apparently melds aspects of traditional, pagan folk culture with the contemporary counter-culture. (2008: 119)

The film engages deeply with power structures and authority, and where that authority comes from in this clash. The idea of power structures and representation of authority is central to Howie's value as a representative of the Crown: 'A man who has come here with the power of a king, by representing the law', as the librarian puts it. And, as Howie points out, when the islanders' murderous ritual proves unsuccessful and the crops fail again, it is their own, direct ruler that they will sacrifice. Power has responsibility and has its costs.

Lord Summerisle's power comes from inheritance, from his ownership of the island and from his power as head of this isolated society; he is not only landowner, but also cult leader. As he states, his grandfather reintroduced a form of paganism to the island to encourage the islanders to work for him, and to adopt his new cultivars and cultivation practices, which led the island to flourish for a while. There is a clear sense of the appeal of a return to the past here that is frequently attached to idealised visions of rural arcadias, where people and nature work together and produce abundance, and the fertility of the people and the land runs in parallel. It appears to be a society where people do not suffer from the restrictions of the dominant culture, where there is greater sexual freedom and a strong sense of community.

However, while it is presented as having returned the islanders to their old gods and old practices, this is actually the imposition of practices developed from book learning, and not native practices either, but a mixture of English, Scottish, Irish and Gallic. This is very much an imagined community, its paganness being non-specific, not organically grown from the land but introduced by an authority: the current Lord Summerisle's grandfather. While the current Lord Summerisle and the islanders may consider themselves true believers, and we can assume that there have been adjustments to the beliefs imposed to make them fit with the islanders' lives, this is as artificial an introduction as the varieties of fruit introduced alongside the belief system. It is also a system that contains the seeds of its own destruction, by empowering the people, and it is worth noting that Lord Summerisle appears to be the end of his line: there is no indication that he has a child to continue this cult leadership. As the crops fail, so we see the religion turning from one of life and fertility to one of murder, and the destruction of direct authority; giving the people power, as in both *Witchfinder General* and *Blood on Satan's Claw*, is ultimately dangerous.

The power of *The Wicker Man* lies in how appealing it makes its alternative culture: these people seem happy, free, and Howie is dour and seeks to impose order, power and authority. Yet Summerisle also imposes order: the islanders have their roles. The Landlord's Daughter, Willow, is feted as such in song, which also refers to her role as a sacred sexual partner, initiating boys into sexual maturity and trying to tempt Howie as part of the tests he must pass to prove himself worthy as a sacrifice. The Landlord's masked role as Punch in the final ritual allows Howie to assume his identity, or believe he has. Summerisle himself takes on a further ritual identity in his wig, dress and makeup, assuming a persona merging man and woman and so the powers of both, in a magical sense. There is certainly a comfort in the idea of a community in which everyone knows their place and their relationship to everyone else, and knows that their role has significance, but this is also a method of control.

Newland (2008) demonstrates how the music of the film works with these ideas of authenticity and control. It merges seemingly authentic traditional music with contemporary folk music, the boisterous community performances with controlled studio sound. The community performances represent the appeal of the folk tradition as bringing people together in shared experiences, including at the final sacrifice, but we also see the same community unity through song in the extended version of the film, where we see Howie singing in community with his own church. As Newland emphasises, music has emotional and physical affect, and it is this that demonstrates the stresses between Howie's more constrained behaviour and habits and the freer behaviour of the islanders, especially because he is clearly himself affected by the music. This is particularly shown by his response to Willow's seduction song, attacking his sensibilities through the senses. But his resistance here confirms him in his role as sacred virgin fitting for sacrifice, where, if he had given in to desire, given in to the rituals of the community, it would presumably have made him unsuitable, or at least less suitable, for sacrifice.

Conclusions

The Wicker Man returns us to the romantic ideas of folk culture as survival of ancient culture linked to a geographical place and to the mutual belonging of people to place and place to people, while showing how much these are constructions to serve present needs. Trish Winter and Simon

Keegan-Phipps summarise the ways that folk revivals have often been constructions presenting what is supposed to be 'a "pure" or "authentic" musical expression of a nation's people that could be harnessed to bolster nationalist sentiment in the face of growing cosmopolitanism and crises of national identity' (2013: 5). Few folk horror communities are depicted as being explicitly concerned with spreading their culture beyond a specific locality, with exceptions such as the Welsh nationalist cult of *Darklands* (see Edwards 2020) or *Witchfinder General*, which suggests that this culture is already the culture of the people. Yet the very linking of folk horror communities to ideas of ancient connections to a particular location, and to practices that exclude outsiders, has an undeniable link to ideas of remaining apart from and different from the rest of the world, and has undeniable links to the roots of nationalism. Blood and soil and the way they intermingle may be common images and concepts in folk horror, but 'blood and soil' was also a Nazi slogan.

And here we see the tension that I think is key to folk horror's multiple appeals: that it recognises the attractions of community, of knowing one's place in the community, of being more connected to nature and life, of being free from the constraints of the State. But it also recognises that those freedoms come at a cost. They depend on a disconnection from the responsibilities and structures of the wider world, and so represent a threat to those power structures. They represent a rejection of other cultures, and the opportunities offered by engaging with them as equals. They represent a desire to escape into the past rather than to face the challenges of the future.

These communities can also be seen as microcosms of wider cultures and societies, though. The individual case studies outlined here suggest how the parallels between the localised society and wider society show structures of power to operate on different scales, but all are based on imagined rituals, and led by individuals whose power can be challenged. Folk horror texts can be read conservatively as dreams to be achieved of independent community where everyone knows their place, or as conservative representations showing the horrifying results of giving power to the people. Authority will be toppled by the power that it has given to the folk.

What is significant is that these narratives often present the challenge to contemporary, dominant society not as resulting in chaos, but as resulting in an apparently stable community and culture, one potentially so stable that it can persist unchanged at its heart for hundreds or thousands of years (though this may be an illusion). These dangerous Others that challenge dominant society are not foreigners, not outsiders, but are actually representatives of a more 'true' national and cultural identity than that of dominant society because of these (perceived/believed) ancient connections. Folk horror, I argue, can be profitably examined through the role of the folk, because that helps us to think about how each text relates to conceptions of ordinary people working as a community. In doing so, it relates to images and ideas of identity, particularly national and local identity. And what many of the classic folk horror texts seem to present is a tension between the appeal of community and connection, and the costs of retreating to the past.

References

Boyes, Georgina (2010), *The Imagined Village: Culture, Ideology and the English Folk Revival*, rev. illustrated edn. Leeds: No Masters Co-Operative.
Cooper, Ian (2011), *Witchfinder General*. Leighton Buzzard: Auteur.
Cowdell, Paul (2019), '"Practicing Witchcraft Myself during the Filming": Folk Horror, Folklore, and the Folkloresque', *Western Folklore* 78:4, 295–326.
Edwards, Cary (2020), 'Identity and Folk Horror in Julian Richards' *Darklands*', *Revenant 5* (March), 74–91.
Evans-Powell, David (2021), *The Blood on Satan's Claw*. Liverpool: Auteur.
Harmes, Marcus K. (2013), 'The Seventeenth Century on Film: Patriarchy, Magistracy, and Witchcraft in British Horror Films, 1968–1971', *Canadian Journal of Film Studies* 22:2, 64–80.
Hunt, Leon (2002), 'Necromancy in the UK: Witchcraft and the Occult in British Horror', in Steve Chibnall and Julian Petley (eds), *British Horror Cinema*. London: Routledge, pp. 82–98.
Newland, Paul (2008), 'Folksploitation: Charting the Horrors of the British Folk Tradition in *The Wicker Man*', in Robert Shail (ed.), *Seventies British Cinema*. London: BFI, pp. 119–128.
Storey, John (2003), *Inventing Popular Culture*. Oxford: Blackwell.
Thurgill, James (2020), 'A Fear of the Folk: On *Topophobia* and the Horror of Rural Landscapes', *Revenant 5* (March), 33–56.
Winter, Trish and Simon Keegan-Phipps (2013), *Performing Englishness: Identity and Politics in a Contemporary Folk Resurgence* Manchester: Manchester University Press.

5

Doomwatch: sacrifice zones and folk horror

Dawn Keetley

Doomwatch (1972) is infrequently cited in the critical conversations about folk horror, and yet it is a key text.[1] Not only does it seem a clear influence on Robin Hardy's 1973 film *The Wicker Man*, but its creators share a strong folk horror pedigree: it is directed by Peter Sasdy, who also directed *The Stone Tape* (1972), while the screenplay was written by Clive Exton, who would go on to write the 1977 *BBC Ghost Story for Christmas* episode, 'Stigma', as well as the 1979 M. R. James adaptation for ITV, *Casting the Runes*. The film was, moreover, produced by Tigon British Film Productions, the company behind the folk horror classics *Witchfinder General* (1968) and *Blood on Satan's Claw* (1971). *Doomwatch* was a spin-off from the BBC science-fiction television series of the same name, which ran from 1970 to 1972 and featured a Government agency called the Department for the Observation and Measurement of Scientific Work, dedicated to tracking down unethical and dangerous scientific research. While the film obviously has science-fiction roots, Tigon decided to market it as horror, seeking to capitalise on its earlier horror successes. The film's US title, *Island of the Ghouls*, makes its positioning as horror clear, as does initial marketing for the film. The poster cast the islanders as 'monsters' by (inexplicably) depicting them as green, and the trailer intones that its protagonist's job on the island is 'to save these people from the pitiable, frenzied monsters they are fast becoming'.[2]

The plot of *Doomwatch* follows Dr Del Shaw (Ian Bannen) as he travels to Balfe, a fictional island off the coast of Cornwall, where he is investigating whether an oil spill has disrupted the island's ecosystem. While there, Shaw must contend with unaccountably hostile locals, who, with the exception of the schoolteacher – fellow 'outsider' Victoria Brown (Judy Gleeson) – do everything they can to get him off the island. *Doomwatch* thus exemplifies the structuring dynamic of folk horror – the often-violent encounter between the local/rural/primitive and the global/urban/modern.

As Shaw investigates the sea life around Balfe, the Doomwatch team back at the lab in London discover that the fish he sent them evince an

Figure 5.1 The 1972 poster for *Doomwatch*

unnatural growth. With the lab instructing him to collect more samples, Shaw remains on Balfe and soon conscripts Victoria to help him discover what ails the islanders. They find out that the islanders are afflicted by a mysterious disease that they (led by their vicar) attribute to inbreeding and a consequent divine punishment. Shaw determines, though, that they suffer from 'acromegaly', usually caused by the over-production of a hormone in the pituitary gland but in this case caused by a toxic brew of radioactive waste and growth hormones dumped off the coast of the island. The islanders are finally coerced off the island to be 'cured' by an extended series of X-rays (possibly lasting up to a year), as the film ironically circles back to the radiation that helped cause the disease in the first place.

With its emphasis on the dire effects of military and industrial pollution, *Doomwatch* fails to offer the typical 'sacrifice' central to folk horror and instead represents the island itself as a *sacrifice zone*: the land and the community that lives on it are ceded to the inexorable processes of the globalising economy.[3] Literally abandoned at the end of the film, the island is in fact positioned throughout the film as already lost to globalisation – and while the islanders themselves (at least at first) appear to be the powerful and even threatening 'folk' of folk horror, they, like their land, also turn out to be already lost, 'wasted humans' rather than 'folk'. It is telling that the opening scene of the film shows the villagers gathering in the woods at night, resonant with the 'pagan' rituals that punctuate so much folk horror. The villagers are there, however, to bury a dead girl. There are no rituals promising fertility, only death. What comes to the surface in *Doomwatch* is not a life-affirming sexuality repressed by mainstream society but deadly barrels of toxins and the life-destroying sickness of global modernity that dooms land and people alike.

Doomwatch and *The Wicker Man*

The status of *Doomwatch* as folk horror is evident not least in the way that it uncannily anticipates the iconic *The Wicker Man* – although its figuring of the island as sacrifice zone, in the end, profoundly diverges from its more famous successor. *Doomwatch* may well have been a direct influence on *The Wicker Man*. The former was initially released in March of 1972 and was playing in London by early June of that year (*Daily Telegraph* 1972). Filming on *The Wicker Man* began in October 1972, and those involved could certainly have seen *Doomwatch* on its release several months earlier. In an uncanny error, a short review of *Doomwatch* in the *Daily Telegraph* on 4 June 1972, upon its opening at the Rialto in London, incorrectly stated that the film is set on 'an off-shore Scottish island' (Hinxman 1972). *Doomwatch*'s Balfe thus uncannily conjures up *The Wicker Man*'s Summerisle.

There are multiple striking similarities between the plots of the two films. Like *The Wicker Man*'s Sergeant Neil Howie (Edward Woodward), Dr Del Shaw is an embodiment of urban modernity who heads across water to a remote island where he finds strange beliefs and superstitions endemic to the isolated villagers. Both films thus immediately demonstrate two of the links in Adam Scovell's 'folk horror chain' – isolation and 'skewed belief systems and morality' (2017: 17–18). Like Howie, Shaw gets the sense that the locals are hiding things from him as they peer from behind curtains and resist his efforts to engage them in what he feels is sensible conversation. Both Howie and Shaw have disturbing experiences in pubs (Howie's involving sex and Shaw's involving an outburst of violence). Both men meet a blonde woman whose motives and allegiances are not entirely clear at first. There is a missing girl at the heart of each plot – the allegedly missing Rowan Morrison in *The Wicker Man* and the dead girl in the woods whom Shaw finds (and then loses) in *Doomwatch*. Both Howie and Shaw go into the local schoolroom, asking questions of the teacher, as part of their 'investigations'. There's even a specific parallel in that both men eat distinctly unsatisfactory meals. Howie enquires why the (tinned) food is so bad when Summerisle is supposed to be famous for its produce, and Shaw asks Victoria 'Is the food always so awful on this island?'. In each film, the 'badness' of the food defies the outsider's expectations about rural locales and actually signals what will be soon be revealed as the barrenness/toxicity of the land.

In their encounter with 'strange' locals, both Howie and Shaw attempt to impose the institutional authority of modern 'rational' society. Realising something is wrong with the islanders, Shaw repeatedly insists that they should seek medical help, just as Howie repeatedly threatens the inhabitants of Summerisle with the law and decries their departures from Christian orthodoxy. The conflicts in the two films resolve quite differently, however. In *The Wicker Man*, the islanders' 'pagan' beliefs ultimately overcome Howie, thus also overcoming modernity, the law and mainstream Christianity. Along with all the 'civilised' values and rules he represents, Howie is burned on the altar of the wicker man, enacting Scovell's fourth link in the folk horror chain – the 'happening/summoning', the 'violent' culmination of the community's 'skewed' belief system (2017: 18). The 'horror' of the film stems largely from this final sacrifice of the avatar of 'normal' society and from the demonstrable power of Summerisle's folk beliefs. In *Doomwatch*, however, the 'strange' villagers and their island are sacrificed on the altar of modern science and medicine, and their sacrifice is not a discrete and sensational event but an integral part of the ongoing temporal processes of global modernity.

The sacrifice zone in *Doomwatch*

In its difference from *The Wicker Man*, *Doomwatch* makes visible what is typically repressed in folk horror. *Doomwatch* shows that beneath the culminating violent sacrifice – the discrete event that concludes much folk horror, and exemplified by the burning of Howie in the wicker man – is modernity's *ongoing* production of 'sacrifice zones'.[4] The creation of sacrifice zones is distinctly *not*, then, an exclusive, bounded event. Chris Hedges and Joe Sacco, in *Days of Destruction, Days of Revolt*, define 'sacrifice zones' as those areas 'that have been offered up for exploitation in the name of profit, progress, and technological advancement' (2012: xi).[5] By this definition – indeed, by any definition – Balfe becomes a 'sacrifice zone' at the end of the film when all of the islanders are transported to the mainland because the island has *already* been sacrificed to the nexus of the military, corporate and scientific-medical establishments. These institutions, collectively, dump radioactive waste and manufactured growth hormones off the island's shores and then insist that the only 'cure' for the islanders lies in their being wrenched from their home, hospitalised and subjected to ostensibly curative radiation. At the end of the film, Balfe is left utterly abandoned, its future lying 'in ruins', as Victoria laments. In *Doomwatch*, then, the land itself – the island – is sacrificed in a final scene that is less melodramatic than the concluding scene of *The Wicker Man* but certainly more quietly devastating.

The geography of *Doomwatch* embeds the imaginary island of Balfe in the multiple processes that constitute it as a sacrifice zone. At a key moment in the film, when Shaw confronts a Royal Navy admiral about dumping waste off the coast of Balfe, the admiral points at a map indicating 'Castle Rock', on Balfe (Figure 5.2). The admiral identifies the area between Land's End and the Isles of Scilly, an archipelago off the south-western tip of Cornwall. Tellingly, this area was the site, in 1967, of the UK's worst oil spill, a disaster explicitly woven into the diegesis of *Doomwatch*. After the opening scene showing the villagers burying a girl in the woods, the credits roll over documentary footage of an oil spill that coats the sea, the land and birds, as attempts are made to wash it off. When the footage shuts off, revealing the Doomwatch lab, Dr Quist (John Paul) remarks that the spill was twelve months ago – and that Balfe bore the worst of it. The explicit reason for Del Shaw's visit to Balfe, then, is to determine, as Quist puts it, 'what effect the oil – and the new detergent they used to disperse the oil – had on seashore life'. The oil spill is thus foregrounded in the narrative, scarcely

Figure 5.2 The 'admiral' points to where the navy dumped radioactive waste. *Doomwatch*, 1972

amenable to being hidden – just like the *Torrey Canyon* itself, which struck Pollard's Rock in the Seven Stones Reef between Land's End and the Isles of Scilly and spilled all 119,328 tons of its crude oil onto the coasts of Cornwall, Devon and Brittany (Marriott and Macalister 2021: 105; Vallero and Letcher 2013: 140).

If folk horror is structured by the local/global conflict, *Doomwatch*'s oil disaster, repeating the catastrophic grounding of the *Torrey Canyon*, perfectly exemplifies both the encroachment of the global and the ways in which it threatens local communities. The *Torrey Canyon* embodied an emergent global Britain: registered in Liberia, sailed by an Italian captain, owned by the Bahamas-based Barracuda Tanker Corporation, part-owned by American Union Oil, the *Torrey Canyon* had been chartered by British Petroleum to carry crude oil to a refinery in Wales. The subsequent oil slick affected local Cornish fishing and tourism industries, as well as devastating bird and animal life along the coast of Cornwall (Barkham 2010; Marriott and Macalister 2021: 105; Green and Cooper 2015). In their book *Crude Britannia*, James Marriott and Terry Macalister describe how the *Torrey Canyon* disaster 'provoked a national debate', as 'oil entered the long conflict between two distinct visions of Britain. Between Britain as rural, natural and traditional and Britain as industrial, technological and modern'. By the late 1960s, these two visions were in increasing conflict, a conflict embodied in tens of thousands of dead seabirds, 'rivers foaming with detergent and the oil on the beaches' (Marriott and Macalister, 2021: 105–106). In their study of oral histories taken from Cornish people who lived through the *Torrey Canyon* spill, Anna Green and Timothy Cooper similarly emphasise that both the wreck and the clean-up 'performed' and hardened what they call 'the power relationship between a metropolitan elite and local people' (2015: 897). As the (national and international) 'political, military and scientific elites took control', they revealed (and perpetuated) a 'subaltern community, often economically vulnerable, whose indigenous knowledge was ignored or devalued' (Green and Cooper, 2015: 892). Five years after the *Torrey Canyon* disaster, the conflict it galvanised between 'Britain as rural, natural and traditional and Britain as industrial, technological and modern', along with the creation of a 'subaltern community', is played out on *Doomwatch*'s fictional Balfe.

While Balfe's problem at first and most visibly seems to be the oil spill and the toxic detergents meant to remediate it, it turns out that there are layers to Balfe's creation as sacrifice zone, that the process began years before Shaw arrives. Indeed, the oil spill is soon discarded as a salient element of the plot. The discovery that the marine life around Balfe is much larger than it should be takes Shaw into the waters on the *other* side of the island from that affected by the oil spill, where he discovers a 'prohibited zone', marked off by bollards. Underwater, Shaw's Doomwatch partner, Dr John Ridge (Simon Oates), discovers barrels of both radioactive waste ('mildly radioactive waste', as the Royal Navy admiral in charge of the project describes it) *and* manufactured pituitary growth hormones.

Doomwatch's images of barrels laden with toxic chemicals is strikingly prescient. Its filming in late 1971 both echoed the worst oil spill in Britain's history and eerily anticipated another environmental disaster.[6] In January 1972, after the filming for *Doomwatch* was finished but before its theatrical release, a Spanish ship sank off the Channel Islands and spilled 750 drums of highly toxic chemicals along the Cornish coast, from Wembury in the east (near Plymouth) to Mount's Bay and Penzance in the west – terrain that had already been affected by the oil spill and that maps onto the imaginary landscape of Balfe, from its filming location in Polkerris to the fictional 'Castle Rock' near Land's End. Like the *Torrey Canyon*, the Spanish ship, the *Germania*, was bound in the web of global trade. The chemicals on board were from 'Union Carbide (Belgium) Ltd', although Union Carbide is a US company, and the ship was sailing from Hamburg to Barcelona.[7] This film about the creation of an erstwhile fishing community as a sacrifice zone is thus temporally entwined, both before and after, in global environmental disasters. Newspaper articles about the 1972 chemical spill even include headlines that reference the 'Doomwatch Beach' and the 'Doomwatch Coast', invoking the TV series and, uncannily ahead of the fact, the film itself.

Unlike the chemicals that spilled from the *Germania*, which were – like the oil from the *Torrey Canyon* – very much out in the open, the barrels poisoning Balfe (radioactive waste and growth hormones) are submerged, underwater, thus figuring the much less visible histories of pollution in Britain, not least its actual underwater disposal of radioactive waste. A report released by the International Atomic Energy Agency (IAEA) in 1999 revealed that the British Government had been continually disposing of radioactive waste at sea between 1948 and 1976 (IAEA 1999: 53–63). In a rather transparent anticipation of the report's release, moreover, the Government finally admitted in 1997 that, contrary to its denials for the prior thirteen years, it had indeed dumped radioactive waste in the Irish Sea, only six miles from the Scottish coast (*Irish Times* 1997). Maps in the IAEA report that show where the waste was deposited, including one that indicates spots close to the coast of Cornwall in the English Channel, uncannily echo moments in *Doomwatch* that map the underwater spread of the toxic brew of radioactive waste and growth hormones (IAEA 1999: 53, 58; Figure 5.3). And the reluctance of the British Government to admit exactly how close to the coastline it had been discarding radioactive waste is figured in the extensive scenes in *Doomwatch* in which Shaw tries to discover who dumped the barrels off Balfe – efforts that are met by initial, knee-jerk denials.

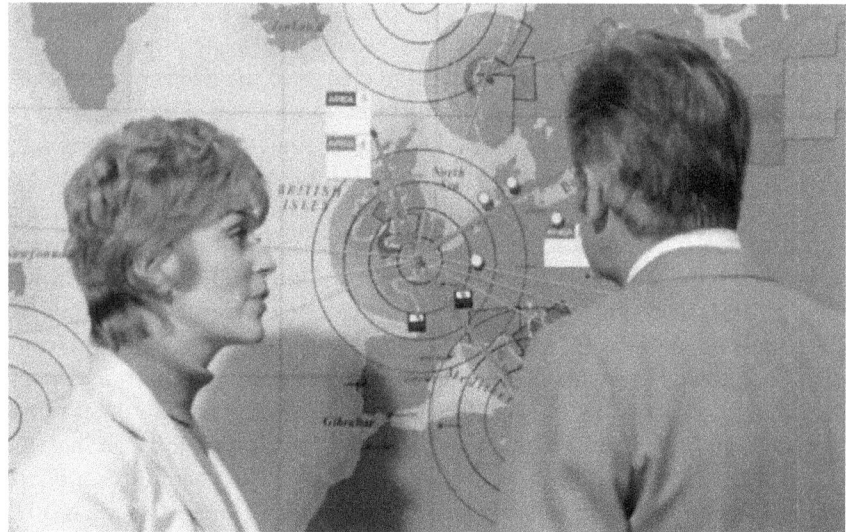

Figure 5.3 The spread of the growth hormones, mixed with radioactive waste. *Doomwatch*, 1972

Of the pollutants encroaching on Balfe, those that most evince the damage of global modernity are the 'pituitary growth hormones' – leaking from their containers underwater, bubbling, foaming, mixing with the water, and ingested by fish and then people. It is this hormonal brew, already composed of 'mucked about' molecules but then mixing with leaking radioactive waste, that is directly responsible for the islanders' acromegaly. The chairman of Doran Chemicals is supremely unabashed by what his company has done, finally admitting that he makes 'a lot of hormones' and that, as Ridge suggests, their prime goal was to create an effective livestock feed additive. The chairman says that, at first, it worked, increasing 'the growth rate of bullocks by 30 per cent'. But, of course, Doran Chemicals needed to produce it in bulk for the global meat market – and that's when things went wrong: 'the animals were in a pitiable state, quite uncontrollable. It seemed to produce in them a kind of frenzy.' As the chairman describes the animals' frenzy, the film cuts to Balfe, where a man, himself in 'a kind of frenzy', jumps to his death from an upstairs window. Animals and humans are drawn together in the space of this cut, bound to each other as equal victims of the effects of mass manufactured growth hormones.

Hormones have been used to increase the size of cattle since the early 1950s, especially in the UK. Even as other European countries began to cease their use in the early 1980s, Britain continued to argue against bans, and as much as 50 per cent of British cattle was being given growth hormones in the mid-1980s, when Britain voted *against* a European Commission proposal to bar the use of all hormones in livestock (Davis 2003: 322–323). Britain had been an integral part of the 'global meat complex' since the mid-nineteenth century, when it began both importing beef products from the Americas and Australasia and attending to ways British farmers could compete on the global market, including the use of growth hormones (Young 2019). Chris Otter has argued that the global meat market turned animals into 'capitalist machines', imbricated within a 'technology of capital accumulation'. The 'intensive meat complex', Otter argues, 'was a global technological infrastructure' (2020: 35, 47). *Doomwatch* shows how the isolated islanders of Balfe become caught up in the web of this 'meat complex', how they became, like cattle, 'capitalist machines', part of a global industry that had been integral to Britain's expanding markets since the Victorian era.

It is critical to the particular folk horror formation exemplified by *Doomwatch* that the conventional 'outsider' and avatar of globalism so central to the folk horror plot (Del Shaw in this case) is positioned as arriving at what only *seems* to be the isolated and rural location, and rather late in the game. From the opening of the film, when he is treated with profound suspicion, to the end, when he is directly accused – 'You're an outsider and you're trying to tell us what to do' – Shaw is treated by the islanders as the conventional intruder of folk horror. But he is preceded in his journey to Balfe by crude oil; radioactive waste; and toxic, chemically altered growth hormones – all products of Britain's global economy. Indeed, I suggest that Shaw must be seen as an *effect*, part of an assemblage of global processes, rather than as, himself, a singular 'outsider'. The environmentalist organisation he represents, created specifically to counter the 'worldwide pollution problem' (as revealed in the opening credits) is similarly an effect of, because profoundly entangled with, the global industrialisation it is designed to remediate. As Marriott and Macalister point out, for instance, the devastation wrought by the wreck of the *Torrey Canyon* 'catalysed' the environmental movement, *an integral corollary to global industry* (2021: 106). Environmental disaster, in other words, bred environmental movements. Tellingly, when Shaw says to Victoria early in the film that he is from Doomwatch, she responds 'the pollution people', to which Shaw adds 'Anti-pollution, I should hope'. This 'misperception' on Victoria's part marks the actual mutually constitutive relationship between 'pollution' and 'anti-pollution'.

Indeed, at several moments, *Doomwatch* depicts how the 'anti-pollution' scientists are very much like the 'polluters' they police – the officers in the navy, the corporate leaders. Not least, they are all remarkably chummy, which is to say they are connected by class, similarly marked as 'elites' whose careers and lives are invested in global capitalism. The chairman of

Doran Chemicals, for instance, who manufactured the devastating growth hormone, breezily says to Doomwatch scientist John Ridge 'I'm not in trouble with you fellows?', to which Ridge, equally lightly, replies 'I don't think so'; then, in the friendly chat that follows, the chairman mentions his 'old friend Quist', adding that they were 'at Oxford together'. This elite group, composed of well-educated scientists, heads of chemical companies and Royal Navy admirals, all end up, moreover, relatively free of blame for what happened to the inhabitants of Balfe. In the end, the buck gets passed to a local company, Keston Disposals, which Doran Chemicals contracted to get rid of its 'mucked about' growth hormones. Keston is located on the mainland of Cornwall, just across from Balfe, and its owner speaks with a regional and working-class accent (*not* the accent of the elite and the well-educated); he alone is the object of Shaw's anger.

Indeed, Shaw himself comes to embody quite overtly the entangled web of pollution and anti-pollution. At the end of the film, Shaw informs the islanders what is wrong with them and tells them that they must leave their home for treatment on the mainland. The islanders immediately blame him: 'You want to kill the island', shouts one of them. Despite his claims that all he wants to do is help, Shaw is indeed implicated in the global modernity that has turned Balfe into a sacrifice zone – and not only because of his organisation's cosy relationship with polluting admirals and corporate chairmen. Shaw tellingly engages in a culpable mystification of what has happened to the islanders, thus shielding those who are responsible for their disease and for the devastation of their island. In his speech to the islanders, Shaw evades explanation while seeming to offer it. He tells the islanders that the acromegaly they are suffering from 'has been caused by the hormone getting in from the outside – probably, we think probably [*sic*], in the fish that you eat'. And that is all he says. Shaw fails to tell the islanders exactly who on the 'outside' is responsible, and he even seems to put some of the blame on them as the only subjects – the only actors – in his explanation (they ate the fish). Despite his avowed 'anti-pollution' efforts, then, Shaw becomes complicit with the forces of global industry and capital by mystifying the causes that led to the sickness that has decimated the community on Balfe. He denies them the ability to understand their situation, and thus they will be forever unable to resist or to protest it.

Despite the film's quite open exploration of what has most recently converged to lead to Balfe's sacrifice, there is still more that is repressed within the diegesis but visible in the *mise-en-scène*. The landscape of *Doomwatch* raises two once-important industries of Cornwall, the pilchard fishery and tin mining. The evocations of both, I argue, intensify the decline evident in Balfe village life and make it clear that the vicissitudes of global trade began much earlier than the mid-twentieth century. Most of the location filming

Figure 5.4   Polkerris, from the hills above the cove, in *Doomwatch*, 1972

of *Doomwatch* takes place in Polkerris, a small village on the south coast of Cornwall by the English Channel, on the east side of the St Austell Bay.

The scenes of arriving at and departing from Balfe are filmed in Polkerris, as are the scenes in the woods (where Shaw finds the dead girl), and the pub in the film is the Rashleigh Inn, still a mainstay of Polkerris village life. Polkerris was one of many ports along the Cornish coast that prospered thanks to the seasonal pilchard migration; the particular geography of the cove at Polkerris, moreover, made it perfect for the popular seine fishing, in which fish were caught by nets draped across shallow waters close to the coastline.[8] There is a visual reference to this particular form of the fishing trade in *Doomwatch*, when one of the islanders is shown folding what looks like a large seine net.

For a combination of reasons, however, both the pilchard and the seine fishing trade – at its height in the middle of the nineteenth century – went into a steep decline through the late nineteenth and early twentieth century. Indeed, seine fishing was almost completely gone by the 1920s after 'a decade or more of unsuccessful seasons which were the prelude to the virtual cessation of the pilchard's [*sic*] visits' (Bennett 1952: 222). A warm-water fish, the pilchard disappeared from the coast of Cornwall by the 1960s because of cooling seas (Pinnegar *et al*. 2002: 387). There were changes in the global market for pilchards, as well as the increasing dominance of motorised and deep-sea boats. Some historians attribute the demise of the local fishing industry to such things as a 'lack of enterprise' on the part of seine fisherman in their failure to adapt (Bennett 1952: 221), and the collapse of the pilchard fisheries has become part of the story of the 'Great Paralysis', a period of 'lethargy and inertia, perhaps even trauma' that stretched from the late nineteenth century (when Cornwall saw its mass emigration) until the decades after the Second World War (Payton 2017: 259–263). Choosing Polkerris as the filming location for Balfe, then, involved selecting a location that exemplifies the demise of the local pilchard fishing industry and the 'Great Paralysis' thesis about Cornish industry. Indeed, the film amplifies this thesis by never depicting the islanders at work: the nearest instance is the brief shot of the man folding (not using) a fishing net. And when Shaw needs a boat to take him around the island and asks Victoria 'Is there a fisherman on the island that will help us?', Victoria can recommend only her friend from the mainland: her response implies there is no fisherman with a motorised boat on the island.

A final part of Balfe's imaginary landscape is indicated by a single intercut shot when Shaw is on the rocky coast of Balfe, early in the film, collecting evidence of potentially toxic wildlife. This shot, from Shaw's perspective, is the abandoned Wheal Coates Mine, a former tin mine in St Agnes in north Cornwall (Figure 5.5).[9] Wheal Coates Mine operated from 1802 to 1889, afflicted by the general collapse of Cornwall's mining industry from the mid- to the late nineteenth century – an inevitable collapse, Bernard Deacon writes, because Cornwall's 'staple industry' depended on 'the extraction of a finite natural resource' (2007: 165). Historian Philip Payton most closely identifies the 'paralysis of Cornish society and economy' from the late nineteenth

Figure 5.5 The abandoned Wheal Coates Mine in St Agnes in *Doomwatch*, 1972

century until the period after the Second World War with the collapse of the mining industry (2017: 259). Indeed, by 1939, when the mine in St Agnes closed, 'tin mining was all but obliterated' (Payton 2017: 262). The *mise-en-scène* of *Doomwatch*, then, integrating a shot of an area of Cornwall that is nowhere near 'Balfe' or Polkerris, seems designed to highlight this collapse and paralysis – all due to the drying up of local resources (tin, along with pilchards) and the vagaries of global markets. Landscape is, of course, one of the links in Scovell's folk horror chain (2017: 17), but it is critical to read not just generic 'landscape' but the actual places of folk horror film, along with their histories – both evoked *and* repressed within the *mise-en-scène*. Reading the places encompassed in Balfe's imaginary landscape discloses the multiple layers of its repeated constitution as sacrifice zone.

Wasted folk

In the culminating scene of *Doomwatch*, the islanders recognise that Shaw's remedy involves the death of their island: 'There won't be any village left', declares one; 'You'll kill the whole island, that's what you'll do', says still another. This culminating sacrifice of the island, its final emergence as sacrifice zone, is prefigured in the villagers themselves, who are, I argue, rendered as what Zygmunt Bauman described as the 'wasted lives' produced by modernity (2004). Bauman describes the increase of lands that are 'sparsely populated or depopulated' because of 'economic progress', which renders 'once effective modes of making a living unviable and impracticable' (2004: 4–5). He says that modernity's creation of 'wastelands' goes on to produce a corresponding 'human waste', or, 'more correctly, wasted humans (the "excessive" and "redundant", that is the population of those who either could not or were not wished to be recognized [*sic*] or allowed to stay)'. This 'production of "human waste"', Bauman continues, is 'an inseparable accompaniment of modernity' – and globalisation is 'the most prolific and least controlled "production line" of human waste or wasted humans' (2004: 5–6). In explicitly not being 'allowed to stay' on the 'depopulated' 'wastelands' created by Britain's emergence into the global economy, the islanders of *Doomwatch* are precisely such 'wasted humans'; they are not 'folk'. It is for this reason that they are unable to mount a challenge to the 'outsider', to the processes and the representatives of modernity, a challenge repeatedly staged by other folk horror texts, from James MacTaggart's *Robin Redbreast* (1970) to *The Wicker Man* and *The Third Day* (2020). Shaw marks this *prior* wastage of the villagers of Balfe when he declares, at the town meeting, 'I'm very sorry, but your community is already damaged. It's perhaps beyond repair.'

Doomwatch is a folk horror narrative, then, that figures its characters as eerily divested of their lore, their traditions and their rituals. Mark Fisher has defined the eerie as a 'failure of presence' – the sensation induced 'when there is nothing present when there should be something' (2016: 61). What is most 'eerie' about the islanders on Balfe is what they lack, what is absent: work, folklore, ritual. In the absence of all of these things, the villagers' status as 'folk' is erased. This is especially striking given the actual pervasiveness and power of folklore and ritual in Cornwall specifically. A little before *Doomwatch* was released, Daphne du Maurier published her *Vanishing Cornwall*, which certainly served as an elegy for much that Cornwall had lost, including industries such as fishing and mining. But du Maurier's book is also filled with the folklore and tradition that served to memorialise especially those things that were lost, describing a 'superstition, forever lurking' in the Cornishman's soul (1967: 121).[10] Yet there is no evidence of folklore and tradition among the residents of Balfe; they are represented as already stripped of the 'old ways'. Indeed, while the landscape continually evinces the depredations of globalisation that have worked to create the 'wasted' humans of Balfe, replacing a thriving community, the *mise-en-scène* marks the villagers as part of a bland and insubstantial British nationalism – clearly another thin substitute for local community. In the scene in the schoolhouse when Shaw tells the islanders what ails them – how their bodies have been wasted by environmental toxins – he stands in front of a photograph of the Queen (Figure 5.6), compounding his linkage to corporate, governmental and national power, and offering the villagers a thin substitute for the folk traditions they lost somewhere along the line.

Both Derek Johnston and Paul Newland have pointed out that the 'folk' – the 'organic' community – of folk horror has a dual political import. The folk can certainly be regressive, but they can also function as a powerful stay against modernity. As Johnston points out, the communities in folk horror represent a 'belonging to something specific, local, not urban, national or even international'. They possess an authority that presents a 'challenge to contemporary dominant society', that results not in 'chaos' but in 'a stable community and culture' (2021). Paul Newland has likewise argued that the folk can figure an 'alternative culture' that is 'not governed and controlled by an increasingly global, glossy, homogeneous, superficial culture industry' (2016: 176). *Doomwatch* enacts the truth of these claims in its stark and eerie absence of the 'folk' at the heart of its folk horror narrative. In the end, the final rendering of Balfe as explicit 'sacrifice zone' is contingent not only on the history of global modernity that has entangled the land but also on a history that has shaped the people who live on it – the 'folk' who are so integral to folk horror and yet so eerily, and tellingly, absent in *Doomwatch*.

Figure 5.6 Shaw lectures the islanders in front of a picture of the Queen. *Doomwatch*, 1972

'This island will be in ruins in two years', Victoria says – the last line of the film. It will be in ruins not least because the same processes of globalisation that ruined it have already erased the island's 'folk'.

Notes

1 Scovell mentions *Doomwatch* briefly, writing that the film 'is the culmination in the trend of modern outsiders entering rural realms for experimental reasons that was arguably started by Nigel Kneale in *Quatermass II*' (2017: 88).
2 The original theatrical trailer for *Doomwatch* from 1972 is available on YouTube: youtu.be/5DdR--F21Vk (accessed 24 April 2023).
3 I discuss the theory of 'sacrifice zones' in folk horror in Keetley (2023).
4 This narrative logic also occurs in a much less evident way in *The Wicker Man*, forging a connection between the two films in relation to the notion of the 'sacrifice zone'. In his 1978 novelisation, Robin Hardy attributes a cause for Summerisle's barrenness that reaches back centuries. He establishes the narrative's location as the West Highlands and the Hebrides, and then describes how they were ravaged by the Clearances between the mid-eighteenth and mid-nineteenth centuries when the residents were moved off the islands and sheep were imported by 'the Scottish lairds and the London bankers who backed them' (Hardy and Shaffer 1978: 31). I discuss the relevance of the Clearances to *The Wicker Man* in Keetley (2021).

5 For more on 'sacrifice zones' see Lerner (2010: esp. 2–3), and Farrier (2019: esp. 52–53). Lerner describes the origin of the term in the 'National Sacrifice Zones' 'coined by government officials to designate areas dangerously contaminated as a result of the mining and processing of uranium into nuclear weapons'. He argues, very aptly in terms of the plot of *Doomwatch*, for the expansion of the term to include 'a broader array of fenceline communities or hot spots of chemical pollution where residents live immediately adjacent to heavily polluting industries or military bases' (2010: 2–3).
6 See Richards and Reynolds (1988: 23), which mentions the filming of *Doomwatch* in Polkerris in October 1971, although it incorrectly identifies the production as an episode of the TV series. An article from September 1971 about the sale of Tigon mentions that a film spin-off from the *Doomwatch* series will go into production later that year (*Daily Telegraph* 1971).
7 For details on the disaster see Owen (1972a, b), and Owen and Small (1972).
8 For a history of Polkerris and its pilchard fishery see Hall (2018).
9 For a useful identification of the locations of *Doomwatch* see www.reelstreets.com/films/doomwatch/ (accessed 24 April 2023).
10 See Krzywinska and Heholt (2022) for a discussion of the importance of Cornish folklore.

References

Barkham, Patrick (2010), 'Oil Spills: Legacy of the Torrey Canyon', *Guardian*, 24 June, www.theguardian.com/environment/2010/jun/24/torrey-canyon-oil-spill-deepwater-bp (accessed 24 April 2023).
Bauman, Zygmunt (2004), *Wasted Lives: Modernity and Its Outcasts*. Cambridge: Polity.
Bennett, W. J. (1952), 'A Century of Change on the Coast of Cornwall', *Geography* 37:4 (November), 214–224.
Daily Telegraph (1971), 'The Tigon Group Limited', *Daily Telegraph*, 13 September, 18.
Daily Telegraph (1972), 'Theatres, Cinemas, Art Galleries', *Daily Telegraph*, 1 June, 31.
Davis, Christina L. (2003), *Food Fights over Free Trade: How International Institutions Promote the Agricultural Trade Liberalization*. Princeton, NJ: Princeton University Press.
Deacon, Bernard (2007), *Cornwall: A Concise History*. Cardiff: University of Wales Press.
Du Maurier, Daphne (1967), *Vanishing Cornwall*. Harmondsworth: Penguin.
Farrier, David (2019), *Anthropocene Poetics: Deep Time, Sacrifice Zones, and Extinction*. Minneapolis: University of Minnesota Press.
Fisher, Mark (2016), *The Weird and the Eerie*. London: Repeater Books.
Green, Anna and Timothy Cooper (2015), 'Community and Exclusion: The "Torrey Canyon" Disaster of 1967', *Journal of Social History* 48:4 (Summer), 892–909.
Hall, Nigel (2018), *Polkerris: A History of the Village and Its Pilchard Fishery*. N.p.: The Pilchard Press.
Hardy, Robin and Anthony Shaffer (1978), *The Wicker Man: A Novel*. New York: Three Rivers Press.

Hedges, Chris and Joe Sacco (2012), *Days of Destruction, Days of Revolt*. New York: Nation Books.
Hinxman, Margaret (1972), 'Mother's Girl: Films', *Daily Telegraph*, 4 June, 16.
IAEA [International Atomic Energy Agency] (1999), *Inventory of Radioactive Waste Disposals at Sea*, IAEA-TECDOC-1105. Vienna: IAEA, available at www-pub.iaea.org/MTCD/Publications/PDF/te_1105_prn.pdf (accessed 24 April 2023).
Irish Times (1997), 'Radioactive Waste Was Dumped in Irish Sea', *Irish Times*, 30 June, www.irishtimes.com/news/radioactive-waste-was-dumped-in-irish-sea-1.86450 (accessed 24 April 2023).
Johnston, Derek (2021), 'The Folk of Folk Horror', www.academia.edu/8327298/Time_and_Identity (accessed 2 May 2023).
Keetley, Dawn (2021), 'Dislodged Anthropocentrism and Ecological Critique in Folk Horror: From "Children of the Corn" and *The Wicker Man* to "In the Tall Grass" and *Children of the Stones*', *Gothic Nature* 2 (Winter), 13–36.
Keetley, Dawn (2023), 'Sacrifice Zones in Appalachian Folk Horror', in Ruth Heholt and Dawn Keetley (eds), *Folk Horror: New Global Pathways*. Cardiff: University of Wales Press, pp. 245–261.
Krzywinska, Tanya and Ruth Heholt (2022), *Gothic Kernow: Cornwall as Strange Fiction*. London: Anthem Press.
Lerner, Steve (2010), *Sacrifice Zones: The Front Lines of Toxic Chemical Exposure in the United States*. Boston, MA: MIT Press.
Marriott, James and Terry Macalister (2021), *Crude Britannia: How Oil Shaped a Nation*. London: Pluto Press.
Newland, Paul (2016), 'Folk Horror and the Contemporary Cult of British Rural Landscape: The Case of *Blood on Satan's Claw*', in Paul Newland (ed.), *British Rural Landscapes on Film*. Manchester: Manchester University Press, pp. 162–179.
Otter, Chris (2020), *Diet for a Large Planet: Industrial Britain, Food Systems, and World Ecology*. Chicago: University of Chicago Press.
Owen, John (1972a), 'Cornish Beaches Menaced by Poisons', *Sunday Telegraph*, 16 January, 3.
Owen, John (1972b), 'Doomwatch Beach Shut in Cornwall', *Daily Telegraph*, 17 January, 1, 22.
Owen, John and John Small (1972), 'More Scientists Sent to Doomwatch Coast', *Daily Telegraph*, 18 January, 1, 26.
Payton, Philip (2017), *Cornwall: A History*, rev. edn. Exeter: University of Exeter Press.
Pinnegar, J. K., S. Jennings, C. M. O'Brien and N. V. C. Polunin (2002), 'Long-Term Changes in the Trophic Level of the Celtic Sea Fish Community and Fish Market Price Distribution', *Journal of Applied Ecology* 39:3 (June), 377–390.
Richards, Paul and Derek Reynolds (1988), *Discover Fowey*. Fowey: Richards and Reynolds.
Scovell, Adam (2017), *Folk Horror: Hours Dreadful and Things Strange*. Leighton Buzzard: Auteur.
Vallero, Daniel A. and Trevor M. Letcher (2013), *Unraveling Environmental Disasters*. Waltham, MA: Elsevier.
Young, Paul (2019), 'The Victorians Caused the Meat Eating Crisis the World Faces Today – but They Might Help Us Solve It', *The Conversation*, 21 January, theconversation.com/the-victorians-caused-the-meat-eating-crisis-the-world-faces-today-but-they-might-help-us-solve-it-109310 (accessed 24 April 2023).

6

My ancestors died here: *Requiem for a Village* and the rural English horror of modernity and socio-cultural change

Paul Newland

In this chapter I will focus on David Gladwell's elegiac *Requiem for a Village* (1975), a film that sits on the periphery of current critical formulations of the folk horror genre, but which nevertheless shares many of the genre's key themes and concerns and much of its iconography. As Adam Scovell points out, 'Gladwell's film deserves to be more widely seen and discussed because it exemplifies a key theme in Folk Horror; the breakdown of the everyday normality that occurs through an obsession with the seemingly normal' (Scovell 2017: 83). The film centres on the experience, thoughts, memories and visions of one old man (Vic Smith), who, while slowly and carefully tending graves in a village churchyard in 1970s Suffolk, talks about his memories of people who now lie buried there, and witnesses (or imagines) these long-dead villagers rising from their graves in two extraordinary slow-motion sequences. Paying close attention to the rich aesthetics of the film, I will argue that through its Soviet-montage-influenced editing scheme, which dialectically collides images of nature and timeless rural activities with images of the uniform architecture of a new suburban housing estate and rural fields being prepared by huge machines for further new housing, *Requiem for a Village* locates horror in an ongoing battle between the 'old ways' which are in danger of being eradicated on the one hand, and modernity and rapid socio-cultural change in rural England on the other. I argue that *Requiem for a Village* develops a complex and fragmented vision of the 'monstrous', which is at once located in the memories and/or visions and experiences of the unnamed old man, but also in modernity broadly conceived, symbolised by the vast digging and earth-flattening machines.

David Gladwell is best known for his work as editor on Lindsay Anderson's *If...* (1968) and *O Lucky Man!* (1973), and on the 1972 BBC Television series *Ways of Seeing*, presented by the art critic John Berger. Gladwell also made the films *A Summer Discord* (1955), *Miss Thompson Goes Shopping* (1958), *28b Camden Street* (1963) and *An Untitled Film* (aka *The Killing*) (1964). The director has made it clear that his influences were drawn primarily from European art cinema: 'Eisenstein, Pudovkin, Prévert, Claire, Buñuel, Cocteau, Fellini, Resnais, Vigo' (Gladwell 2011: 14). I will demonstrate that there is clear evidence of the influence of the work of Eisenstein and Pudovkin on display in *Requiem for a Village*. But Gladwell has also signalled the fact that the main inspiration for the film was the English painter Stanley Spencer: 'People emerging from graves as embodied spirits in the clothes they wore in life, waking from a long sleep, yawning and rubbing their eyes: stretching and catching sight of friends and relatives among the living' (Gladwell 2011: 15). Some of the camerawork in the film is by Walter Lassally, a key figure in the Free Cinema and British New Wave movements. The music in *Requiem for a Village*, by David Fanshawe, plays a crucial role in conjuring up the sense of a deep communal past in one rural location. As Elisabeth Sussex put it, Fanshawe's music is 'evocative of a once immovable faith' (Sussex 1975/1976). But the music also creates a profoundly melancholy atmosphere in the film, which, when juxtaposed with the images, evokes a communal, shared sadness at what is being lost from rural England, while at the same time evoking the ghostly voices of the long dead. The formal qualities of *Requiem for a Village* pose problems for straightforward genre classification, because, while the images often seem to be like documentary footage, linking the film to the earlier Free Cinema movement, the use of a fragmentary, intercutting, Soviet-montage-influenced editing style lends the film a modernist aesthetic, problematising, as it does, linear time and space. But there is plenty in the film, visually, thematically and performatively, to consider it within the critical contexts of folk horror. Funded by the British Film Institute Production Board, *Requiem for a Village* was shot on location in rural Suffolk and features the villagers of Witnesham and Metfield. After fading into obscurity, the film was released as a dual DVD/Blu-ray by the British Film Institute in 2011 as part of its 'Flipside' series. This package included a booklet with contributions from the director, David Gladwell, as well as Shona Barrett and Rob Young, among others. This BFI release has further enshrined the cult status of the film.

Several films of the late 1960s and early 1970s depict historical rural British communities in which evil stirs. Examples include *Witchfinder General* (Michael Reeves, 1968), *The Plague of the Zombies* (John Gilling, 1966), *Blood on Satan's Claw* (Piers Haggard, 1971) and the portmanteau horror film *And Now the Screaming Starts!* (aka *Fengriffen*) (Roy Ward Baker, 1973). But other films of the period depict horror unfolding in contemporary rural British places. Key examples include *Doomwatch* (Peter Sasdy, 1972), *Neither the Sea nor the Sand* (Fred Burnley, 1972), *The Wicker Man* (Robin Hardy, 1973), *Straw Dogs* (Sam Peckinpah, 1973),

Killer's Moon (Alan Birkinshaw, 1978) and *The Shout* (Jerzy Skolimowski, 1978). These films depict strange or disturbing activity on the remote edges of mainstream 1970s British socio-cultural experience. As such, all these films fit within (or at the very least on the periphery of) most extant critical formulations of folk horror. After all, as Scovell usefully remarks, the folk horror cannon is not rigid (2017: 81), and is best seen 'not simply as a set of criteria to be read with hindsight into all sorts of media, but as a way of opening up discussions on subtly interconnected work and how we now interact with such work' (2017: 5–6). Moreover, Simon J. Bronner has advocated that while 'folk' on the one hand can suggest a community, it can 'also be construed as an adjective meaning "traditional"', bound up in the processes of 'intergenerational transmission and localized culture' (2017: 1). *Requiem for a Village* certainly focuses on the experience of 'folk': of rural, common people, across time.

Folk horror films are often spatially complex. Indeed, it is often 'anxieties about modernity and modern social change' that explain the appearance of what Peter Hutchings (2004: 29) terms an uncanny 'British anti-landscape'. What comes across in Hutchings's important work is how far rural horror in British films often develops out of a distinct spatial tension between proto-modern, modern and postmodern urban centres (and London and the Home Counties particularly) and distant, seemingly backward peripheral places in which things/cultures/ideas that lie buried might rise at any time. In a recent article on space, place and the horror of rural landscapes, James Thurgill usefully argues:

> Existing writing on folk horror has presented the *topophobia* of rural landscapes as *a priori*, suggesting that pastoral spaces are conceived of in the popular geographic imagination as inherently threatening. This suggests that, at their core, 'countryside' geographies are read as problematic spaces due to their perceived isolation and backwardness, supporting the idea that modernization is both oppositional to the identity of rural communities and rejected by them. In this context, folk horror demonstrates a co-opting of the (largely) metropolitan understanding of rurality as a homogenous [*sic*] spatiality. Observed through the lens of the 'urban gaze', the nuance of pastoral landscapes is lost in reductive articulations of rurality as singular and static. (Thurgill 2020: 34)

While several folk horror films depict rural places as threatening and dangerous (the most obvious example being *The Wicker Man*), this threat tends to be most obviously felt by unwanted incomers or socio-cultural outsiders. However, in *Requiem for a Village*, any sense of threat or danger is instead experienced by locals and insiders: people who are evidently fearful of the rapid and uncontrollable change being brought to their rural English village by faceless mechanical harbingers of modernity.

Writing about the growth of suburbia in the USA in the 1950s, Lewis Mumford argued:

> In the suburb one might live and die without marring the image of an innocent world, except when some shadow of evil fell over a column in the newspaper. Thus, the suburb served as an asylum for the preservation of illusion. Here domesticity could prosper, oblivious of the pervasive regimentation beyond. This was not merely a child-centered environment; it was based on a childish view of the world, in which reality was sacrificed to the pleasure principle. (Mumford 1961: 494)

In the decades after the end of the Second World War, England saw many new housing developments built, which allowed young families to move out of bomb-damaged and often dilapidated cities to brand new, clean, controlled, safe environments such as suburbs and new towns. Such new environments saw the development of a new way of life in England, caught between the agrarian and the urban worlds, often defined by socio-cultural conformity and an embrace of the growing practice of consumerism. The new housing estate seen in *Requiem for a Village* – and the fields being prepared for further development – speaks, in rich, poetic ways, of tensions at the heart of the identity of a 1970s England undergoing profound socio-cultural changes and struggling through the tensions brought about by processes of modernisation. Anthony Alexander points out that 'Environmental determinism – the notion that crime and immorality were created or amplified by the urban environment – led to a tacit view that a better environment would therefore produce a better society' (Alexander 2009: 72). The growth of the new housing estates in postwar England was pushed by planners along balanced and healthy lines, and primarily sprang from a moral imperative (Saint 1988: 147). Suburbs have much in common with new towns, architecturally and socially. They are, after all, places that have become synonymous with family values and community (Short 1991: 50). Suburbs and new towns also resist stable and separate spatial categories such as 'urban' and 'countryside', instead suggesting that socio-cultural tensions could develop between new and old ways of maintaining personal and community identities. Interestingly, Short points out that 'By the 1970s the suburbs had become part of the psyche and intellectual landscape and supporters of the suburbs began to emerge' (Short 1991: 52). But the geographer David Matless recognises that the suburb became a 'contentious English landscape', 'valued by some as essentially English in its modest scale, domestic values and humdrum life, and castigated by others for the same characteristics' (Matless 1998: 34). Comfortable suburban life certainly became a fixture in some notable British television sitcoms of the period, in which it was celebrated and critiqued. These include *Happy Ever*

After (BBC, 1974–1978); *The Good Life* (BBC, 1975–1978); *The Fall and Rise of Reginald Perrin* (BBC, 1976–1979); *Butterflies* (BBC, 1978–1983); and *Terry and June* (BBC, 1979–1987). But these representations of suburban life were often marked by dramatic tension fuelled by differences in class, race and differing levels of socio-cultural conformity. Suburbs also featured widely in sex comedy films of the 1970s, such as in *Confessions of a Window Cleaner* (Val Guest, 1974), in which a level of sexual depravity or sexual freedom (depending on your viewpoint), previously hidden from view behind closed curtains, was thrust onto the surface of suburban English life.

The opening shots of *Requiem for a Village* feature images of the roofs of a new suburban housing development (shot on the Stoke Park estate in southern Ipswich), with television aerials prominently visible, signalling the flow of mass culture and consumerism into the living rooms of the families living here. The close-up images of architectural details of the houses emphasise their uniform nature: all clean lines and fresh bricks, clearly symbolising socio-cultural conformity. Over these images, on the soundtrack we hear the quotidian sounds of a transistor radio, overheard conversations and babies crying. This is a new space, then, designed for new family life. But the film nevertheless shows that for one older resident, this new life has invaded the fields of an old England he has always known. The old man (Vic Smith) lives in a house on this new suburban development, but he appears to be an incongruous figure here, with his scruffy hair and his unkempt demeanour. He rides his bicycle slowly through the quotidian architecture of this new, modern, suburban England; cars neatly parked on the side of the street. There is an overwhelming sense of newness here, of a place where a brand new culture is developing, and where any trace of an ancient rural English past has been erased.

Gladwell cuts from this image of an archetypal, 1960s- or 1970s-built suburban English street to a shot of a cultivated field with mature trees in the distance. The visible juxtaposition between these spaces is made clear. The agrarian past is still evident in this rural field in a way that it is not obviously present in the housing estate. We see a leafy old country lane. Gladwell then cuts to a shot of an old cottage, and then to an old village graveyard, lichen covering the weathered headstones. We also see shots of well-trodden rural paths. The old man then arrives on his bicycle at a busy dual carriageway. He is also an anachronistic figure at this modern roadside; cars swerving, roaring past him as he wobbles slowly along on his bicycle. Gladwell cuts again to another shot of the new housing estate. Here, a bright pink ice cream van waits in the centre of the frame. The jarring juxtaposition between old and new is further continued through the editing scheme, as Gladwell then cuts to a shot of old cottages, and a series of close-up images of their architectural specificities. This is followed by the first of several shots of the huge land-flattening equipment in a field: giant, yellow vehicles in the livery of the Wimpey Homes construction company.

Developed by Soviet filmmakers and theorists such as Lev Kuleshov, Dziga Vertov, Esfir Shub, Vsevolod Pudovkin and Sergei Eisenstein, montage theory stems from the idea that connecting a series of images through film editing can allow a filmmaker to convey complex ideas and elicit an intellectual response from the audience. For Sergei Eisenstein, montage was a highly political form of filmmaking. Montage could contribute massively to the ideological and intellectual power of a film. Inspired by the Marxist theory of dialectical materialism (the process by which social and political change occurs), Eisenstein famously introduced montage to his films *Strike* (1925) and *Battleship Potemkin* (1925). This montage had the effect of creating a synthesis out of two sets of images: a synthesis that conveyed an unmistakable political message by affecting pathos and emotion in the audience (see Eisenstein 1987: 3–6, 198–199; 1998: 93). In *Requiem for a Village*, Gladwell primarily employs a Soviet-style intellectual montage in order to communicate to the audience that radical and violent changes to this ancient rural English landscape are being brought about by faceless, gigantic mechanical leviathans. These huge machines are represented here, then, with the aid of the dialectical editing scheme, as monstrous invaders and destroyers of an old England, laying waste to the old ways, brutally digging up the earth and flattening trees and shrubs.

The montage continues. Gladwell cuts again to the old man, now tending a grave, with Fanshawe's haunting music returning. This is the beginning of one of the most remarkable sequences in *Requiem for a Village*, a sequence that perhaps most obviously marks the film as an example of folk horror. The old man looks up. His attention has been drawn to something. As Gladwell cuts to a point-of-view shot, we see that the old man has spotted the surface of a grave moving. Hands appear out of this grave, and gradually, in slow motion, a man rises up, wearing his Sunday best. Elsewhere in the graveyard, other villagers in period clothing subsequently start to shake off the earth and lift themselves out of their graves, slowly making their way into the church. The old man eagerly follows them, still holding his shears, and with another cut we see him, young again, arriving at his own wedding. This is followed by striking images of the villagers' faces in the church, communicating the fact that this is a close-knit community. Then Gladwell cuts to some painterly shots of rural folk making hay in the fields, as they would have done for generations. These images are intercut in a montage with the

Figure 6.1 *Requiem for a Village*, 1975

marriage ceremony, which functions as a kind of folk ritual, bringing the community together for a shared celebration. Thurgill argues:

> Time and history are integral components of folk horror, emerging as either a survival of the past, a returning of the past, or a returning to the past. The tripartite organization of time in folk horror, while often displaying overlap, offers a useful way of thinking about how spatial experience is inflected and unsettled by the passing of time. (Thurgill 2020: 45)

Thurgill also usefully notes that analyses of folk horror have turned to ideas of spectrality and hauntology, a concept initiated by Jacques Derrida (1994) to describe the haunted political situation at the end of the twentieth century, 'and specifically the haunting of and by Marxist political thought, hauntology shares its lineage with a number of "endist" writings that emerged between the late 1970s and early 1990s' (Thurgill 2020: 45). As the writer Mark Fisher claims: 'Haunting can be seen as intrinsically resistant to the contraction and homogenization of time and space. It happens when a place is stained by time, or when a particular place becomes the site for an encounter with broken time' (Fisher 2012: 19). *Requiem for a Village* is a profoundly hauntological text, centrally concerned with broken time, with distant memories of a place informing this place as it rapidly changes in the present day.

In order to communicate the buried nature of much of English history and culture, and what can happen when this history and culture breaks through into contemporary life, folk horror films often focus on the symbolic materiality of the earth as a surface through which elements of this long-dead past might reappear. This is particularly the case in *Blood on Satan's Claw* (Piers Haggard, 1971), in which one sequence has the camera placed in a field at ground level (Newland 2016) in order to emphasise the human relationship to the earth itself, and to signal the fact that disturbing secrets might lie beneath the surface of things. Dawn Keetley makes an important point about how this sense of a culture lying buried but with the potential to resurface can have a dramatic effect on events unfolding in the contemporary moment in folk horror films: 'If folk horror often serves to "re-enchant" the world with belief in the supernatural, its evocation of a prior and now vanished enchanted world can also serve to emphasize exactly how profoundly disenchanted the contemporary world is' (Keetley 2020: 16). *Requiem for a Village* is also a film that explores 'potential pasts under the surface top-layer of the landscape', as Scovell puts it (2017: 46). Rob Young employed the folklorist George Ewart Evans's phrase, 'the pattern under the plough', to describe what he calls the 'sense of the past lying just behind the present' in Gladwell's film (Young 2010: 18).

Gladwell gives us shots of blacksmiths at work, taking pride in their labour, their traditional, ancient craft. But then, in a strange sequence reminiscent of several period-set, location-shot British horror films of the early 1970s, we see a child capture a small frog and hang it by its leg from a tree near a stream. A sudden cut takes us on through time, eliminating weeks or even months, and now we see nothing but the frog's skeleton remaining. The bones are broken into pieces by hands in close-up and tossed into nearby water. In a continuation of the dialectical editing pattern, we see a shot of a horse captured in slow motion. The film then cuts to shots of a small dog on a lead, walking across the paving stones in a pedestrianised shopping precinct. The relative freedom of the horse in nature is thus symbolically and dialectically juxtaposed with the image of the domesticated pet animal being led through a modern space of consumerism. Offering evidence of the influence of European art cinema, Gladwell has written that his interest in incorporating slow-motion shots came from his love of sequences such as the pillow-fight in *Zéro de conduite* (Jean Vigo, 1933), the funeral procession in *Entr'acte* (René Clair, 1924) and the boy's nightmare in *Los olvidados* (aka *The Young and the Damned*) (Luis Buñuel, 1950) (Gladwell 2011: 14–15).

Other sections of the film locate us firmly within the everyday lives of the past villagers in a more naturalistic way. Indeed, the charming longer sequence that covers the events around the wedding breakfast also has a documentary or Free Cinema-type feel to it. The gathered villagers sing old songs such as 'Daisy, Daisy', and show themselves to be an organic 'folk' community. Theirs is a simple, rural existence. A newly married couple's first night together is also captured as a slow-moving, fumbling, nervous ritual, silent but for the sounds of rustling clothes being discarded, tentative footsteps taken on creaking wooden floorboards. Gladwell then cuts to the scream of a woman in childbirth; her baby is seen emerging from her body. Time passes rapidly again via a cut, and this child, now an adult woman, watches her father (the old man) leave the suburban house with his bicycle. At this moment in the film, a biker gang enters the new landscape. This gang performs a complex symbolic function in the film, evoking a US-influenced rebellious youth subculture, lawlessness and modernity. Gladwell certainly exaggerates the aggressive nature of their faceless movements through space, and the monstrous roar of the motorbike engines. They burn off down a country lane under looming electricity pylons, which operate as symbols of the modernity of a new England.

In a key sequence in the film that works through the old man's view of changes occurring to the village, he enters a field in which one of the huge yellow earth-moving machines stands idle. He slowly circles it – a process that makes its monstrous size abundantly clear – and then attacks it with a clump of earth. Robin Wood has argued that in horror films, 'normality is threatened by the Monster' (1986: 78). In this sequence, the giant machinery, as we have seen through the previous montage, is violently bringing change to this rural landscape, and as such operates as a demonstrably monstrous presence. The 'monster' in horror can be manifested in things a society represses or oppresses. In other words, the monster can operate as society's 'other'. David Bell explores 'articulations' of the rural through horror films in which he argues that the 'victim' is coded as urban and the setting and the 'monster' are coded as rural (Bell 1997: 95). Wood argues that through the figure of the monster, horror films stage 'the struggle for recognition of all that our civilization represses or oppresses' (1986: 75). In Wood's understanding of the monster, a vision of contemporary sociocultural 'normality' is set against the repressed or oppressed 'other'. The boundaries between normality and the monstrous are transgressed, generating horror. But here, in *Requiem for a Village*, the monster is not simply coded as rural. Instead, the monster is coded as a vision of modernity that threatens the rural.

Requiem for a Village features disturbing moments of horror reminiscent of more obviously canonical folk horror films. In the visions of connections between the past and the present constructed in the film, things occur in the film that are morally repugnant. This is particularly the case with the

My ancestors died here: Requiem for a Village

Figure 6.2 *Requiem for a Village*, 1975

rape sequence. The scene begins with an idyllic painterly country scene of farm labourers cutting corn on a warm day. Children bring lunch. We see fresh bread in close up, the hands of a woman cutting an onion, hunks of bread and cheese being shared. As the relaxed lunch unfolds, two of the men present follow a young woman away from the assembled villagers, and subsequently brutally force themselves on her and rape her. This sequence is intercut with shots of the male bikers raping a young woman in the graveyard in the contemporary moment. While horrific and disturbing, the montage here appears to suggest that Gladwell intends this extreme sexual violence to operate on a symbolic level as well as an intellectual and emotional level.

As the film moves towards its final moments, the old man leaves his day at work in the graveyard and walks his bicycle out through the gate. Meanwhile, we see intercut images of the biker gang careering at speed down country lanes. The montage here indicates what is about to happen. The old man is violently struck by one of the bikers, and falls, twisted, onto the road. But the old man – and this time the gathered villagers – witnesses (or imagines) the dead rising slowly up from their graves again. During this sequence, the soundtrack features a haunting musical refrain – ghostly lines sung by a lover as if from beyond the grave: 'God will give you to me again.' The film cuts to an empty rural wasteland, an area cleared for a new development. Now the singers join in on the lines 'The Lord gave and the Lord hath taken away.'

For the final shot of the film, Gladwell cuts again to the new housing development, with the biker gang roaring towards the camera, down the street. This is 1970s England: a nation poised on the cusp of modernity but also unable to forget past traditions, a nation in which the past is ever-present even if it is not always visible in the new developments springing up across the countryside. The spatial and socio-cultural tensions between newness and immaturity on the one hand, and oldness and maturity on the other, are explored by other films of the period that utilise the *mise-en-scène* of similar, new town or suburban-type locations. For example, *Psychomania* (aka *The Death Wheelers*) (Don Sharp, 1972) tells the story of a biker gang that hangs out at a pagan stone circle situated in the English countryside. They commit suicide so they can return as the 'undead', and then take trips into town in order to wreak havoc on the living. The bikers in *Psychomania*, led by Tom (Nicky Henson), call themselves 'The Living Dead'. A key sequence in this film features the gang terrorising shoppers in a provincial 1960s-built shopping precinct (shot in Walton-on-Thames, near Shepperton Studios). Here, as in *Requiem for a Village*, we see the fresh newness of the building development: the sleek, modern lines of the shops, and the colourful, abundant, ordered piles of mass-produced consumer goods on display in the supermarket. By 1974, ASDA had opened twenty-seven 'superstores' of more than 25,000 square feet in Britain. The Co-op had opened twenty-three, Fine Fare twenty-one, Tesco twenty and Morrisons eleven (Sandbrook 2011: 339). In 1970s films such as *The Offence* (Sidney Lumet, 1972), starring Sean Connery, it became clear that despite the promise of a safe new life offered by such new suburban housing developments, they would ultimately not always guarantee safety, security and happiness. In *The Offence*, set on a new housing estate, a young girl is abducted and raped. In Vincent Canby's words, this abduction takes place 'where lawns fade into scrubby fields that don't give one a feeling of space as much as [of] emptiness' (Canby 1973: 5).

Requiem for a Village is an example of 'rural cinema'. For Catherine Fowler and Gillian Helfield, rural cinema can be distinguished from heritage cinema. As they point out, 'the heritage film may demonstrate a harmonious relationship between man and nature and between peasant and fellow members of the rural community ... Within rural cinema, however, the mood is not always nostalgic, nor are the films' representations of the rural inhabitant necessarily positive' (Fowler and Helfield (2006): 5–6). Furthermore, rural cinema is concerned primarily with the relationship between the land

and its inhabitants, and how this relationship develops in terms of a merging of physical and social landscapes (2006: 6). As we have seen, *Requiem for a Village* certainly displays aspects of Fowler and Helfield's formulation of rural cinema, not least through one important feature that provides structure to the lives of rural inhabitants (but also to the film itself): natural cycles. These films take us through the seasons, linked cycles in agriculture, but also cycles of birth and death, and long-held cultural cycles (witness the religious events and folk rituals). Sarah Cardwell points out that 'Landscapes in heritage films are controlled, peaceful, unthreatening' (2006: 26). But in contrast to this, there is an unremitting state of threat in *Requiem for a Village* – the threat of change, of newness, of modernity.

In conclusion, *Requiem for a Village* displays some of the generic markers of folk horror. It might be a folk horror film because it so obviously locates horror in the threat of change to a distinct rural location. But ultimately the film resists any easy generic classification. It functions as Soviet-style political film of ideological and intellectual force; as a rural drama; as a neo-modernist exploration of memory, time and place; as a rural documentary; and as a poetic meditation on changes to rural England. Overall, *Requiem for a Village* is a rare film about an English agrarian conservative impulse and the ongoing tensions between this impulse and the changes brought about by modernity, consumer culture and globalisation.

References

Alexander, Anthony (2009), *Britain's New Towns*. London: Routledge.
Bell, David (1997), 'Anti-Idyll: Rural Horror', in Paul Cloke and Jo Little (ed.), *Contested Countryside Cultures: Otherness, Marginalisation and Rurality*. London: Routledge, pp. 94–108.
Bronner, Simon J. (2017), *Folklore: The Basics*. New York: Routledge.
Canby, Vincent (1973), 'The Offence', *New York Times*, 12 May.
Cardwell, Sarah (2006), 'Working the Land: Representations of Rural England in Adaptations of Thomas Hardy's Novels', in Catherine Fowler and Gillian Helfield (eds), *Representing the Rural: Space, Place, and Identity in Films about the Land*. Detroit: Wayne State University Press, pp. 19–34.
Derrida, Jacques (1994), *Spectres of Marx*. Oxford: Routledge.
Eisenstein, Sergei (1987), *Nonindifferent Nature*. Cambridge: Cambridge University Press.
Eisenstein, Sergei (1998), *Eisenstein Reader*. London: British Film Institute.
Fisher, Mark (2012), 'What Is Hauntology?', *Film Quarterly* 66:1, 16–24.
Fowler, Catherine and Gillian Helfield (2006), 'Introduction', in Catherine Fowler and Gillian Helfield (eds), *Representing the Rural: Space, Place, and Identity in Films about the Land*. Detroit: Wayne State University Press, pp. 1–14.
Gladwell, David (2011), 'David Gladwell Discusses His Work, *Requiem for a Village*', in *Requiem for a Village* DVD booklet. British Film Institute, pp. 14–16.
Hutchings, Peter (2004), 'Uncanny Landscapes in British Film and Television', *Visual Culture in Britain* 5:2, 27–40.

Keetley, Dawn (2020), 'Introduction: Defining Folk Horror', *Revenant* 5 (March), 1–32.
Matless, David (1998), *Landscape and Englishness*. London: Reaktion Books.
Mumford, Lewis (1961), *The City in History: Its Origins, Its Transformations, and Its Prospects*. New York: Harcourt, Brace and World.
Newland, Paul (2016), 'Folk Horror and the Contemporary Cult of British Rural Landscape: The Case of *Blood on Satan's Claw*, in Paul Newland (ed.), *British Rural Landscapes on Film*. Manchester: Manchester University Press, pp. 162–179.
Saint, Andrew (1988), 'The New Towns', in Boris Ford (ed.), *The Cambridge Guide to the Arts in Britain*, Vol. IX, *Since the Second World War*. Cambridge: Cambridge University Press, pp. 147–159.
Sandbrook, Dominic (2011), *State of Emergency. The Way We Were: Britain 1970–1974*. London: Penguin.
Scovell, Adam (2017), *Folk Horror: Hours Dreadful and Things Strange*. Leighton Buzzard: Auteur.
Short, John Rennie (1991), *Imagined Country: Environment, Culture and Society*. London: Routledge.
Sussex, Elizabeth (1975/1976), '*Requiem for a Villlage*', *Sight and Sound* 45:1 (Winter), 60.
Thurgill, James (2020), 'A Fear of the Folk: On *Topophobia* and the Horror of Rural Landscapes', *Revenant* 5 (March), 33–56.
Wood, Robin (1986), *Hollywood from Vietnam to Reagan*. New York: Columbia University Press.
Young, Rob (2010), 'The Pattern under the Plough', *Sight and Sound* 20:8, 16–22.

7

Outsider history, or outside of history

K. J. Donnelly

History is haunted by marginal and unwritten versions of the past, perhaps even by all the events of the past that are discarded from 'history' in order to make a coherent and simple narrative. British folk horror films have an abiding concern with the past, either depicting events in the past or portraying rural activities as in some sense connected essentially with the past more than the present. They allow for a return or persistence of elements discarded or ignored. Folk horror on film might be understood not simply as history, as an agent of history, but more as a form of historicism. This loose process can mark a seemingly irrational alternative to the 'official version' of history or histories. In a way, it is a vernacular history but not simply a 'folk history' from below as approached in the work of historian Raphael Samuel (1994), for example, but something far more fragmented, ambiguous and ambivalent towards Britain and its past. It is more like a history from the unconscious, not necessarily in the strict Freudian sense common to accounts of horror films, but more in the sense of a forgotten – and happily forgotten – heritage. As such, British folk horror is fundamentally about the present's relationship with the past, and often articulated obliquely through a sense of place and landscape. Two very different films made a quarter-of-a-century apart illustrate this temporal-spatial process. *The Lair of the White Worm* (1988) is about legend, while *A Field in England* (2013) addresses magic, both explicitly engaging with rural landscapes as an agent for historicism.

Dawn Keetley makes an important point about how this sense of a culture lying buried but with the potential to resurface can have a dramatic effect on events unfolding in the contemporary moment in folk horror films: 'If folk horror often serves to "re-enchant" the world with belief in the supernatural, its evocation of a prior and now vanished enchanted world can also serve to emphasize exactly how profoundly disenchanted the contemporary world is' (Keetley 2020: 16). Perhaps this is part of the urge to historicism, of finding something lost in the past. Gail-Nina Anderson sees the folk horror revival as a resurgent part of the spirit of Romanticism, 'wanting to connect with the unrationalized and instinctive' (Anderson 2019: 39). These films augur a strong sense that something important has been lost, allied with the notion that the overwhelming instrumental logic of contemporary Britain is something worth escaping. The answer might be found in the past, although not the 'official versions' of history. Yet it is an uncertain question posed by these films, and an answer that might not constitute an answer as such. If culture makes an ongoing discussion of Britain as an entity, which takes place 'in the mind's eye', as Homi K. Bhaba notes (1990: 1), then these films are an underside to the so-called 'heritage films' that have become an important means of conceptualising Britain's past, as noted by Higson (1996: 232–234). The two films under scrutiny here invoke feudalism, pagan worship, therianthropic shapeshifters, the English Civil War, alchemy and gnostic transformation. While some of these are accepted parts of history, other elements are part of a subterranean sense of the past as not 'simple' but dealing with forgotten complexities and using gnostic knowledge. These elements, rather than being reassuring and nostalgic, are fraught and beset with anxieties that are located in the seemingly permanent residual terrain and its mysteries.

What is underneath history?

The landscape is the stage upon which these folk horror dramas are acted out, and as such it retains memories not only of the events of the past, but of their re-enactment in folklore as well as in more recent media (Hutchings 2004; Newland 2016, this volume; Thurgill 2020; Evans-Powell, this volume). In the case of *The Lair of the White Worm*, whilst it depicts baronial mansions in the classic gothic mode, the significant disruptions are beyond that, coming from the bowels of the earth in a classical folk horror manner. *A Field in England* promises hidden truth under the pastoral surface – and it is a moot point as to what is revealed there. Like many British folk horror films, both of these engage with a spatial psychology, accessing things that are hidden in deep, dark and inaccessible locations, or underneath the normality of the land's surface. Behind the walls of old castles and mansions, joined by secret passages, or under the seemingly calm and normal surface of the rural topography, Britain's unconscious, the unconscionable past waits to return.

In both films, the past takes on a spatial character, as a geographical 'underneath'. Of course, this is a pervasive idea in culture generally, and is embodied by the process of archaeology. In this era of obsessive, almost pathological historicism, these films are about our obsession with the past, too. An excessive interest in the past risks a constant 'return of the repressed', and Britain's past affords much scope for this. This folk history is a long way from the 'big history' of the ruling classes ('kings and queens') or the 'abstract large-scale movements' of academic history, or social histories 'from below' that focus on 'the people' and 'their culture'. Folk horror history is more of a returning memory, or a partly reliable half-memory, so-called recovered memory, a legend, or simply wishful or fearful imagination. More superstition, perhaps, than record of actual past events, but, significantly, a vision of the past or fabulation of the way things were. These films address and gesture towards the past in a way that is outside the bounds of conventional and 'accepted' history, while at the same time they seem to be an eccentric and exceptional version of the past (an 'outsider' version). British folk horror films pose a particular relationship between the past and the present. According to Richard Fortey, rock formations are:

> a tangible message from a deeper level than our present landscape. Its faults supply a metaphor for our human deficiencies, inliers [isolated pieces of different more ancient rock] might stand for the collective unconscious. Deeply buried beneath the fossil-bearing rocks of England and Wales there is a foundation of rocks from mysterious times; a more deeply hidden history, yet one upon which everything else is built. (Fortey 1993: 83)

The surface is the symptom of the 'reality' underneath, yet it is the underneath that *defines* the surface. Literally or metaphorically, we expect buried truth to be hidden underneath, or at least to gain access to an unacknowledged reality. It is no accident that archaeology currently is one of the dominant popular concepts of Britain's past. Television programmes such as *Time Team* (1994–2014, Channel Four) also dramatise the discovery of past dimensions through digging underneath the ground to access the past. Both films under discussion in this chapter dramatise this: *The Lair of the White Worm* has the threat from the past in caves underneath the Peak District, while *A Field in England* is about a search for an elusive treasure buried under the field, and includes some digging for it. There is a clear spatio-temporal drama with both. In the former, there are spatial (and probably also temporal) 'wormholes' between the caves and the mansion, the present and past visions, whereas in the latter the eponymous field is outside, indeed totally cut off from, the noisy battle at the film's start.

The underneath is analogous to the idea of the unconscious in psychodynamic psychology. The 'unconscious' of the landscape becomes visible, even tangible. Yet what is the 'unconscious' of what both films create? Both exhibit a strong sense of historicism as magical and irrational. In both, threats (and mysterious compulsive desire) come from underneath the rural landscape. Both are illustrative examples of a renegade, unofficial historicism. Instead of coupling the relation of past to present with notions of 'history', particularly in its official versions, they each build directly on the seemingly timeless English landscape. Yet this landscape is one that bears scars of history and has many stories to tell.

Hidden in *The Lair of the White Worm*

Directed by Ken Russell and based loosely on Bram Stoker's short story, as well as the legend of the Lampton Worm, *The Lair of the White Worm* is about a legendary gigantic snake and its adherents, which are hidden away in the present. An archaeologist (played by Peter Capaldi) believes a skull he finds is connected to 'the d'Ampton worm' (a gigantic white snake), the legend of which tells it was killed by John d'Ampton centuries earlier in the Stonerich Cavern. The nearby Temple House is a mansion owned by Lady Sylvia Marsh (played by Amanda Donohoe), who is a priestess to the ancient white snake god, Dionin, which still exists as a gigantic physical presence hidden in the cave system. These caves can be accessed from the house via underground tunnels. The geographical structure of the film involves the Stonerich Cavern, Temple House, the local manor house (where Hugh Grant, as the current d'Ampton, lives), and the bed-and-breakfast accommodation where the archaeologist is digging. These mark four broad locations matched to the film's important characters: the cavern for the giant snake (a god), Temple House for the aristocratic snake-woman, the manor for the local landowning aristocrat, and the bed-and-breakfast hotel and adjacent archaeological pit, which is where the two young women (Mary and Eve) and the archaeologist (Angus) are located. These spaces differentiate classes (and underline the importance of the landowning aristocracy).

The Lair of the White Worm is founded upon the historical procedure called 'Euhemerism', the process of proving that mythology is founded in real historical event. This validates the folk stories, making them into 'real history' rather than folk hearsay. Old, sometimes seemingly ridiculous traditions are shown to be based on retaining a memory of something important that is needed for contemporary society to deal with a forgotten problem. Ultimately, the film appears very much in favour of tradition, with social structure shown as symbiotic and functional, and finally reassuring. But reassuring in the face of what? Perhaps, on the one hand, that Britain is a viable entity where people from different social backgrounds can unite against a common enemy, or, on the other, that there are perpetual gigantic problems hidden beneath the surface that constantly need addressing. One way or another, with Dionin as a metaphor for perpetual hidden problems of great magnitude.

As a Ken Russell film, *The Lair of the White Worm* is characteristically camp and bold, mixing comedic and extremely shocking elements with a fairly weak narrative drive. Russell wields a series of archetypal characters: an archaeologist; an aristocrat; a powerful and sexually confident woman; a demure, good-hearted woman; etc., forging a matrix of relations that enables striking events if not gripping narrative.

Rather than being set in an agricultural landscape, the film moves between big country houses and caves in the Peak District, but remains rural. Its folk horror aspect is clear, as it is based not only on myth and legend but also on its situation within the English landscape. In classic gothic manner, evil is hidden away in country mansions, but more importantly it is situated underneath the ground. Consequently, the archaeologist unearths something that would better be left buried.

Lady Sylvia's intermittent transformations into a snake woman engage with the prominent worldwide legend of the snake woman. Although there is perhaps little British tradition of snake woman mythology, it reminds of TV sports presenter turned mystic David Icke's declaration that the English royal family are shape-shifting lizards (Lewis and Kahn 2005; Austin 2017). Indeed, anti-aristocratic myths and stories retain a certain amount of currency. *The Lair of the White Worm* also loosely engages with a small tradition in British cinema, with antecedents such as *The Snake Woman* (1961), and Hammer's films *The Gorgon* (1964) and *The Reptile* (1966).[1]

The Lair of the White Worm includes startling flashback visions as protean bursts from the past. These display the past not as a dull, indifferent and straightforward thing from school history books but rather as 'hot' and shocking outbursts of sex and violence. They consist of a static long take, reminiscent of early cinema's tableaux, and with something of the character of *tableaux vivants*. The first ensues when Lady Sylvia steals the skull and spits venom onto a crucifix on the wall. Eve then touches this and has an 'acid' vision, where she is with nuns praying to Jesus on the cross. Roman soldiers enter and attack and rape them, the snake wraps around Christ and Lady Sylvia appears in half-snake form. This daydream flashback has something of the character of a memory, or a collective memory, perhaps. Rather than history, the past becomes an incoherent burst of anachronistic violence. The aesthetics are strident and confrontational, with a strange and singular fiery background created by greenscreen effect, which confuses space in the frame. This sequence is startling both in its content and its rendition, with disturbing images alongside the fiery background that cuts through and around the images. The second vision appears when Mary's mother-snake bites her. The single-shot tableau has snake men come out of the mouth of a large face of Lady Sylvia. With knife-like penises they attack Mary violently, again with the fiery special-effect backdrop but also this time with the skull superimposed on the screen and moving forward in front of other images. The third occasion is when Eve snaps out of being hypnotised while on the telephone and warns Mary. This vision has Lady Sylvia in half-snake form, licking a phallic blood-covered spike, while surrounded by spikes impaling nuns. This scene is reminiscent of images of Vlad the Impaler, and rather than the fiery superimposed background of the previous visions, on this occasion the background is mountains and plains, which could well be Romania/Wallachia. It is accompanied by a strident burst on the church organ to underline the blasphemous images. Unusual audiovisual techniques provide a window to the unrepresentable.

Each vision belongs to a character yet they are all caused by snake venom, and rather than individual reverie they are collective flashbacks to a coherent past of images. These are all outbursts from history, heavily sexualised, shockingly violent and aesthetically audacious. In a way, these 'hot aesthetics' of the past are reminiscent of musical song sequences, and indeed, not so far from some of Ken Russell's striking musical set-piece song sequences in films such as *The Music Lovers* (1971) or *Lisztomania* (1975). Indeed, like Russell's other films, these violent outbursts are startling and highly memorable set pieces that often appear to 'step outside' of the film's narrative and diegetic world. They lack dialogue but have significant sound and music.

The Lair of the White Worm pulls apart the distinction between humanity and the animal kingdom, taking great interest in the aesthetic possibilities, exploiting the constant use of fish-eye lens, confusing perspectives, strident imagery and wry humour. The film's cinematography was by Dick Bush, who had photographed not only many of Russell's other films, but also a number of Hammer Horror films, Peter Watkins's TV drama *Culloden* (1964), the celebrated BBC *Whistle and I'll Come to You* (1968) and the canonical British Folk horror film *Blood on Satan's Claw* (1971). Despite the folk horror narrative, the epicentre of the film is the 'folk horror tableaux', which condense shocking images of violence as phantasmic glimpses of the past. Whether they are real images of history or fantasies of the past is open to question, but these pull with them the rest of *The Lair of the White Worm*'s concepts about the past's relationship to the present. The film suggests the past won't go away, even if we pretend it is not there; and what's more, it is far more horrifying than we ever imagined. As a populist form of history, the film suggests that negativity resides in big country mansions, or remains hidden away underground, but endures. Furthermore, the social divisions of the past persist and are natural. Feudal and religious structures remain, and for good reason, as the local aristocrats continue a timeless battle, one where old religion (Dionin) ultimately loses out to landownership (the d'Ampton dynasty).

Burrowing underneath *A Field in England*

A Field in England has some similarities to *The Lair of the White Worm*, most notably in the idea of important hidden truth being underneath, and the intermittent use of unconventional tableaux that break the narrative drive of the film. Popular writing about British folk horror appears to have all but forgotten *The Lair of the White Worm* but lauds *A Field in England* as canonical of the new 'revival' of folk horror on film. Not only does the latter's iconography remind of and connect with *Witchfinder General* (1968) but the film was also directed by Ben Wheatley, a director with a palpable interest in the possibilities of folk horror. At the centre of *A Field in England* is a confrontation between alchemist, O'Neil, and alchemist's assistant, Whitehead. Whitehead (played by Reece Shearsmith) enters the field with Cutler, Friend and Jacob, all of whom are absconding from an English Civil War battle. O'Neil (played by Michael Smiley) is pulled from nowhere on a rope by the others. He tells them there is some treasure hidden in the field, which is sought but not found as they have their experience altered by hallucinogenic mushrooms.

The film is open to multiple interpretations, and indeed, seems to challenge the audience to rethink it, asserting the past as a bearer of ambiguity and mystery rather than event and fact. *A Field in England* has a strong feeling of being an allegory or metaphor, or at least of having a resonance beyond its immediate representations. On one level, it appears like a drug-induced dream, while on another it might be understood as a reworking of the traditional schools historical 'narrative' of the English Civil War, as a group of 'ordinary people' unite to destroy a despotic king. However, other interpretations offer themselves. For instance, that the field represents purgatory. Whitehead, Cutler, Jacob and Friend are all dead and are intent on reaching an ale house (which is heaven), traversing the purgatorial field. They encounter Satan (O'Neill), who compels them to dig a pit as an entrance to hell, but ultimately they defeat him and have a triumphal exit from the field. Another compelling interpretation is that the different characters are all fragments of Whitehead's psyche, which are unified by the end of the film.[2] This 'gnostic journey' interpretation makes much sense.[3] The far from straightforward status assigned to events and their representations becomes apparent late in *A Field in England*, engendering a reappraisal of the film's earlier events.

The aesthetics of *A Field in England* mark it out as distinctive. A couple of strategies align it more closely with art cinema. The film is shot in black and white, lacking colour, but dynamic in its shading tonalities. It also lacks sound at times, and intermittently includes the startling use of static images as *tableaux vivants*. These are unnervingly ambiguous. They appear to lack any function for narrative development and comprise characters halting for a moment, dallying inexplicably. Reminiscent of Roy Andersson films, but perhaps more like paused video games or animated DVD opening menu screens, these intermittent *tableau vivant* sequences are confounding in their function for the film. However, their stasis chimes with the relatively static character of the film's action – which is literally held within a field. *A Field in England*'s extensive dialogue scenes often appear aimless and incidental to the succession of events, and perhaps even at times distantly resemble modernist drama such as the works of Harold Pinter or Samuel Beckett. In terms of antecedents, clear forerunners are Peter Watkins's remarkable docudrama *Culloden* (1964), about the 1746 battle in the Jacobite rebellion, and Kevin Brownlow and Andrew Mollo's *Winstanley* (1975). This was a biopic of the social reformer Gerrard Winstanley, who, at roughly the same time as *A Field in England*'s setting, founded 'the Diggers' or 'True Levellers', an egalitarian farming community who were suppressed by the establishment during Oliver Cromwell's protectorate. Both films were shot in black and white. *A Field in England* follows suit. It has become a convention that the past is depicted in black and white; however, on a metaphorical level this might also suggest a time when thinking was 'black and white', following a division into two well-differentiated sides of conflict. Yet, if *A Field in England* appears to begin from this premise (the two sides of the Civil War), it is overwhelmed with ambiguity (which side are they fighting on?) and ultimately the seeming resolution of division in the film's perplexing ending.

While perhaps in some ways *A Field in England* is not obviously a folk horror film, it is steeped in folk mysticism secured firmly in the British landscape. The company pull O'Neil out of a mushroom circle – although in some ways the reverse: it makes more sense that he was actually pulling them into it. Mushroom circles, or fairy rings, are enchanted spaces that are exceptions to normal time and space. Similarly, the extremely strange rope-walking sequence is signalled as very different from the rest of the film so far by its aesthetics. A very different type of music signals that this is 'semi-outside' the film's existing frame of reference. Indeed, the grotesque character of the events presented is underscored by the slow-motion effect on the images as a homology to the strident piece of drone music.[4] The sequence is preceded by harrowing off-screen screaming from Whitehead, who is inside the tent with O'Neil. This sets the audience's imagination into overdrive, as the sounds are extreme, but we are denied the images to accompany them and confirm events. Whitehead emerges from the tent tied to a rope, walking out from the tent with a wide-eyed and disturbed look on his face, as he is being manipulated by O'Neil as a divining device, a human dowsing rod, to 'see underneath' the field magically. Like a human metal

Outsider history, or outside of history 125

Figure 7.1   *A Field in England*, 2013

detector, Whitehead illustrates how we are no longer on a normal plane of existence and 'underneath' is more important. The disturbing divining ropewalk sequence moves the film squarely onto a more extraordinary level. The ensuing psychedelic sequence is the conclusion of this trajectory.

The film immerses us in Whitehead's confusing and psychedelic experience. It appears partially to be a regurgitation of his memory, and in terms of aesthetics derives a number of its visual aspects from 1960s psychedelia (inverted screen, strobe effects, a mirrored screen effect, hallucinations and discontinuity) (Donnelly 2015: 38–42). Actually, the strange aesthetics start before he eats the (presumably hallucinogenic) mushrooms. Whitehead appears to see upside down, and then the black sun image materialises accompanied by a large deep gong sound. O'Neil looks for him and Whitehead eats mushrooms, alternating a big close-up of mushrooms with his eating face. Images blur; the screen divides with a mirror effect down the middle; there is a shot of a running beetle, images shot through a spider's web, and the grass blowing in the field. Sound is no more coherent or continuous. We hear some of the song 'Baloo My Boy', wind and electric guitar feedback. These images culminate in a mirror image of O'Neil, as we gradually realise that this sequence is predominantly a 'remix' of previous images from the film, a reorientation of Whitehead's memories of events in the field leading up to this point. Diegetic sound drops out to leave silence, and a succession of discontinuous images proceeds: a smiling Whitehead, heavy wind and smoke speeded up, the tent blowing away, occult papers being blown, O'Neil's scrying mirror smashed. This seems like an extended play of unmotivated sound and image, or at least an esoteric and cryptic succession of images, sounds and actions.

The dramatic but ambiguous image of the black sun, like an eclipse, is intercut with a close-up of Whitehead's eye, and echoes the shape of O'Neil's scrying glass. Such images suggest that the film is not about reality but about perception. Indeed, in an interview Ben Wheatley discussed how he was interested in perceptual aspects such as the persistence of vision, and mental processing of repeated images (Colegate 2013). This is evident in the use of black-and-white photography, discontinuous editing, upside-down images, mirror images, blurred focus, absent sound, the use of extreme close-ups and the bizarre 'time halted' tableaux suggesting that physical reality (as film knows it) has broken down, all of which appear to question what we see and hear. This interest in perception (underlined by the psychedelics) questions what we see and hear, and problematises the status of what is represented in the film more generally, making *A Field in England* difficult to take at face value. It appears to be hinting at things not being what they seem, while almost asking us to interpret them. Early on, Cutler tells Whitehead: 'you're as good as dead to them this side of the hedgerow', while Whitehead tells him he has only seen 'only shadows' in the field. The implication is that everyone has been intentionally conjured into the field by the alchemist – or are dead. This transition through the hedge seems to be supernatural, a little like traversing the wardrobe to enter the land of Narnia in the books of C. S. Lewis. The sounds of the battle recede to the point where quickly it feels as though they have totally disappeared, bolstered by Commander Trower's bizarre appearance in the hedge but apparent inability to traverse it and enter the field. It seems the company have escaped from a battle, of which we see nothing. We hear it briefly, then it is gone. All the aesthetic signals suggest they might be dead and journeying into the afterlife.

A Field in England had an extraordinary multi-platform release – simultaneously in cinemas, online, on DVD and Blu-ray, and on the Film4 television channel – which mirrors the character of the film as an ambiguous object open to re-viewing and many different interpretations – and a longer shelf life. The film resembles a classical *katabasis*, where the hero makes a journey into the underworld, and probably the most convincing interpretation of *A Field in England* is that it depicts a journey of gnosis, where all the characters are aspects of protagonist Whitehead. Its climax sees Whitehead shoot O'Neil in the head from behind, destroying his face, and then seemingly merging with him. Jacob tells Whitehead that he'll 'try to save him from himself', and O'Neil later confirms to him that 'we're two halves' of the same person. The final images include a frontal tableau shot of Whitehead, flanked by the apparently reanimated Friend and Jacob, and looking confident and resembling a mixture of the two antagonists. The aesthetics suggest transcendence and unattainable experience, grasping at the birth of something new.

Engaging with recent British cultural history, *A Field in England* is directly connected to one of the canonical British psychedelic films, Donald Cammell and Nic Roeg's *Performance* (1970). One of the most occult British feature films, *Performance* culminates in a dramatic and aesthetically bold hallucinogenic sequence, after which one character shoots the other in the head and then the two seemingly merge into one in the final shots of the film. The same happens here. Engagement with earlier history is not straightforward. The concept of the English Civil War is a resonant idea, yet the film's representations appear inconclusive. Indeed, we don't even know which side the group of men have been supporting. The sounds of the battle melt away once we are through the hedgerow, and upon returning back at the end of the film there are no battle sounds. Does this suggest it is a metaphorical battle? *A Field in England* poses the English Civil War as 'alternative' to the psychic magnet of British representation: the First World War. This war has become an increasingly worn-out shorthand for emotional and psychic trauma of the nation. The English Civil War is now almost forgotten in the deep past, but is revived as a way of portraying being at war with the self, emblematised by the paralleling and conflict of Whitehead and O'Neil, apparently inspired by Civil War re-enactments, a traditional British form of cosplay, which suggests the past has never quite left Britain. Indeed, perhaps is 'doomed to repeat the past'. The English Civil War is a clear metaphor for modern divided Britain, although perhaps less intent on addressing two sides than outlining a situation of instability and confusion.

If Wheatley is portraying a 'divided Britain', this sense of schism is hardly a new thing in Britain but is merely the latest and perhaps most visible incarnation.[5] The film is rife with metaphors for tensions that remain unresolved and part of British society. How does the past serve the present here? Not a burst from the past but in a continuum of the same social relations as in *The Lair of the White Worm*, where the Civil War embodies an unavoidable sense of division as deep backdrop for a narrative of the split of the English psyche that strives to (re)unify the person and so to unify the nation.

Conclusion

Rather than being 'history' these films are premised upon a process of historicism, a present discussion of past events and ideas about what has happened before. British folk horror films allow for a return or persistence of elements from the social (and cultural) past, where *The Lair of the White Worm* is built around a perpetual but covert conflict that holds social structure in place, while *A Field in England* looks back to an extremely significant but culturally marginal conflict, one that involved a radical rethink of the nation amid extreme political and social instability. While on the surface perhaps this relates the overt radicalism of historians such as Raphael Samuel, or E. P. Thompson's (1963) 'histories from below', it is far more ambiguous and incoherent. In a way, it marks a willingness to engage the past and the legacies of the past on their own terms rather than integrated into a package of 'meaningful' historical discourse. British folk horror films are not 'history' as such, but are more a phantasmagoria of the past, interested in allowing the depiction of perennial anxieties and hidden magic processes, both of which are considered to remain firmly alive today but hidden.

Both films are concerned with the past. *The Lair of the White Worm* appears to depict images from the past through its startling intermittent *tableau vivant* vision sequences, which erupt violently into the film's present day. It also confirms that the past of legend remains alive in the present, where the hidden truth of the white worm Dionin and its species-hybrid priestess is revealed. *A Field in England* depicts England in the mid-seventeenth century, seemingly during a battle in the English Civil War. Despite its historical importance, though, this period remains ambiguous or oversimplified for the British public. Both films are metacultural, in that they engage with traditions of representing the British past. *A Field in England* looks like, and apparently was inspired by, a society that re-enacts battles from the English Civil War (Colegate 2013), and *The Lair of the White Worm* includes a ritualistic festival re-enactment of the past at the start.

These two films are very different. *The Lair of the White Worm* is jokey, camp and baroque with shocking outbursts. *A Field in England*, on the other hand, is colder and less emotional, with a feeling of distance from the proceedings. Both films include static tableaux that 'step outside' the films, halting the diegetic illusion. *Lair* offers hot moments of set-piece shock from the past, while *Field* offers 'dead' moments of repose that seem to underline the time and space of the film as fantastic and psychological rather than as a representation of a believable diegetic world. Both films contain strong 'hallucinogenic' influences, making shamanistic cinematic visions of Britain's past but also engaging them with late 1960s 'psychedelia'. This functions as a metaphor for a 'different way of seeing', allowing access to an alternative version of Britain and its past. Consequently, aspects of style dominate any sense of historical veracity, with images and sounds exploiting their own materiality to render a sense of returned past as primarily emotional and textural in character.

Like a number of British folk horror films, these two resurrect unresolved conflicts that have become the unrepresentable parts of history.

They offer an alternative to consensus, to 'official' history, providing an image or at least a sense of the past where marginalised aspects are ceded weight and significance. While we might think we will find the truth hidden underneath, perhaps we are more likely to find a psychic truth. This tallies with Mark Fisher's description of hauntology's oblique addressing of the future: 'When the present has given up on the future, we must listen for the relics of the future in the unactivated potentials of the past' (Fisher 2013: 53). British folk horror films engage these unactivated aspects of the past in a manner that makes the past uncertain from the present's point of view. They make the foundation of modern Britain seem less stable, less done and dusted. This is built directly on the seemingly timeless and permanent British landscape, making an interest in the past also a concern for the eternal. That both of the films use tableaux suggests history not as narrative but as a static snapshot, a disconnected fragment against a continuum of permanence rather than change. Landscape is static but its effects are not in terms of space as much as in terms of time, where past meets present in a superimposed time rather than the linear, rational cause-and-effect development we might expect from traditional history. This is folk horror as static time, holding a simultaneity of past and present, which is embodied by the landscape. Emphasising people as utterly transitory, this landscape is one that bears scars of past events and is wreathed in the ineffable. As my title suggests, on the one hand these films speak of the past in a way that is outside of conventional history, and on the other they mark something of an 'outsider' version of Britain's history. In either case, the emphasis is on an 'unofficial' version of Britain's past, which is held in marginal memory and half-remembered as a trace in folk-inflected culture, most particularly in folk horror films such as these.

Notes

1 A staple of Aztec, Indian and Jewish legends among others, snake women have been well represented in cinema. Examples include *Cult of the Cobra* (1955), *The Seventh Voyage of Sinbad* (1958), Hong Kong film *Madam White Snake* (1962), American film *Sssssss* (1973), Indian film *Nagin* (1976), Hong Kong film *Green Snake* (1993), American film *The Secret of Lizard Woman* (1995), Indian film *Devi* (1999), Thai film *The Curse of the Lizard* (2004), American film *Queen Cobra: Snakes on a College Campus* (2007), and Indian film *Hisss* (2010).
2 Interpretation: O'Neil as Catholic occultist outsider; others as divided and different although nominally the same. Ben Wheatley registered a number of different interpretations in a Film4 interview: www.youtube.com/watch?v=bgwnlM4q pEU&ab_channel=TEC (accessed 26 April 2023).

3 This 'journey' is arguably very distantly reminiscent of John Bunyan's allegorical *The Pilgrim's Progress* (of 1678); indeed, naming the character 'Friend' seems to reference Bunyan and confirm the allegorical status of the film.
4 This is the only piece of licensed music in the film: *Chernobyl* from Blanck Mass's eponymous debut album of 2013 (which also includes a piece called *Icke's Struggle*).
5 The film's characterisation suggests a trace of a significant historical Protestant–Catholic divide in the UK, with O'Neill as the Irish outsider dismissed as 'not Christian' (a common charge made by Protestants against Catholics in the past) and 'the devil'.

References

Anderson, Gail-Nina (2019), 'The Old Ways', *Fortean Times* 381 (July), 36–43.

Austin, Jon (2017), 'David Icke Explains His Infamous Theory Why "Queen IS a Shape-Shifting Reptile"', *Daily Express*, 17 February, www.express.co.uk/news/weird/768800/David-Icke-queen-shape-shifting-lizard (accessed 26 March 2022).

Bhaba, Homi K. (1990), 'Introduction: Narrating the Nation', in Homi K. Bhaba (ed.), *Nation and Narration*. London: Routledge, pp. 1–7.

Colegate, Mat (2013), 'Pulling the Veil from the Mysteries: Ben Wheatley Talks *A Field in England*', *The Quietus*, July 5, thequietus.com/articles/12754-a-field-in-england-ben-wheatley-interview (accessed 20 July 2021).

Donnelly, K. J. (2015), 'The Psychedelic Screen', in *Magical Musical Tour: Rock and Pop in Film Soundtracks*. London: Bloomsbury, pp. 31–44.

Fisher, Mark (2013), 'The Metaphysics of Crackle: Afrofuturism and Hauntology', *Dancecult: Journal of Electronic Dance Music Culture* 5:2, 42–55.

Fortey, Richard (1993), *The Hidden Landscape: A Journey into the Geological Past*. London: Jonathan Cape.

Higson, Andrew (1996), 'The Heritage Film and British Cinema', in Andrew Higson (ed.), *Dissolving Views: Key Writings on British Cinema*. London: Cassell, pp. 232–248.

Hutchings, Peter (2004), 'Uncanny Landscapes in British Film and Television', *Visual Culture in Britain* 5:2, 27–40.

Keetley, Dawn (2020), 'Introduction: Defining Folk Horror', *Revenant* 5 (March), 1–32.

Lewis, Tyson and Richard Kahn (2005), 'The Reptoid Hypothesis: Utopian and Dystopian Representational Motifs in David Icke's Alien Conspiracy Theory', *Utopian Studies* 16:1 (Winter), 45–75.

Newland, Paul (2016), 'Folk Horror and the Contemporary Cult of British Rural Landscape: The Case of *Blood on Satan's Claw*', in Paul Newland (ed.), *British Rural Landscapes on Film*. Manchester: Manchester University Press, pp. 162–179.

Samuel, Raphael (1994), *Theatres of Memory*, Vol. I, *Past and Present in Contemporary Culture*. London: Verso.

Thompson, E. P. (1963), *The Making of the English Working Class*. London Victor Gollancz.

Thurgill, James (2020), 'A Fear of the Folk: On *Topophobia* and the Horror of Rural Landscapes', *Revenant* 5 (March), 33–56.

8

Anglo creep and Celtic resistance in *Apostle*

Beth Carroll

A sense of regionality in horror films is not a new phenomenon. It is not uncommon to see films shift action from the urban to the more rural for moments of horror and for sites of violence, whether this is Marion Crane's driving from the city of Phoenix, Arizona, towards an off-the-beaten-track motel in *Psycho* (1960), or Canadian nurse Betsy Connell's dislocated experience in the Caribbean in *I Walked with a Zombie* (1943). This contrast between two locations and geographies seems particularly apropos in the folk horror genre, in which sites of difference and, perhaps, *potential*, appear central not just to the narrative, but to the horror itself. Examples of this can be found in some of the most seminal folk horror films, such as *The Wicker Man* (1973) and *Blood on Satan's Claw* (1971). These two examples demonstrate regionality on a number of levels: first in terms of the national, and second in terms of the rural within a nationally specific, and temporal, context. In the folk horror genre, the senses of regionality and the rural often become synonymous ideas, the rural being reduced to and coded as having a particular regional identity the viewer is probably familiar with, if only superficially. As Louis Bayman and K. J. Donnelly make clear in their introduction to this volume, Britishness holds a unique place within folk horror. However, Britishness is so fraught with ambiguity and contradiction that it becomes too vague an idea with regard to folk horror. Instead, it is within the contrast among regions within the British Isles that insight can be found. For it appears that it is distance from the watchful eye of the centre and the institutions therein that enables unorthodox thinking to develop, particularly in terms of religion. England, and arguably even more specifically the south of England and London, are assumed to be the cultural constant and standard by which the unfamiliar is compared. By this measure, anything that is different permits a space for horror to occur, and this is true of the regions and nations of Britain beyond England.

Though it is generally accepted that there is as yet no clear and agreed-upon definition of folk horror, regionality does appear to be a key component: more specifically, regionality that directly evokes and engages with the past. For, as Adam Scovell argues, it is the clash between the past and the present that enables the horror to develop and is important to the genre. The gap is between the modern and the old, between the known and the unknown or imagined (Scovell 2017: 7). In folk horror, rural areas represent the past and feature ways of life that may now have been lost to the country as a whole. As Joshua B. Tuttle states, 'folk horror [is grounded] in the experience of those who interact with it' (Tuttle 2020: 344): in effect, with people who are often isolated, geographically and socially, engaging in old ways of doing things, often related to paganism. The folk horror genre thus tells a story of difference: difference from the status quo that has had the ability to manifest itself by virtue of isolation. Britain has made seminal contributions to the folk horror genre from its earliest elicitation. It is striking that a country so geographically small can conjure such sites of difference and isolation that lead to such violence. Within the British Isles, certain areas are returned to within folk horror with regularity, including Wales, Scotland and Cornwall: areas with a clear sense of their own identity and to whom the term 'region' is problematic, revealing the southern English lens through which Britain is understood. These locations may be overtly named within the narrative, as with the use of Scotland in *The Unkindness of Ravens* (2016), or may be used as a landscape. *The Dark* (2007) is an example of the latter, wherein the film is set in Wales but shot on the Isle of Man. Alternatively, as in the 'Cornish folk horror' *Enys Men* (2022), they may even form part of the film's marketing.

This chapter explores regionality in folk horror through a focus on Wales, specifically as it relates to an evocation of Celticness, which the country is associated with and often embraces (see Visit Wales (n.d.)). It argues that the Celtic looms large in the *English* imaginary as a location for the rural, and as a site of difference and danger. The contrast assumes an English viewpoint to folk horror that makes use of such regionality. Using Wales as its case study, the chapter examines how folk horror can evoke an ambiguous Celticness, culturally, religiously, and aesthetically, to make strange what was once more prevalent across the British Isles more generally. In folk horror, the Celtic represents the arcane past, found only in isolated and rural communities. More pointedly, this Celticness is ambiguous by virtue of being seen through an English lens, and, more pointedly, one that is more specifically framed by the south-east. This is not to say that the Celtic is an English creation: on the contrary, the English imaginary of the Celtic provides a dominant, albeit warped, representation in audio-visual media and folk horror more particularly. It is a profoundly and deliberately nebulous concept, so as to be suitably malleable and useful for the folk horror genre's depiction of the Celtic as an othered stereotype, found in locations such as Wales, Scotland and Cornwall. This English dominance over the image is seen even within a Welsh film such as *Apostle* (2018), which will be the filmic focus of this chapter. This, then, prompts the question as to the extent that a Welsh film such as *Apostle* supports such a system of English imagining, and, furthermore, how the film uses the Celtic as a way to represent horror and, at times, attraction.

Apostle and celtic representation

To begin the exploration of how Wales, the Celtic and *Apostle* intersect to provide a site of both horror and promise, it is important to outline the film more broadly, before focusing on three key areas of Celtic representation and how it intersects with folk horror: namely the rural, the culture and its relationship with religion. Set in 1905, the film follows an Englishman, Thomas, played by English actor Dan Evans, in his search for his sister, who has been kidnapped and is being held to ransom. The audience travels with Thomas as his investigation leads him to a rural and isolated island that, whilst lacking geographic specificity, is dominated by people with Welsh, and to a lesser extent, Scottish accents, in contrast to Thomas's own English one. It is revealed that the island hosts a community of people who follow a religion led by Malcolm, played by the Welsh actor Michael Sheen. Malcolm offers his congregation absolution and freedom from the tyranny of the English Crown. He appears to be a self-proclaimed prophet who has formed this religion to worship 'Her/She', the goddess of the island. While her power and status are ambiguous, she does take the form of an elderly woman. Thomas hides himself as a member of the congregation as he seeks his sister. He discovers that the community partake in bloodletting, the blood being fed to the restrained goddess: a form of sacrifice submitted in the hope of bountiful harvests. Malcolm and his lieutenants have held the goddess captive since their own arrival on the island, yet Thomas appears to see her in what could be interpreted as visions. Human mastery over the goddess has not been achieved. Thomas's sister is discovered and, as befitting a folk horror film, after several bloody altercations she escapes in a boat, presumably back to the mainland and the safety of England. Thomas and Malcolm, however, are not so fortunate; they remain on the island, with their bodies and energies becoming one with the land, perhaps replacing the goddess, who has by this point been killed.

Apostle sets up several dichotomies, three of which are apposite here: the contrast between the rural and urban, the tension between personal liberty and institutional power, and religious nonconformity versus Anglicanism. These contrasts can more broadly be placed within the wider comparison between Wales and England, with Wales representing freedom from the urban, ecclesiastical bureaucracy that England is tacitly accused of signifying. In order to strike the contrast efficiently, Welsh writer and director Gareth Evans evokes the Celtic as a cultural shorthand. Celtic iconography and references define the rural landscape: the island is not a dangerous place just because it is rural; it is dangerous because it is Celtic. As with other folk horror films, such as *Blood on Satan's Claw*, in *Apostle*, in part, the Celtic represents an old-world paganism, now only found in isolated rural communities that have cut themselves off from modernity – in this case, specifically England and its legal and religious institutions.

To understand the ambiguity of the term 'Celtic', it is worth providing some background to it, and the context in which I am using it, as well as considering how and what appears in the shared cultural imaginary. The archaeologist Barry Cunliffe provides an engaging breakdown of the different approaches to understanding the term 'Celtic', or 'Celts' (Cunliffe 2011). He surmises that the word 'Celts' has become so argued over that many theorists would claim it has become redundant as a term, especially as it has been used politically. This misuse of the term, he points out, is a result of over 300 years of theorising that has always rather erred on the side of vagueness, whether that be a lack of geographic specificity (broadly the west of Europe) or a definition based on language, whereby linguists ascribed the name 'Celtic' to a family of languages (such as Scottish Gaelic, Welsh, Breton and Cornish). Approaching the nineteenth century, there was a focus on the art and material culture of these peoples: what has been termed 'Celtic art', the precursors of what many of us may well be aesthetically familiar with today in existing popular culture (Cunliffe 2011: 190–191). Even before this interest by archaeologists and linguists, the Celts were written about in terms of relative barbarism. The Romans, for example, saw them as peoples who did not reflect the Romans' own dominant, contemporaneous thoughts on gender, war and personal attire.[1] As J. H. Williams argues, key to the Roman understanding of the Celts was the codifying of them as non-urban, essentially rural (Williams 2001). For the Romans, as Cunliffe states, 'created the classical stereotype of the Celt – the Celt as "Other" – the antithesis of the civilised human. Celts are "wild beasts", "war mad", excitable, easily dispirited, loud and boastful, unlike we, who are civilised, controlled, steadfast, and sober' (Cunliffe 2011: 194). The animalism associated with the Celt is obvious here, and is in direct contrast to the Romans (broad a category as that may be), with whom we, as a society, have come to identify (see Hingley 2000). In part, the Celts are these things *because* their landscape and geography are rural, because they follow different rules.

Several things are clear from this: first, that a stereotype of the Celts appeared early on and persists today, particularly in terms of the revival in popularity of Celtic art; second, that much of the understanding of the Celts and the Celtic has historically come from external, non 'Celtic' sources; and third – and following on closely – that the Celts are what we might broadly term 'anti-establishment'. This othering of the Celts is not synonymous with a negative view, however. For many of the Romans, the Celts represented a rustic virtue, associated with many qualities that 'civilised' Romans were deemed to have lost (see Tacitus 1996; Laurence 1997). Many of the views of the Celts follow a framework commonly found in orientalist discourses: namely of an othering that is to be disavowed whilst being simultaneously enticing; of offering a primal freedom that the establishment has little space for. The folk horror genre makes use of these ideas associated with the representation of the Celts via its use of Wales, particularly as viewed through an English lens. In *Apostle*, the Celtic offers the onscreen community freedom and redemption from English law, whilst in parallel, and arguably as a result, becoming a site of barbarism and brutal violence. Here we have the rural Celtic space offering both opportunity and violence.

Changing landscapes

An early example of this contrast between the rural and urban can be seen in the opening of the film. It opens on a rural scene with a steam train in the distance, foregrounding the move from the urban towards the rural, from 'modernity' to parochialism. There is no immediate clarity as to where this is within the British Isles, other than through the contrast to places that it is clearly not. For example, this opening idyll is intercut with a scene in a large house in England. The house suggests old money, and through it a sense of the establishment and institutionalism, supported by the revelation that this is the house of an industrial business owner, the father of Thomas. The urban is quickly placed in visual contrast to the rural, encouraging a distinction that calls to mind the impact of the industrial revolution and how it was not felt evenly everywhere. The camera follows Thomas as he moves about the room. An over-the-shoulder shot shows that the house is attached to a now quiet and abandoned factory. Interestingly, the *mise-en-scène* and framing illustrate that Thomas is not entirely at home in these surroundings, despite this being his father's house. His clothing is worn and drab in comparison to the lawyer he converses with at the house; he is unkempt in appearance; and he is initially small in the frame, almost collapsing in on himself. After Thomas is told details of his sister's kidnap and perilous situation, and is entrusted with bringing her home, he travels via train and boat to get to the isolated island. The further Thomas travels away from his English home, the more unfamiliar the surroundings and people. The landscape is mountainous and surrounded by water, calling to mind both the Welsh coast and Snowdon (Yr Wyddfa in Welsh). These are people who have clearly and deliberately separated themselves from the mainland, who, in order to enter the religious community, must leave 'corrupting' influences and personal belongings behind, including printed material. This calls to mind paganism, which broadly represents a turning away from religions of the book, as well as from the rules of property ownership so embedded in the Victorian mindset. Malcolm's henchmen carefully vet the people for contraband before permitting them onto the boats. 'Clothing and heirlooms only' are allowed – items associated with a dead past – while books are shown to be burnt in a close up shot. The lack of access to the printed word is suggestive of control and paganism, as well as a turn towards isolation.

The first appearance of the island, however, is one of beauty. A medium long shot reveals small rowing boats approaching the shore, framed by mountains. The scene starts silently, with quiet droning strings slowly increasing in volume. There is an echo to this sound, depicting the vastness of the space, but also Thomas's anxiety. Aural close-ups of footsteps and luggage being unloaded punctuate the scene, providing a sonic contradiction. The camera shows close-ups of Thomas repeatedly looking over his shoulder juxtaposed with long shots of the mountain range, with a cross standing upon the top. This familiar Christian imagery is undermined by the revelation that rather than being religious in nature, the cross is in fact the rigging of a boat. That the rigging is assumed to be a cross is not surprising, considering both the English eyes through which we see them – Thomas's – and the religious framing that the audience have had up until now. This landscape not only makes the familiar *un*familiar, it also holds surprises. The rural features the unexpected and, through it, potential. This place is unfamiliar by virtue of being regionally different from England.

It is notable that Malcolm is played by Michael Sheen, who has, in recent years, taken great pains to embrace his Welshness publicly and to support the country both artistically and politically, in so doing becoming a figure of resistance. In the documentary series *Jennifer Saunders' Memory Lane* (ITV, 23 December 2020), Saunders dedicates an episode to Sheen's years spent in Port Talbot when he was a youth. Port Talbot, a town on the south coast of Wales, is described by Saunders as famed for its landscape; its industrialism; and its cultural exports, such as Sheen, Richard Burton, and Anthony Hopkins. Sheen, on the other hand, describes it as a 'working-class steel town'. Port Talbot is viewed by Sheen as a place that wins your love, that is industrial but surrounded by scenery – a place of memory and personal journeys, and, importantly, a place of the people. Interestingly, whilst Saunders describes Sheen as the best 'Welsh' person he could be, in the context of a conversation about his adolescent desire to fit in Sheen is more specific. He describes himself as someone from Port Talbot. Saunders, the English actress, has generalised and homogenised Welshness, whereas Sheen is keen to promote a sense of regionality and difference.

Welsh resistance to English Anglicanism

Though I have used the term 'regional' in this chapter already, there should be some wariness of using the term unproblematically in a Welsh context, in part because of the liminality of the country and the differences that exist between its margins and centre, as well as Wales's relationship with its border with England. As Kate Woodward makes clear in her discussion of *On the Black Hill*:

> Wales, without the political apparatus of the traditional nation-state and with a border (partially straddled by the Black Mountains) that remained legally unconfirmed until 1972, has long been considered an 'imagined' and 'invented' nation, and the Welsh landscape has sat at the heart of discourses of philosophy, politics, painting and poetry in Wales. (Woodward 2016: 105)

Put simply, Wales and England have long been in a relationship with one another, often viewed from the English perspective as a core–periphery relationship, whereby England draws resources from Wales and 'charitably' shares its culture in return. This cultural offering can be seen in numerous ways, including with regard to law and religion. It has frequently been met with Welsh resistance. As Dorothy Sylvester elucidates:

> The two Welsh [parliamentary] Acts popularly known as the Acts of the Union (1536 and 1542) were framed with the aim of absorbing Wales into the English realm and applying the English political, administrative and judicial systems to the government of Wales. They brought to an end the power of the marcher lords as independent rulers and henceforth the king's writ ran throughout England and Wales. (Sylvester 1969: 129)

One way we can see resistance to this lies in how Anglicanism does not dominate the Welsh religious landscape as it does the English. In 1662 the Act of Uniformity, passed by the English Parliament, dictated the nature of worship and ecclesiastical structure within the Church of England, including within Wales. Despite this diktat, however, as Moelwyn Williams makes clear, the Anglican Church could not maintain its dominance in Wales, particularly in the countryside. Williams states that:

> Other factors, such as the inability of the bishops to use the Welsh language, absenteeism, pluralism, and alienation of revenue, all contributed in varying degrees to undermine the influence of the Anglican church. A wide gap,

therefore, existed between the Established Church in Wales and the peasantry of the countryside. The position was further exacerbated by the positive failure of the Church to respond effectively to the changes in population that were taking place in the industrial areas. (Williams 1975: 164–165)

In short, part of the reason why Anglicanism was replaced by nonconformism as dominant in parts of Wales is that the former failed to appreciate the differences that existed in Wales: culturally, geographically and demographically. Wales is not England, and neither is it a uniform other. As Williams states, 'It is estimated that by 1851, the Nonconformists had *captured* nearly eighty per cent of the population'(Williams 1975: 165). The growth of nonconformism had a direct impact on the landscape of Wales. As Sylvester claims, 'The Nonconformist churches by using remote situations for many of their meeting places and chapels, added a further stimulus to hamlet growth (and sometimes provided a prime nucleus)' (Williams 1975: 145). Fundamentally, nonconformism grew in rural areas, and these rural areas grew as a consequence of nonconformism: a cycle that placed nonconformism at the heart of many Welsh communities and presents an essential difference from England, where Anglicanism dominated, and arguably still does on a cultural level. Nonconformism is part of a dissenting movement that began in Wales in 1639. As Sylvester describes:

> Discontent with the clergy and the state of churches was rife in Wales, pluralism was common, and many churches were either rarely or never used. The way was thus open for the rise of the numerous dissenting societies which arose, at first slowly, then rapidly, especially from the 1730s. (Sylvester 1969: 185)

Principally, nonconformism in Wales was marked by a move away from the previously dominant Anglicanism and towards independent religious communities, each with their own minister and individual doctrine. Isolated, non-Christian religions found in rural locales are prevalent in folk horror, but it is more specifically from the marriage of paganism with this independent nonconformist religious context that much of *Apostle*'s horror derives. The first suggestions that the religious community that have taken Thomas's sister is not of the Anglican Church arrives early on. As Thomas is gathering details of his sister's kidnap, the lawyer providing him with information states that 'These people ... they're blasphemers, a cult, a disease; be careful, be smart, bring her home.' The rhetoric associated with these people clearly places them at odds with the English lawyer's religious beliefs, which are used as a moral barometer, a baseline to which other religious beliefs are compared. Whereas his Anglicanism brings truth, the religion of the island is presented as barbaric and base. The lawyer's language clearly positions the islanders as participating in non-religious practices that actively offend God. Whilst the audience will have opportunity to see more of the 'cult', this does initially frame its practitioners as different, as other, and through a specifically English lens.

As Thomas surreptitiously tricks his way onto the boat to the island, he overhears the people being described as 'brothers and sisters' as a church bell tolls in the distance. Here we have religious language used to provide ambiguity. This is language actually shared by Anglicanism, whereby the congregations are often described in terms of a 'flock'. Prayer meetings are discussed by the boat passengers. There is just enough Christian rhetoric and similarity as to prove uncanny, but whereas Anglicanism is *heimlich*, this 'disease' represented by Malcolm's religion is *unheimlich*. As with many nonconformist groups, there is enough reference to the forms of Protestant Christian worship, but it is distinctly not Anglican. In part, its danger lies in its deceptive closeness to 'acceptable' religion. It is like the echo of a lost memory of an old religion that Christianity once emerged from but that has now been made strange by time in terms of ceremony and familiarity. As Thomas is on the boat, the space is depicted as claustrophobic and dark, the camera makes use of close-ups, and the rate of editing increases. The use of low-key lighting and sudden camera movements successfully depicts a boat being rocked by the elements. The danger of the boat crossing is palpable, and there is heavy use of ambient sounds, such as the sail flapping in the wind and the waves lashing at the boat. The lack of music during this moment makes it more than a little uncomfortable, as the sounds of a sheep's bleating slowly quieten as it is lost to the sea. Thomas failed to save the sheep, which the other passengers threw into the sea as a deliberate impromptu sacrifice, saying only that 'It was as intended. Only She decides whether to give or take. We do not intervene', followed by a chant of 'Amen'. The camera returns to a centrally framed close-up of Thomas. He is the audience's conduit into this strange, rural space; he is an English lens onto the rural community.

This persistence of non-Christian imagery continues upon Thomas's entering the island community. The camera reveals an eyeline match cut to a medium close-up of a pale, stone statue, looming from the left of the screen. This, presumably, is the 'She' previously referred to. The camera returns to this statue a few moments later in a series of shots that show the statue from various angles, but never in its entirety. It presents a fragmented and unknowable 'She' to the audience, unlike the familiarity of Christ told through parables and gospels. The female imagery is at odds with the social system in place on the island, with men in charge not only of who comes and goes from the community, but whether they are allowed absolution from their previous crimes. This becomes clear during Malcolm's introduction. The scene starts by providing diegetic communal hymn-singing. The choice of hymn, 'Broad Is the Road that Leads to Death', is an interesting one. It was written by the English nonconformist Isaac Watts, who was born in Southampton in 1674 and became an independent minister (Sotonopedia (n.d.)). This extra-textual knowledge further supports the contrast overtly being made by the film between nonconformism and Anglicanism. The echo of the Reformation is still being heard, along with the intolerance that accompanied it.

As the hymn fades away and Thomas walks towards the meeting-house-cum-ministry for the community, a Welsh male voice shouts:

> Radicalist, conspirator, traitor, enemy of the king ... those are the words they attributed to me as they shackled my hands and the hands of my brothers ... before they imprisoned us on a charge of treason. Sentenced to death. But for what? My only crime was to dare dream of a world where each waking day we rise equal. Compassion is no crime.

This is our introduction to Malcolm, and he is immediately positioned not only as a figure of authority, shown by the central framing as he stands afront the seated listeners, but as one who is at odds with the Crown, with England. The island, shaped by Malcolm and the religious beliefs of the followers of 'She', is inherently nonconformist and anti-English. His strong Welsh accent makes this point, but so too does Malcolm's positioning of his crimes as 'reasonable', as not *morally* wrong. He is on the side of good, unlike the law shaped by England and its institutions. This suggestion, of a religion built upon a moral code different from that of Anglicanism, evokes a dichotomy between the rural and the urban, between truth and overworked doctrine. Malcolm's emotive use of language is at odds with the transcendent language usually associated with Anglicanism. As Malcolm argues, this religion is one moulded by core or base principals of compassion and equality, rather than the teaching of scholars and priests: people who provide religious direction externally, from the top down. Here, *Apostle* provides an engaging contradiction: on the one hand, this is a religion that is a direct threat to England's authority, legally, institutionally, and religiously or morally. Conversely, it also offers simplicity and freedom from overbearing complexity of scripture and historical teachings. This isolated religion, geographically and spiritually, is both threatening and appealing. This is a trope of folk horror more generally. As Scovell argues in relation to *The Wicker Man*, 'Folk Horror is equally about muddying the morals of community as it is about portraying them ... it has been said on many occasions ... that there is great potential in Summerisle's more liberal elements' (Scovell 2017: 22–23). He further points out that Summerisle's religious depictions and practices are 'other' by virtue of comparison, both textually and extra-textually, the latter in relation to Edward Heath's Conservative Government at the time of the film's release (Scovell 2017: 23).

In *Apostle*, though the absolution offered by the island's religion comes at a cost (bloodletting for the majority and death for a few), it is no different from what Anglicanism is offering. This is made clear when the now seemingly atheist Thomas reveals that he was once a Christian missionary in China who suffered violence and escaped death during the so called Boxer Uprising (the Yìhéquán movement). Here the film clearly portrays the danger of religious imperialism and the lack of protection offered to its parishioners. As Malcolm's daughter notices scars on Thomas's back, she asks what has happened to him. His reply is 'My faith. I once held fast a belief in the divine.' As Thomas tells his story in voiceover, the camera cuts to a close-up of his eye, shrouded in low-key lighting and with a cross aflame reflected in it. It becomes clear that this is a flashback to his time in Peking. The violence is extreme. Thomas tries to pray for divine intervention, but rather than being saved by his Christian god, he is instead branded with the mark of the cross on his back as the region burns and others are killed. Thomas states that 'The promise of the Divine is but an illusion'; his belief in God has been rocked, and his belief in family and his sister is all that remains. However, when questioned by Malcolm's daughter, he responds by describing her father using Matthew 7:15: 'Beware false prophets which come to you in sheep's clothing but inwardly they are ravening wolves.' Thomas's faith may have gone, but he still uses the Bible as a vernacular that he assumes all will understand. It reflects the Anglican worldview that he expects to predominate but does not find on the island.

Figure 8.1 Christian imagery used in flashback in *Apostle*, 2018

Druidic beliefs and nonconformism

The spiritualism of the island community ties together elements of both druidic belief and nonconformist Christianity, both of which have very close ties to Wales and the Welsh landscape. Although a tradition more widely associated with the Celts, druids have a particular association with Wales, dating back at least as far as the Roman author Tacitus and his descriptions of the Roman conquest of Anglesey, the last part of Wales to maintain druidic culture. Of the druids, Tacutus wrote that '[t]hey deemed it indeed a duty to cover their altars with the blood of captives and to consult their deities through human entrails'; however, his works would also come to define the druid as a symbol of resistance to the imperialist onslaught.[2] Initially this onslaught was wrought by Rome, but could be seen as equally valid in the rejection of Englishness of later centuries. Druidism became part of Britain's consciousness with the druidic revival started by William Stukeley through works such as his 1743 essay 'The Theology of the Druids' (Stukeley 2011 [1743]). In the public imagination, druidism becomes a form of homegrown orientalism. As Lewis Spence stated in 1928:

> The Secret Tradition of Britain! Does not the very name stir the heart and appeal to the imagination of the true son of Albion with a thrill more mysterious and romantic than any allusion to the magics of Egypt or Hind? ... I am heir to a lore as exalted, as sublime as these, inherited from Druid sires, and in the main restored by pious searching. (Spence 1928: 192)

The film suggests that this druidic other is as fallible as the Anglican imperialism. This is made clear by the ways in which man (and in this case it is specifically the men of the village) uses the religion in corrupting ways. Whilst the true nature of the community's goddess is left somewhat ambiguous, it is human anger and greed that cause most of the horror. The first overt discussion of how the island's religion has been corrupted is when Malcolm attempts to stop his close friend and his son from leaving the island for good. In a tense conversation, the friend, Frank, tells Malcolm how chaining up the island's goddess has wrought disease and despair. Running almost concurrent to this conversation is perhaps the most overt example of the fallibility of the island's religion and followers. Malcolm's lieutenant, Quinn, upon finding out that his daughter is pregnant, brutally kills her and blames her fiancé, Jeremy, for her death. Quinn, dressed all in black and covered in blood, attaches Jeremy to a torture device that involves essentially drilling a corkscrew into his head. The camera lingers over the equipment in close-up, with a dolly shot tracking sideways along the length of the drilling device. Tremolo strings play non-diegetically as the island community stand closely watching the torture, with Quinn surrounded by men dressed in black garb, the statue of 'She' centrally framed between

Figure 8.2 Non-conformist imagery in *Apostle*, 2018

them. The shape of the surrounding men's outfits is akin to those of Catholic penitent hoods, often associated with the Spanish Inquisition. As with the nonconformist imagery, the outfits borrow from Christian imagery, whilst being distinctly non-Anglican and hinting at other familiar horrors. While many of the islanders look sickened by the scene, others watch proudly. Upon killing Jeremy, Quinn takes what appears to be a rose petal and places it in the boy's head, stating: 'I grant unto you this symbol of purity, may it guide you.' Quinn uses the religious rhetoric disingenuously. He is not a believer, but rather someone who has identified that using religious symbolism can grant him power and permit him to take Malcolm's place. His violence becomes a testament to his faith, however false it may be. The statue of 'She' looming over the scene becomes an ironic statement; she offers no protection to Jeremy, just as none was offered to Thomas in Peking. The religions, no matter where they are practised or the differences between them, have both wrought violence upon their followers. In the case of 'She', Malcolm and his followers have acted violently towards her also, leading her to ask Thomas to end her suffering, which he does using fire, echoing the burning crosses during his time in China.

Conclusion

Though scholars may argue over definitions, the folk horror genre plays with difference: difference between the rural and the modern, between the arcane and the known religious text, between the individual and the institution, and between the past and the present. These dichotomies exist in *Apostle*, making it an engaging modern example of the genre. In this chapter I have not provided a taxonomy of ways in which the film fits the genre's categories, but rather I have argued that its horror derives from a focus on a *cultural* understanding of the Celtic: an understanding that is no doubt lacking nuance and is reliant on stereotype and shared cultural imagining. More specifically, I have argued that Wales, despite all its variety, has been reduced to a representation of the Celtic and, more specifically, the druidic. In *Apostle*, the Celtic is a site of difference exactly *because* it is understood through an English – specifically southern English – lens. It comes to represent the past, and through it a combination of paganism and nonconformist Christianity, and a threat to established law and order. All these things assume an English framework and mode of viewing, made explicit by Thomas's being the audience's onscreen conduit. However, despite the horror and violence inflicted on Thomas and others by Malcolm's religious community, there is much to covet on this island. Anglican religion has demonstrably failed Thomas, whilst there is no doubting the supernatural abilities of the island's goddess, though she is not as infallible as the Christian God. This is a community that, because of its isolation (geographically rural, socially distanced and with a rejection of private property), provides opportunity for redemption and freedom from English law. In *Apostle*, nothing is simple, however. The idyll of the landscape comes at a cost of violence and other forms of tyranny, and ultimately leads to death. Yet, the alternative that it is framed against – Anglicanism, English modernity and law – is also shown to be deficient. Its tyranny is ultimately what led Malcolm to the island and the formation of its community. Its dogmatic insistence on moral and lawful authority, and for this to be the truth across the British Isles, forces rebellion and a suffocation of difference. In short, the idea that these are dichotomies is a fallacy. *Apostle*, and folk horror more generally, make use of the regional as a shorthand to highlight both horror and potential.

Acknowledgements

Many thanks to Adam Chapman and Peter Girdwood-Carroll for their thoughts on this chapter.

Notes

1 Adding to the ambiguity of the term 'Celt', the Romans were quite happy to use the Greek term *Keltoi* and the Latin *Galli*, or 'Gauls' in English, quite interchangeably, seeing all peoples to their north-west as a more or less homogeneous group. See Woolf (2010).

2 Cornelius Tacitus, *The Annals*, 14.30, in *Complete Works of Tacitus*, ed. Alfred John Church, William Jackson Brodribb and Sarah Bryant (New York: Random House, 1942), available at www.perseus.tufts.edu/hopper/text?doc=Perseus%3Atext%3A1999.02.0078%3Abook%3D14%3Achapter%3D30 (accessed 11 May 2023).

References

Cunliffe, Barry (2011), 'In The Fabulous Twilight', in Larissa Bonfante (ed.), *The Barbarians of Ancient Europe*. Cambridge: Cambridge University Press, pp. 190–201.
Hingley, Richard (2000), *Roman Officers and English Gentlemen: The Imperial Origins of Roman Archaeology*. London: Routledge.
Laurence, Ray (1997), 'Writing the Roman Metropolis', in Helen M. Parkins (ed.), *Roman Urbanism: Beyond the Consumer City*. London: Routledge, pp. 1–20.
Scovell, Adam (2017), *Folk Horror: Hours Dreadful and Things Strange*. Leighton Buzzard: Auteur.
Sotonopedia (n.d.), 'Watts, Isaac,' sotonopedia.wikidot.com/page-browse:watts-isaac (accessed 6 March 2022).
Spence, Lewis (1928), *The Mysteries of Britain; or, The Secret Rites and Traditions of Ancient Britain Restored*. London: Rider.
Stukeley, William (2011 [1743]), 'The Theology of the Druids', in *Abury, a Temple of the British Druids, with Some Others, Described*. London: printed for the author, available at www.gutenberg.org/files/64626/64626-h/64626-h.htm (accessed 11 May 2023).
Sylvester, Dorothy (1969), *The Rural Landscape of the Welsh Borderland*. London: Macmillan.
Tacitus (1996), *Agricola; Germania; Dialogus*, Vol. I, ed. R. M. Ogilvie and I. A. Richmond. Cambridge, MA: Harvard University Press.
Tuttle, Joshua B. (2020), review of Adam Scovell, *Folk Horror: Hours Dreadful and Things Strange*, *Gothic Studies* 22:3, 344–346.
Visit Wales (n.d.), 'Caernarfon's Military Might', www.visitwales.com/things-do/attractions/castles-and-heritage/castles-and-forts-caernarfon (accessed 12 March 2022).
Williams, J. H. (2001), *Beyond the Rubicon: Romans and Gauls in Republican Italy*. Oxford: Oxford University Press.
Williams, Moelwyn (1975), *The Making of the South Wales Landscape*. London: Hodder and Stoughton.
Woodward, Kate (2016), ' "Here is Wales, there England": Contested Borders and Blurred Boundaries in *On the Black Hill*', in Paul Newland (ed.), *British Rural Landscapes on Film*. Manchester: Manchester University Press, pp. 103–118.
Woolf, G. (2010), 'Saving the Barbarian', in E. S. Gruen (ed.), *Cultural Identity in the Ancient Mediterranean*. Los Angeles: Getty, pp. 255–272.

9

Women's folk horror in Britain: history, industry, style

Amy Harris

Introduction

Using Hélène Cixous's essay 'The Laugh of the Medusa' (1976) and the notion of *écriture féminine* (or 'women's writing') as a framework, this chapter argues that although the generic form of folk horror is historically rooted in androcentric traditions, women filmmakers have a special ability to subvert established tropes and return agency onto the women subjects of such films, and therefore offer unique takes on the genre via access to more significant creative roles. The purpose of this chapter, however, is not to attack the historical basis of this gendered imbalance, which is well discussed in scholarship, but to shift focus from generic conventions to the new forms of subjectivity that come by having women in major creative roles. Cixous, writing to an imagined female audience, proclaims that 'writing is for you, you are for you; your body is yours, take it', encouraging them to reclaim creative agency and explore new takes on established generic forms (Cixous 1976: 876). As such, this chapter considers women creatives who use filmmaking to push back against dominant formats of folk horror.

I will consider two microbudget films that are currently outside the folk horror canon. Arguably, work by independent filmmakers, operating outside industry paradigms, has reconfigured the tropes of historically masculine genres encouraging counterhegemonic narratives that challenge the upkeep of prevailing power structures (Williams 2012). In the UK, the post-2000 British horror boom has allowed women's voices to be heard for the first time, thanks to emergent funding opportunities, independent distribution channels, dedicated film festivals and scholarship on the changing dynamics of the industry (Harris 2022). Despite exciting developments in women's horror filmmaking and the developments in the pertaining scholarship, approaches to women's British folk horror have been overlooked. This chapter offers a springboard for further investigation into women's British folk horror. The first case study is Jacqueline Kirkham's *Following the Wicca Man* (2013), an independently financed film that had limited terrestrial release before being distributed by Amazon US. Kirkham worked as a professional photographer before trying her hand at filmmaking, meaning that she lacked formal training in film practice – a further marker of independence. The second case study is K. Pervaiz's *Maya* (2021), mostly self-financed by Pervaiz with the support of private investment. *Maya* had its world premiere at Renegade Film Festival (formerly Women in Horror Film Festival) where it won Best Feature Film. At the time of writing, *Maya* is currently touring film festivals, most recently Portland Horror Film Festival, as Pervaiz seeks wider distribution. Employing these films as examples, this chapter will explore how recent women's folk horror in Britain has pushed back against the established androcentric forms of the subgenre, offering new avenues of representation that challenge, subvert and deviate from traditional folk horror.

Cixous and women's style

Cixous establishes the notion of an *écriture féminine* to discuss women's writing and writing styles, although her framework can also be applied to non-literary texts. She argues that women's literary forms deviate from a historically masculine style because they 'always surpass the discourse that regulates the phallocentric system' (Cixous 1976: 883). I would suggest that the presence of women authors in the literary horror canon who incorporate women's experiences into their writing, including Mary Shelley, Ann Radcliffe and Vernon Lee, supports Cixous's point that when women write, something different happens. Turning specifically to horror, then, recent publications identifying women's contributions to, and unique take on, the genre's tropes and archetypes include *Women, Monstrosity and Horror Film: Gynaehorror* (Harrington 2016), *New Blood in Contemporary Cinema: Women Directors and the Poetics of Horror* (Pisters 2020), and *Bloody Women: Women Directors of Horror* (McCollum and Clarke 2022). Arguments made by these scholars often begin by identifying an industry-wide gender imbalance before going on to address the issues of gender and genre through a series of specific case studies. In *Women Make Horror* (Peirse 2020), the first all-women-edited collection on horror, questions of style, content and purpose are discussed. Quoting Christine Gledhill, Peirse writes that the construction and performativity of gender and identity encourage scholars to approach the production of genre films and the cultural-textual work of generic conventions differently, noting that horror is 'particularly valuable' for exploring questions surrounding women-made horror because the genre often focalises received notions regarding 'gender, sexuality, identity, and the body' (Peirse 2020: 9). Peirse concludes that it is difficult to identify what makes these films different, as there is no such thing as a singular framework for approaching women's work. There seems, however, to be a collective agreement among scholars that when considering women's horror the identity of a filmmaker precedes the generic style of horror and its subgenres.

The notion that there is an inexplicable difference between the work of men and that of women resonates with this chapter's aims, but also highlights a pitfall in the discussion of women's horror. Cixous writes broadly about generic literary forms, and at times the nuance to her argument – that women's liberation can be achieved via writing – is lost amid her unwavering passion. Indicative of her placement within feminism's second wave, Cixous also prescribes an essentialist view of the body that relies on sexual difference, which leaves no space to consider non-binary people and other marginalised genders. Nonetheless, it is important to think about women-made folk horror as evidence of Cixous's direction that 'woman must put herself into the text – as into the world and history – by her own movement', to explore her own individual experiences through creativity (Cixous 1976: 875). Therefore, this chapter acknowledges the plethora of styles influenced by individual experiences and identity formations, so while Kirkham and Pervaiz both engage with generic forms of folk horror their outcomes are completely different, which provides evidence that there is no single representation, theory or idea about women and what they create.

Folk horror: its histories and its present

This section argues that existing definitions of folk horror, however vague, construct it as a masculine mode of filmmaking that the *écriture féminine* framework might push back against. The vague outline of what can be taken as a folk horror film, discussed by Louis Bayman and Kevin Donnelly in the introduction to this collection, has resulted in an expansion of a narrow number of forms that now make up the folk horror canon. Definitions of folk horror have therefore been informed by a select number of films from this canon, meaning that women-made folk horror has been excluded from definitions of the genre.

The 'birth' of folk horror from the late 1960s to the early 1970s has been attributed by scholars to three mid-budget British films, *Witchfinder General* (1968), *Blood on Satan's Claw* (1971) and *The Wicker Man* (1973), all of which featured men in primary creative roles as writers, producers and directors. At the time of production, the industrial limitations of filmmaking in Britain meant that primary roles in production remained in the hands of men. Cixous describes an 'imbecilic capitalist machinery ... that works against [women] and off [their] backs' (Cixous 1976: 877), a pessimism towards economic imbalances in the creative industries that is still justified today. Although she is concerned chiefly with publishing houses that 'worked for man's profit', her sentiment can also be mapped onto the UK film industry, particularly during the 1970s, when folk horror was on the rise (Cixous 1976: 883). At this time a small number of women were making experimental, avant-garde films, but none of them could be described as folk horror filmmakers; and, on larger-scale productions, women's roles behind the camera were also very limited. Although women were not a targeted exclusion, the canonised 'unholy trinity' quickly became shorthand for critics and folk horror scholars to describe the first wave of folk horror in Britain, and, by virtue of its set of characteristics produced in a masculine tradition, it is not surprising that women's work in this genre has struggled to find recognition thus far.

Bayman and Donnelly point out that discussions of early British folk horror films remain concerned with whether certain films conform to the 'particular aesthetic choices' of equally specific, and androcentric, texts. Scholarship has long considered the ways in which folk horror has a history of objectifying women in front of the camera, with these canonical texts serving as examples of this. Indeed, the foregrounding of women's bodies and sexuality in British folk horror is a double-edged sword that historically presents violence towards women as horrifying while circulating unflattering representations of women and denying them agency over their emancipation. The onscreen representations of women in these films are equally unflattering. While somewhat positive motifs – including the powerful matriarch; feminine sensuality; and earth-centredness in the representation of witchcraft, wicca and paganism – prevail (explored in Tanya Krzywinska's *A Skin for Dancing In* (2000)), ultimately women serve as objects rather than subjects in these films. In this collection, Laurel Zwissler explicitly makes the point that *The Wicker Man* is an example of 'androcentric art' that

> may still be feminist if it exposes contradictory constructions of masculinity, which *The Wicker Man* certainly does ... It is solidly androcentric, but not misogynist. It portrays a ritual community built on gender complementarity reliant on biological essentialism, but that structure includes power for women. (pp. 49–50)

Folk horror aligns with ideas that powerful women are monstrous; threatening; overtly sexual; hysterical; and need to be contained, controlled, and punished, per Barbara Creed's (1993) seminal work on the 'monstrous-feminine'. Ultimately, and with the benefit of hindsight, the masculine style of preceding works is one that invites or necessitates a counterhegemonic rebuttal.

Contemporary, or second-wave, folk horror, has proven a more fruitful arena for the production of women-made folk, which may suggest that updated definitions of folk will include or make reference to women's work. Despite intimating 'new incarnations' of the mode, lists of notable revival texts are once again androcentric and make no mention of women's British folk horror films (Keetley 2020). Additional influential work on folk horror by Adam Scovell (2017) and Diane A. Rodgers (2019) also overlooks women-made folk horror, yet there are a number of examples that might have been considered, such as *Urban Ghost Story* (1998), *The Daisy Chain* (2008), *The Love Witch* (2016), *Curse of the Scarecrow* (2018), *Blood Runs Down* (2018), *The Other Lamb* (2019), *Relic* (2020), *A Banquet* (2021), *You Are Not My Mother* (2021) and *Woodlands Dark and Days Bewitched: A History of Folk Horror* (2021). These examples, although anglophonic, demonstrate that women are actively experimenting with the folk horror genre, and yet these films are not included in recent scholarship on folk horror.

Notably, many second-wave folk horror films that encompass the tropes of folk horror, identified by Bayman and Donnelly, are larger productions that had UK theatrical and/or UK terrestrial release, including *The Fallow Field* (2009), *Amen Island* (aka *Unhappy Birthday*, 2011), *Outcast* (2010) and Ben Wheatley's folk trilogy (*Kill List* (2011), *Sightseers* (2012), *A Field in England* (2013)). However, there are many films among those released since 2000 that have not been distributed via theatrical channels. Arguably, the difficulty of databasing British films is in part due to their mode of release. Most of the UK horror films released since 2000 are made on low budgets and released through video-on-demand services or straight to disc. Consequently, many films sail under the radar of both critical assessment and industry statistics, which still, anachronistically, identify theatrical release as an index of validity.[1] By considering the changing production dynamics of the film industry to account for small studio and independent productions, there are many women-led folk horror films that have thus far been overlooked by scholarship, including the work of Kirkham and Pervaiz.

I have written elsewhere that specific economic environments affect film-making and can provide a novel opportunity to highlight examples of women's unique and undervalued work in contemporary horror (Harris 2022). Nonetheless, in 2013 Kirkham's micro-budget film *Following the Wicca Man* was, at the time of release, in competition with Ben Wheatley's *A Field in England* (2013), the third instalment of his folk horror trilogy. Kirkham raised £3,185 via fifty-two backers, as well as contributing her own funds to make *Following the Wicca Man*. In a personal conversation, Kirkham revealed 'we kind of lost our legs with the marketing; we really needed help but didn't have any money left to pay to help us get the film out. There was a facility online which made it easy to set up with Amazon and it happened to be USA.'[2]

In contrast, Wheatley had already established a name for himself after the success of *Kill List* (2011) and *Sightseers* (2012). Although his production had a meagre budget of £300,000, it was released on multiple platforms simultaneously, including cinemas; home media, including Film4; and video-on-demand services. In short, Kirkham's independently financed and distributed film did not stand a chance against Wheatley's. Although it might seem unusual to compare these films, the production of women-made films as independent, micro-budget and arguably obscure reflects women's marginal status in the horror industry and even sometimes reflects their experience of filmmaking in films that comment on industrial precarity and marginality (Harris 2022). In support of this, Eddie Falvey writes that 'there is a difference between the independence of a [small] studio … and the independence of a [microbudget filmmaker], who makes films without access to institutionalized production, distribution, and exhibition networks' (2021: 72). Simply, the groundswell of support for Wheatley's film highlights the precarity of competing filmmakers and provides further evidence that the folk revival is male-led.

Exploring small-scale productions is a good starting point for identifying and discussing women-led British folk horror because a common feature is that they are usually financed and distributed independently, particularly in the UK. Cixous directs women to move beyond historical binds into a future that is 'no longer determined by the past' where they might return to that which has been 'confiscated' from them (1976: 875, 880). Since 2000, the British film industry has seen an unprecedented boom in small-scale women-led horror productions (Harris 2022). Since then, women filmmakers, almost totally absent from the pre-millennium British horror landscape, have used funding and distribution opportunities made available to them to produce horror in distinctive ways (Harris 2022). In the UK, a combination of easy access to cheap equipment and independent distribution channels has broadened the range of people making horror films. Independent modes of filmmaking and distribution also allow for more creative freedom without the constraints of production budget, release deadlines, industry-controlled marketing and so on. For Kirkham, this meant that she could star in her film as well as write and direct it. She describes the fun process of having this creative freedom: 'it was our first ever film and we hadn't even made a short before. It was something that just started small, and we mainly just did it for fun.'[3] Pervaiz expresses similar appreciation for the creative autonomy of independent filmmaking. In conversation she expressed the liberation of being able to have full creative freedom with her film, emphasising that 'the audience is left to their own devices to figure out [the film] ... that's how I wanted to present the film'.[4] Both Kirkham and Pervaiz express how independent production dynamics allowed them the creative freedom to experiment with their filmmaking. Although both filmmakers faced the challenge of successfully distributing their films, the changing production dynamics allow for the sort of creative autonomy that Cixous was championing.

What we can ascertain from discussing British folk horror so far is that, first, definitions of the genre have been informed by a small selection of male-directed, androcentric folk horror films; second, women's contributions to the genre in the UK, although sparse, have not been considered; and third, because of the latter, generic forms of folk horror remain defined by androcentrism. Therefore, revising the landscape of British folk horror opens a space to the experiential basis for making films differently depending on a filmmaker's subjectivity, framed here by gender. As such, the final sections of this chapter will explore how women's folk horror style illustrates women filmmakers returning agency to the women subjects of their films.

Women's folk horror style in *Following the Wicca Man*

Although the film's title, *Following the Wicca Man*, suggests parallels between Kirkham's film and *The Wicker Man*, beyond having a protagonist investigate a town's local cult the films have little in common. *Following the Wicca Man* tells the story of Clayton Stone (Gaz Elliot), a successful filmmaker with the world at his feet. When conducting research for his latest film about modern-day witches, he tries to infiltrate a secret coven with disastrous consequences for his loved ones, including his pregnant girlfriend, and those who try to save his soul. The film's tagline asks: 'Has his research gone too far?'. Whilst the plot centres on Clayton's journey to find the witches, a subplot focuses on his troubled relationship with his girlfriend. Although supportive at first, Clayton's girlfriend is apprehensive about his involvement with witches. Clayton ignores her angst and later also ignores the advice of a good witch (played by Kirkham herself) in favour of getting a better story for publication. Despite continuous warnings from the good witch, who proclaims he is an 'innocent fool' venturing into dark and unknown territory, Clayton persists, and uses aggressive tactics to infiltrate the coven – even going as far as engaging in sex rituals to obtain information for his story. When Clayton successfully meets the coven, he receives a mysterious power from them, although this is at the expense of his girlfriend's life. Towards the end of the film, he attempts to hide evidence of his girlfriend's death and couples up with the good witch. Clayton reminds the good witch of the power the coven has over her family, encouraging her to align with him. Although the purpose of this plot-point is unexpected (or perhaps poorly signposted, a further marker of the potentially haphazard construction of the micro-budget film) there is a sense that Clayton is panicked by his alignment with the coven. However, the film ends with Clayton discussing his next film venture as he toasts the success of his previous one.

As with the films that came before, *Following the Wicca Man* makes use of images synonymous with folk: tarot cards, runes, cats, tarantulas and owls act as signifiers of witchcraft, pagan rituals and spirituality throughout the film. But, like most folk films, such images have little meaning outside the film's context, and are designed to indicate a realm unknown to the protagonist and in which he is unwelcome. Indeed, the focus here is less on the accuracy of authentically depicting witchcraft (evident in the notion of the good witch and bad witch that runs through the film), and more on the women's revenge against a man who forces his way into their sacred space. After all, the price of Clayton's power is his girlfriend's death. After the incident, a family friend reveals to Clayton that his girlfriend was pregnant at the time. He appears visibly distressed by the news, perhaps having a sudden realisation that this might not have happened if he had listened to advice. The film ends with a close-up of Clayton's hand as he raises a toast to his success; the shot reveals a tattoo of the coven's symbol, which indicates membership of or ownership by the coven.

Kirkham does not encourage sympathy for her protagonist. In fact, Clayton is not a likeable character, as he seems set on creating the next award-winning film about witches, ignoring the needs of his girlfriend and advice from the good witch. Echoing traditions in women's horror writing, there is something Frankensteinian about the film's commentary on male hubris, where the triumph of ambition at the cost of responsibility must ultimately be condemned. When Clayton's girlfriend describes a time when she was sexually assaulted at a college afterparty he does little to support or even acknowledge her, and is quickly occupied by a telephone call concerning his film. Later, we see his girlfriend pondering when she should reveal the pregnancy. Meanwhile, Clayton is occupied with blood rituals, using the juices from raw steak to attract the coven. When his girlfriend prepares a romantic dinner in the hope of revealing her pregnancy, Clayton abandons her to seek out the witches instead. He is often seen using a laptop, reading or talking on the telephone. He pays little attention to his girlfriend unless he wants her for sex. Throughout the film Clayton is misogynistic. The relationship appears unbalanced, and the girlfriend explains to her friend that she cannot tell her parents she is living with him. Although it is never revealed why, there is a sense that she is trapped in the relationship. After she dies at the hands of the coven, Clayton attempts to cover up the murder, lies to her friends and family, and even kisses one of her friends. His behaviour is self-centred, and his actions are selfishly motivated; when his girlfriend finally dies, his true intention to become part of the coven and share in their power is revealed.

Following the Wicca Man presents a narrative that focuses on the ignorance of a male reporter towards the power of a coven of witches and pays brief homage to early folk horror films by engaging with the themes of sex, violence and witchcraft that are central in them. However, a key difference is the freedom given to the women, whose rebelliousness and sexual prowess never result in their own punishment. When Clayton finds the coven, he is tied to a tree and stripped naked by two witches. Later he has sex with a witch as part of a ritual. Notably the sex is consensual, and the witch is shown straddling him as the camera adopts Clayton's point of view by looking up at her, emphasising her power. Interestingly, sex here is either shown with women in a position of power or not at all. When Clayton and his girlfriend have sex, a short montage of natural imagery plays out coupled by the sounds of sexual activity and orgasm. It seems that Kirkham is more interested in showing sex when a woman is in control. Her choice to focus on women's sexual power *and* sexual pleasure is at odds with folk horror traditions. Arguably, Kirkham demonstrates an awareness of the genre's archetypes, recognising the limiting representations of femininity and women's sexual autonomy in horror that are so often bound by patriarchal models of sexual difference.

Throughout its narrative, *Following the Wicca Man* provides a dichotomy wherein men are ignorant while women are knowledgeable and powerful, which, while reductive, challenges notions of gendered power in such works. That said, the girlfriend's murder by the coven complicates the representation of women as strong and independent. When Clayton's girlfriend chases after him she is captured by the coven, who quickly invite her to have sex with one of the men. She refuses and is promptly killed. Although her death serves as a reminder to Clayton that the coven is in control, his girlfriend is disempowered against the witches, which could suggest that women require supernatural support to survive. Overall, *Following the Wicca Man* offers commentary on the gendered dimensions of the folk horror subgenre and invites a more nuanced reading of women's agency, especially regarding witches, who, it argues, can be powerful without needing to be punished. That said, the film also demonstrates an uneasy depiction of womanhood through the girlfriend, who falls prey to familiar tropes, in this case the sacrificial woman.

Women's folk horror style in *Maya*

In its first incarnation *Maya* started as a rough-cut feature film, and then later Pervaiz developed it into a short film before she was eventually able to raise finances of £50,000. Pervaiz remains passionate about her film, explaining that it was born out of her desire to navigate and work through her own personal trauma, coupled with an aim, as a British-Pakistani woman living in the United Kingdom, to understand better her relationship to Pakistan and its culture. Like her previous film, *Black Lake* (2020), Pervaiz inserts herself and her experiences into the narrative and, in doing so, into the historical landscape of British folk horror, which perfectly illustrates the notion of the *écriture féminine* being applied here.

The film tells the story of a young woman, Maya (Madiha Hidayat), who has a supernatural experience as a child while playing games with her younger sister. It is believed by her family that this is a jinn possession – jinn being a form of spirit-demon, a belief which is prevalent in Islam – and that the demon will haunt the bloodline until the family are separated. For her protection, or so she is told, she is taken away from her birth parents to live with another family. The film follows her development as a young woman, moving through early childhood to puberty. As Maya grows up, her past begins to haunt her through fever dreams and hallucinations. She receives phone calls from a mysterious voice claiming to be her mother, sparking a desire to return home. With the support of her adopted sister, Maya unpacks the memories of a fractured childhood and tries to face her demons. She travels back to her family home to find out what happened to her as a child. The film's narrative is slow-paced and abstract, leaving the audience to decide whether Maya is possessed or experiencing psychological symptoms of childhood trauma.

Pervaiz uses folk horror as a way of navigating through the trauma of adverse childhood experiences, positioning herself and her experiences directly in relationship to the film's narrative. As a child, Pervaiz was fascinated by horror stories concerning possession, and evil folktales. In conversation she reflected on how many of these stories were used as a warning not to misbehave, explaining that some areas of Pakistan believe strongly in jinn possession, which can result in children being taken away from their families at a young age. Pervaiz describes how:

> the film uses nightmares to distort Maya's memories and so what is presented to the audience is not a true account of events. The real trauma in *Maya* is childhood trauma. Maya is separated from her family from a young age, which occurs after a jinn attack. She isn't sure why she has been taken away as she has no recollection of anything – except through her nightmares. These

nightmares occur when Maya menstruates and so a link is made between menstruation and dreaming. The menstrual blood is used almost as a portal into the dream world which connects to the drawing of blood during the jinn attack. However, Maya's memory is distorted. We are drawn to Maya's bloodied clothes, more so than her sister's now scarred face. Later, we see an open facial wound, which becomes the real site of trauma because this is where demonic transference happens. It is typical for jinn attacks to stay within families, and so Maya experiences death time and again throughout the film. The jinn consume within a specific bloodline and so it transpires that Maya was sent away as a child to keep her safe. Unable to overcome her trauma, Maya is drawn back to the childhood home where she is consumed.[5]

Pervaiz creates eeriness through the film's sound design, which is supported by Tatsujiro Oto. They layer guttural audio, taken from real-world recordings of what are believed to be jinn possessions, with soft melodies to create an eerie sense of foreboding. In an interview with *Horror Obsessive* Pervaiz states that 'the most exciting thing for horror fans might be knowing that the film contains authentic demonic sounds' (Parker 2021).

It is worth noting that a supernatural presence is often signalled sonically in films, and in the real world strong sonic manifestations often occur more than visual manifestations. In *Maya*, these sounds often occur when Maya is alone, left to ponder what happened to her in her childhood. Pervaiz favours aural horror over visual horror, and so there are few scenes that depict demonic possession visually. In this way the narrative is ambiguous, and the audience are left to decide whether Maya is possessed or not.

Pervaiz uses the horror of jinn possession to interrogate complex issues that exist in Pakistani culture, with a particular focus on the treatment of women. Research shows that 'possession worldwide is found more commonly in women and marginalised groups and may be a vehicle through which they can express their complaints in a context in which they can be heard' (Dein and Illaiee 2013: 290).

Maya's supposed possession usually occurs at times when she is unable to express her confusion over her fragmented childhood memories. In this way, it can be understood that her 'possession' is intermingled with her childhood trauma, rather than the sexual difference that usually prefaces abuse in other folk horror films (it should be noted that the film's scenes of menstruation are not a site of horror; instead they are used as an indication of Maya's age). *Maya* offers a fresh perspective on how one can represent possessed women in folk horror by offering subjectivity that asks the audience to identify the causes of her possession/abuse, both personal and cultural. By subverting the tropes of the genre, and specifically a trope common in folk horror, *Maya* challenges the assumption that women's possession/abuse is due to their sexual difference, instead attributing it to a wider cultural inability to recognise and respond to the experiences of marginalised groups. In *Maya*, jinn possession also serves to articulate an anxiety about identity, particularly as Maya feels like an outsider in her own community. In this way, *Maya* provides an intimate and personal perspective of possession that links it to a manifestation of childhood trauma.

Conclusion

This chapter has argued that micro-budget, women-led folk horror productions offer entirely new ways of exploring British folk horror in relation to women's style borrowed from Hélène Cixous's notion of the *écriture féminine*. Using Cixous's essay 'The Laugh of the Medusa' as a framework, the chapter has made a case for understanding women's folk horror as existing outside historical paradigms defined by a narrow canon of texts, and explores how women-led folk horror films have an identity that is informed directly by the identity and experiences of the filmmaker.

Cixous is adamant that women have been misrepresented as 'uncanny stranger[s] on display' by men, so she persuades her reader to imagine herself, to write for herself, to better represent herself and her experiences in her chosen medium (1976: 880). *Following the Wicca Man* and *Maya* demonstrate, in one way or another, that women's creative autonomy invites new and exciting possibilities within the context of a historically bound mode such as British folk horror, and can provide a space for women to explore their own sense of self through generic styles. Kirkham explores new-age witchcraft in a narrative in which she imagines a powerful female sexuality that can destroy men. For Pervaiz, who had already crafted several short films and a feature-length film, the genre offered a way to explore her own cultural heritage, as well as ideas about trauma transposed onto the subject of jinn possession.

A final point to consider, although hard to cover at length here, is that Cixous also notes a resistance towards women who challenge the status quo in their works. She states that when a woman writes, her words almost always fall upon male ears 'which [hear] in language only that which speaks masculine' (1976: 881). In line with this, it is interesting that Kirkham's film was subject to harsh criticism before its release. She was trolled on the internet after the trailer was uploaded onto YouTube, and although comments have since been removed by Kirkham – after its release, Kirkham made her film private on YouTube to avoid further trolling – the backlash she received speaks to Cixous's idea that *écriture féminine* is not necessarily welcomed by audiences. Although we cannot assume the backlash was from men alone, it is interesting that Kirkham's film was reviewed so negatively. *Starburst*, on the other hand, praised *Following the Wicca Man* as a 'low-budget self-financed film … worth seeking out if you fancy something a bit different to the norm' (Unsworth 2014). Perhaps by 'norm' the reviewer is referring to the androcentric films to which viewers are accustomed.

Pervaiz also experienced rejection of her work when she hosted a private screening of *Maya* in Pakistan. Pervaiz uses folk horror to navigate difficult topics relating to jinn possession, but it was the scenes of menstruation that met disapproval from the Pakistani audience, who turned away from the screen, refusing to engage with the content. Pervaiz says that 'luckily everyone did stay in their seats, but it was so notable how uncomfortable everyone was about the menstruation scene. You couldn't hear anyone breathe!'.[6] However, *Maya* later had its global premiere at Renegade Film Festival in 2022, which was held in person for the first time after a hiatus due to the COVID-19 pandemic. Dedicated to spotlighting the work of marginalised filmmakers, this international festival helped Pervaiz garner critical attention from popular horror outlets. including *Fangoria* and *Horror Obsessive*. Pervaiz was awarded Best Feature Film – an accolade that can be used to help market her film further on the festival circuit. The positive response to Pervaiz's folk horror film reflects a shift in the reception of women-led folk horror and a celebration of women-led horror more generally, as evident in responses to the works of Melanie Light, Alice Lowe, Rose Glass and Prano Bailey-Bond. Certainly, this chapter calls for closer attention to the style of women-led folk horror films, and argues that such films have potential to revise and expand on androcentric examples of the genre.

Acknowledgements

I'd like to thank Eddie Falvey for his continuous support in helping me to develop this chapter.

Notes

1 With thanks to M. J. Simpson for this point.
2 Jacqueline Kirkham, personal conversation with the author.
3 Jacqueline Kirkham, personal conversation with the author.
4 K. Pervaiz, personal conversation with the author.
5 K. Pervaiz, personal conversation with the author.
6 K. Pervaiz, personal conversation with the author.

References

Cixous, Hélène (1976), 'The Laugh of the Medusa', trans. Keith Cohen and Paula Cohen, *Signs* 1:4, 875–893.
Creed, Barbara (1993), *The Monstrous-Feminine: Film, Feminism, Psychoanalysis*. London: Routledge.
Dein, S. and A. S. Illaiee (2013), 'Jinn and Mental Health: Looking at Jinn Possession in Modern Psychiatric Practice', *The Psychiatrist* 37:9, 290–293.
Falvey, Eddie (2021), '"Art-Horror" and "Hardcore Art-Horror" at the Margins: Experimentation and Extremity in Contemporary Independent Horror', *Horror Studies* 12:1, 63–81.
Harrington, Erin (2016), *Women, Monstrosity and Horror Film: Gynaehorror*. London: Routledge.
Harris, Amy (2022), '"They've Got Something You Haven't. A Cock": Exploring the Gendered Experience of Women Directors of Horror in Britain', in Victoria McCollum and Aislinn Clarke (eds), *Bloody Women: Women Directors of Horror*. London: Rowman, pp. 97–113
Keetley, Dawn (2020), 'Introduction: Defining Folk Horror', *Revenant* 5 (March), 1–32.
Krzywinska, Tanya (2000), *A Skin for Dancing In: Possession, Witchcraft and Voodoo in Film*. Trowbridge: Flicks Books.
McCollum, Victoria and Aislinn Clarke (eds) (2022), *Bloody Women: Women Directors of Horror*. London: Rowman.
Parker, Sean (2021), 'K/XI's Maya Heading to Film Festivals This Fall', horrorobsessive.com/2021/05/28/k-xis-maya-heading-to-film-festivals-this-fall/ (accessed 29 April 2023).
Peirse, Alison (2020), *Women Make Horror*. New York: Rutgers University Press.
Pisters, Patricia (2020), *New Blood in Contemporary Cinema: Women Directors and the Poetics of Horror*. Edinburgh: Edinburgh University Press.
Rodgers, Diane (2019), 'Something "Wyrd" This Way Comes: Folklore and British Television', *Folklore* 130:2, 133–152.
Scovell, Adam (2017), *Folk Horror: Hours Dreadful and Things Strange*. Leighton Buzzard: Auteur.
Unsworth, Martin (2014), 'DVD Review: FOLLOWING THE WICCA MAN', www.starburstmagazine.com/reviews/dvd-review-following-the-wicca-man (accessed 29 April 2023).
Williams, Linda (2012), 'Film Bodies: Gender, Genre and Excess', in Barry Keith Grant (ed.). *Film Genre Reader*, 5th edn. Austin: University of Texas Press, pp. 159–177.

Part III

Folk horror's cultural landscapes

10

Ritualistic rhythms: exploring the sensory affect of drums in British folk horror cinema

Lyndsay Townsend

Whilst dating back millennia, the use of drums in ceremonies and rituals is a practice still demonstrated by religious communities to this day. For some groups, the beat of a drum acts as a gateway to connecting with spiritual realms, with the steady rhythm inducing a trance-like state and complete concentration on the ceremony at play (Henderson 2014). Whereas for others, the drum brings energy and life to a celebration, encouraging joyous movement and a combination of spiritual, physical and emotional connection with those around them. Drums are also tactile objects, traditionally made using the furred hide of an animal, and require a physical meeting of hand and instrument to produce an effective sound; they demand human contact, and it is crucial to analyse this tangibility when drums are represented in visual and aural media. Concerning itself with small communities of 'folk' and intertwined with a combination of eerie landscapes, strange happenings and demonstrations of the 'old ways', folk horror is a pivotal example of media that take advantage of this physical relationship between drums and ritual, particularly through the medium of film. Compared to the increasingly polished drumbeats heard on popular studio soundtracks, however, the drumming in folk horror is distinct. Typically played by a character *within* a ritual or community onscreen, the folk horror drumbeat is often heard as a dull thud, reverberating organically through the scene. It can be irregular in rhythm as opposed to a steady, modern pulse, and adapts to the movements of others, changing tempo and volume to reflect the activity of individuals onscreen. The folk horror drumbeat is *intuitive*, played by ordinary members of the folk community (rather than a trained professional), and reflects an organic return to the instrument's early, authentic use. However, it is not simply a blended layer of the soundtrack, but a distinct *sensory* technique that has three crucial roles in the genre – establishing a sense of folk community, representing the corporeality of endangered bodies onscreen, and signalling a greater level of threat and fear that is crucial to the wider genre of horror.

Before examining the way in which drums are used in folk horror cinema to conjure a wealth of varied meanings, I first want to turn to the main theoretical framework that is threaded throughout this chapter – sensory, or phenomenological, theory. Folk horror is an inherently sensory subgenre, and to truly unpick the unsettling 'ambiance and aesthetic that more often can be felt intuitively rather than defined logically' (Paciorek 2018: 15) (the feeling that something is *not quite right* with the world onscreen), a turn to sensory film theory is integral. Aiming to understand the 'meaningful relation between cinema and our sensate bodies' (Sobchack 2004: 54), sensory film theory explores the ways in which the formal elements of a film can make the audience *feel* a certain way, particularly in evoking physical, bodily responses. Certain genres, including the horror film, benefit greatly from this analysis, and by examining a film's aesthetic elements, such as sound, cinematography and *mise-en-scène*, we can understand how a film can raise the hairs on an individual's arm, make them flinch in empathetic pain or cause them to raise a cushion over their eyes in fear. Similarly, many elements of folk horror benefit greatly from phenomenological analysis; from the eerie, rural landscape that feels familiar yet strange, to the emotional alignment that pulls you closer to the innocent protagonist trapped within the confines of a small, outdated community, folk horror is full of *feeling*, and requires an active viewer fully to appreciate and experience the unsettling affect that it aims to conjure. One of the multiple ways in which folk horror cinema achieves such a phenomenological affect, moreover, is through the sound of a drumbeat – a recurring sonic motif of the subgenre. Through primary focus on *Kill List* (2011), amongst secondary examples, this chapter will examine the distinct sound of a drumbeat in folk horror cinema and argue for its effective role in conjuring three crucial notions that define the genre – community, bodily affect and fear.

Acting as a springboard for the chapter, Ben Winters's article 'Corporeality, Musical Heartbeats, and Cinematic Emotion' (2008) explores the relationship between sound and sensory affect, particularly illuminating the affective relationship between film music and horror film. Beginning by outlining how cinematic music and sound are effective in reflecting the emotional state of the characters onscreen, Winters notes the ways in which, as an active audience, we can empathise with these emotions, adapting our own moods to match those of the characters within the film. For example, if a protagonist is chased by a masked killer onscreen, our hearts may skip a beat if the character trips and falls, or we may flinch if the killer narrowly misses the protagonist's body when brandishing a weapon. Winters then develops this idea through attention to the relationship between music and embodiment, observing the power of a heartbeat when it is present through a film's score or sound effects. He notes that the 'presence of the heartbeat helps us achieve [emotive engagement] by encouraging us to equate a fictional character's endangered corporeality with an awareness of our own sense of bodily precariousness' (Winters 2008: 4) – in essence, the presence of a heartbeat immediately creates a sensory connection between the audience and the characters within the film, encouraging us to take on feelings of thrill or fear. Building on Winters's argument that sound in horror film (particularly a heartbeat) strengthens emotive engagement, I will now examine the use of drums in folk horror cinema, starting with its role in identifying and establishing a strong sense of a folk community.

Establishing a 'folk' community

Released in 2011, Ben Wheatley's *Kill List* remains a crucial addition to the folk horror canon, following Jay (Neil Maskell) and Gal (Michael Smiley) as two ex-military friends who take on a job as contracted hitmen only to find themselves soon rooted in a sacrificial nightmare. A gritty thriller throughout, it is only in its final twenty minutes that the film truly exhibits folkloric horror. After successfully crossing off two victims from their hitlist, Jay and Gal make their way to the home of 'the MP' (the final person on their list) and, whilst observing the house, begin to hear a strange happening in the woods nearby. Following the noise of chanting and, particularly, drumming, Jay and Gal move closer to the trees, where they witness a torch-lit procession of people, some naked and some dressed in long, white gowns. Uniting the followers in the parade, moreover, is an incessant drumming that establishes a sense of community among the group, as each member's steps match the beat of the instrument and a steady pace is communally sustained. Joined by clashes of cymbals and high-pitched singing, the unsettling sonic cacophony provides an unnerving atmosphere, and positions Jay and Gal as outsiders to this 'othered' community of unknown individuals dressed in masks and gowns.

A community of 'folk' is an integral theme to the genre of folk horror; it is where archaic beliefs thrive uninterrupted and threat is cultivated towards outsiders. Made up of individuals who present views different from the stereotypical norm, the communities in folk horror are the root of the fear, with the dangerous collective power of breeding sinister beliefs. As the main way in which Adam Scovell's notion of 'skewed belief systems and morality' (Scovell 2017: 18) is expressed, a small community of people (or folk) in folk horror is the physical source of terror – the individuals who perform rituals; parade eerily in costume; and, more often than not, sacrifice the innocent protagonist, who finds themselves isolated within the community's domain. Whilst Matilda Groves has described folk horror as central in expressing the 'horror of the people' (Groves 2017), Dawn Keetley pushes further to unpick the community in folk horror, likening them to a *tribe* 'bound together by shared (folkloristic) beliefs, traditions and practices' (Keetley 2020: 11), particularly through 'ritual [and] folklore' (Keetley 2020: 12). To build on Keetley's argument, a further element that binds the tribes of folk horror is an emphasis on repetitive rhythms. Including the chanting of mantras; synchronised group movement; and, most particularly, the beat of a drum, repetitive rhythms in folk horror serve to unify the community both physically and symbolically, focusing the group and ensuring that each member of the folk community is working together. Furthermore, through the steady and unsettling beat of the drum, the tribes of folk horror narratives are *bound* together and given power from within, differentiating themselves from those who are not members of the folk community. *Kill List* exemplifies this in the aforementioned forest scene, where the strange behaviour of the folk community is united through the sound of the beating drum, alienating Jay and Gal (and also us as viewers) from the parade.

The use of a drumbeat to reflect and strengthen a folk community is also heard in *The Wicker Man* (1973). In the scene of the May Day parade, where Sergeant Howie (Edward Woodward) hides in the Punch costume unbeknownst to the other group members, the community begin to play instruments as the parade begins, and a steady drumbeat acts as a sonic guide to the group's movements. Leading the parade is Lord Summerisle (Christopher Lee), and it is crucial to observe the ways in which his actions coincide perfectly with the beating of the drum – his grand movements, which include leaping, spinning and waving his props, are synchronised with the drumbeat, and he moves, along with his fellow parade members, in time to the rhythm. In comparison, Sergeant Howie moves in an oppositional way, messily waving his arms and bumbling along; he cannot feel the rhythm of the drum, as he does not *belong* in the parade. As Lord Summerisle heads the parade with a strong, majestic presence, it is as if the drumbeat follows him specifically as he leads the group along – despite not playing the drum, he is in control of the beat, and his followers are in synchronisation with their leader. This is illustrated further when the drumbeat gathers speed as Lord Summerisle enters into the frame, and then ceases abruptly as the character stops in his tracks. Here, the drumbeat encourages us to *feel* the coordinated movements of the Summerisle community, whilst simultaneously aligning viewers emotionally with the frantic movements of Sergeant Howie as he desperately tries to blend in. Consequently, this disconnected relationship between the drumbeat and the unsynchronised movements of Sergeant Howie illustrates the power of the Summerisle community as a collective, and emphasises the sonic nature of their rituals and traditions.

Here, both *Kill List* and *The Wicker Man* work to reflect the togetherness of a folk horror community as expressed *through* the drumbeat, and the relationship between drums and ritual is strengthened. Whilst this relationship can be seen in other films of the genre, such as *The Devil Rides Out* (1968), where a frantic drumbeat emphasises the chaotic movements of a sinister ceremonial ritual in the woods, the drumbeat can also be used to signify different *types* of folk communities. Whereas the three aforementioned films focus on regressive folk communities, with their wicker masks, fire torches and wyrd beliefs, the drumbeat can also be used to unite increasingly modern folk communities and reflect the ever-changing British landscape. With the bleak backdrop of postindustrial Wales, *Darklands* (1996) follows a journalist as he falls deeper into researching a sinister religious cult, and is a pivotal example of how the drumbeat can be used to express the space in which the folk community resides. In a scene where journalist Frazer (Craig Fairbrass) is sedated by doctors, he has a vision that shows members of the religious cult dancing to a steady beat. Rather than performing on a traditional drum, however, the cult members repeatedly hit hanging metal tubes to produce a clashing beat: an industrial rhythm to reflect the postindustrial town in which the folk community live. Reminiscent of the industrial music scene, this clashing drumbeat particularly evokes the work of Einstürzende Neubauten and Test Department – two musical groups who used organic materials and industrial objects to create a jarring, powerful sound. From scrap metal to construction machinery, these unlikely instruments conjured a beat that fuelled the punk rock movement and enabled themes of the deep past and postindustrialisation to be combined with provocative, aggressive rhythms. Taking place in an abandoned car factory in Cardiff, Test Department's collaborative performance of their album *Gododdin* in 1989, with the Welsh theatre company Brith Gof, further serves to exemplify this idea. By accompanying the dramatisation of an early moment in Celtic history with 'found' instruments and an environment reflective of a dying era, *Gododdin* uses industrial drum rhythms and a community of performers to reflect a cultural zeitgeist: postindustrial Wales, as seen in *Darklands*. Much as *Kill List*, *The Wicker Man* and *The Devil Rides Out*, *Darklands* continues to encourage an automatic connection between the drumbeat and folk communities, and shows the ways in which the behaviour and movements of folk horror tribes are sonically united through the beat of a drum. Therefore, whilst we are made to feel alienated from the community onscreen (viewers are regularly positioned with the isolated protagonists, as with Jay and Gal in *Kill List*), this strengthened connection between sound and image simultaneously positions us to *feel* their rituals and practices through the steady beat that rings through the scene. Through the drumbeat, audiences are encouraged to *join* the folk horror tribe affectively and *feel* the rhythmic pulse that binds each folk individual together. The drum therefore acts as a tool both to reflect the folk community and to beckon the audience *into* the folk community, creating an unsettling sense of false security and uncertainty as to whom our empathy should be aligned with.

Understanding the bodies onscreen

Returning to *Kill List*, as the folk community marches forward to a clearing in the woods (with Jay and Gal watching from behind the trees), a woman from the procession is led forward to a platform and a noose is placed around her neck – at this point, all sound has ceased. But as the woman waves eerily to her fellow parade members, an isolated drumbeat fills the soundscape once again and the audience are presented with close-ups of sacrificial masks and fire from the torches. The folk community is once again united by the drumbeat, and the connection between drums and rituals is reinforced. However, as the hollow beat rings through the scene, the sound takes on a secondary meaning. As we are faced with close-up shots of the group members, particularly of their costumes and bodies, the corporeality of the figures onscreen is emphasised and the drum adopts the role of a heartbeat, building steadily as the scene progresses. This role is further exaggerated when the woman steps forward from her platform (thus hanging herself) and the drumbeat comes to an immediate stop, creating a direct connection between the drumbeat and the activity of the body onscreen. Whilst acting as a signifier for the sacrificial ceremony taking place and uniting the folk community, the drumbeat reflects the corporeality of the characters within the narrative – it ceases to be heard when the woman steps down from her platform, acting as a sonic cue to identify the character's moment of death.

This use of sound to represent corporeality is not a new cinematic technique, and phenomenological film analysis has articulated the ways in which cinema itself is embodied, in order to account for the affect felt by audiences. Drawing focus on certain affective genres, it is in horror that phenomenological film analysis has more recently centred, and Xavier Aldana Reyes's *Horror Film and Affect* (2016) is one of many crucial investigations into bodily affect and the horror genre. However, as Reyes admits, these studies have focused primarily on a certain *type* of horror – one that is gory and visceral, and directly attacks the viewer's senses. In contrast, folk horror is subtle, hosting an unnerving sense of peace and isolation, and whilst it *is* distanced from 'torture-porn' horror, its portrayal of corporeality is still worthy of examination. Folk horror relies on our engagement with the bodies onscreen, and whether it is to align us with the isolated protagonist or to make viewers understand the collective power of a folk community, the use of sound to reflect corporeality (and particularly a heartbeat) is a significant technique in drawing audiences phenomenologically closer to the world onscreen. As Vivian Sobchack notes, 'we do not experience any movie only through our eyes ... we see and comprehend and feel films with our entire bodily being, informed by the full history and carnal knowledge of our acculturated sensorium' (2004: 63), and it is this level of bodily experience that is conjured through the drumbeat in folk horror. Using our 'acculturated sensorium', thus using our *own* bodies to understand the movements and corporeal activity onscreen, we can truly be aligned with the characters in a folk horror narrative and *feel* the physical affect that the drumbeat provides, through its positioning as a heartbeat. By explicitly representing a beating heart, moreover, the drum becomes more than a simple aural signifier of ritual or folk community, but exists as a physical connector between us as viewers and the characters who are crucial to the genre of folk horror.

The distinct use of a drumbeat to substitute a human heartbeat is not only observed within *Kill List*, and this technique can also be seen within many films of the genre, including *Blood on Satan's Claw* (1971). In the film's penultimate ritual scene, when ploughman Ralph (Barry Andrews) is taken from his farmhouse and struck down in the woods by Angel Blake (Linda Hayden), the village's satanic followers begin to march around the fire and steadily beat their drum – here, as soon as the drumming begins, Ralph is revived back to consciousness, drawing a link between the steady drumbeat and his beating pulse. As Ralph continues to rise from the ground, the beat gets stronger, reinforcing the link between the drumbeat and his character's corporeality and creating a physical alignment between us and Ralph onscreen – we can make the connection between a strengthening pulse and Ralph gaining the energy to rise from the ground, through the knowledge and history of our own 'acculturated sensorium'. Similarly, in *The Wicker Man*, when the community of Summerisle is playing a game of 'Chop!' (where an individual's head is placed amongst an arrangement of swords), this link between corporeality and a drumbeat is illustrated again. Whilst members of the May Day parade take turns in positioning themselves within the swords, a drumbeat echoes through the film's score, reflecting the quickened heartbeats of each nervous character. Many escape with their heads still intact; however, as a villager dressed as a rabbit enters the trap, the drums build in anticipation and suddenly come to a halt as the rabbit is instantly decapitated. Although we soon discover that it was only the rabbit's *costume* that was decapitated by the swords, the link between the silence of the drumbeat and the character's mortality is strengthened in this scene, and further emphasises the importance of understanding characters onscreen. For viewers, it is shocking to see the decapitation of an innocent villager, but this further serves to exaggerate the sinister spirit of the folk community. Lord Summerisle and his followers celebrate the 'winners' who escape the arrangement of swords; however one unlucky follower is always excluded from the group through their loss of life. Here, the ritual decides who is included and excluded from the folk community, and through the striking use of a drumbeat to signify the rabbit's (presumed) death, we are positioned with Sergeant Howie to experience the shock of such an outdated practice; through the drum, we understand the endangered corporeality of the rabbit and the sinister nature of the community who inflict the danger.

By not only representing the collective folk community, but further aligning viewers with the physical bodies within a folk horror narrative, the drumbeat can again be seen as particularly crucial in constructing the genre's unsettling sensory affect. Through the distinct connection between the drumbeat and the human heartbeat of characters within the narrative, audiences are given the opportunity to use knowledge of their own bodies and *understand* the level of danger onscreen, thus reacting accordingly. Whether this reaction is fear or concern, it is certainly strengthened through the sound of the drumbeat and fulfils folk horror's aim to unsettle its audience.

Feeling the fear of folk horror

A third way in which folk horror film utilises the drumbeat is to achieve a feeling of fear: the ultimate goal of horror as a wider genre. As Jay and Gal cautiously observe the parade from behind the trees in *Kill List*, curious as to *why* the group are in the forest and *what* they are gathering to do, the film often cuts to the faces of both characters, showing their confused expressions and paranoid movements. Here, the sound (and ceasing) of the isolated drumbeat that plays throughout the scene can be seen not only as representing the united community in the woods and corporeality of the woman in the parade, but also as indicative of Jay and Gal's individual heartbeats as they nervously watch the scene unfold. Whereas the drumbeat originally signifies their quickening pulses as both men try to make sense of the ritual before them, the sudden end to the beat also represents the gut-wrenching moment of shock when the woman kills herself in front of their eyes: the moment they both freeze in horror. As Winters notes, the presence of the heartbeat in a film 'draws the spectator's attention to a character's endangered corporeality' (Winters 2008: 13), and within this scene we can certainly understand Jay and Gal's fear as they observe the ritual. Even as the drum ceases when the noose is placed around the woman's neck, this is representative of Jay and Gal's sudden point of realisation – the heart-stopping moment that reveals the sacrificial nature of the event they are observing. The drumbeat does not simply reflect the folk community and physical corporeality of characters in folk horror, then, but also indicates the *fear* embedded into each character's emotions and, consequently, our *own* fear as we witness the woman step down to her death. Through an alignment with the drumbeat, and the subsequent heartbeats of Jay and Gal, the sudden ceasing of the drum signifies a moment of horror and causes our own heartbeat to freeze automatically in empathy. We *feel* the fear illustrated through the beat, and sudden halt, of the drum.

As Winters continues to note, '[if] we hear a heartbeat and recognise it as such, ascribing it to a particular character, we are naturally drawn to considering our own heartbeat and therefore share the concern expressed by the character in a state of fictional fear for her/his own corporeal precariousness' (Winters 2008: 13). Here, Winters draws upon the ways in which audience members can use their own bodies to empathise with a character onscreen and particularly regulate their own heartbeat in accordance with the heartbeat highlighted though the film's soundscape. Using this phenomenological framework, we can then begin to understand the ways in which folk horror uses a drumbeat to connect sensorially with us, as viewers, and create a feeling of building fear and discomfort. Through the strengthened presence of a drumbeat, not only do we take on Jay and Gal's feelings of wariness and caution as they observe the ritual from afar, but consequentially we also feel their terror as the event takes a sinister turn, using our *own* bodies to empathise with the heartbeat onscreen. This level of phenomenological engagement with the drumbeat onscreen also means that our own heartbeats pick up the pace when we are placed in the centre of the ritual, surrounded by masked individuals and fiery torches, and are encouraged to *become* part of the folk community through the unifying beat of the drum. Our heartbeats also cease in horror when we witness the woman in the forest step down to her brutal death; we actively *feel* the fear that folk horror aims to conjure, through the beat of the drum.

When Jay realises that something very sinister is taking place at the ceremony, he takes matters into his own hands and fires a gun at the folk community. After delivering a fatal shot to one of the group's leaders, the ritual attendees proceed to shriek and run forward to Jay and Gal, intent on revenge, and in the background (amongst familiar sounds of cymbals and chanting) a frenzied drumbeat enters the soundscape. In this scene, not only is a *steady* drumbeat used to indicate corporeality and a persistent building of fear, but a *frenzied* drumbeat is then also introduced to indicate when that fear is intensified. Depending on the tempo and rhythm of the drumbeat, therefore, the level of fear that we are encouraged to align with changes: slow to indicate developing danger, frenzied to show panic and stress, or frozen to show complete horror. This technique of changing the speed and style of the drumbeat to reflect the desired emotional affect can also be observed in the film's final scene, where Jay is forced to fight a mysterious hunched figure. Stripped naked, dressed in a sacrificial mask and handed a knife, Jay is pushed to the centre of a clearing, where a figure in white linen and a wicker mask is moving around him. As the pair brandish knives at each other, a rolling, frenzied drumbeat can be heard in the soundscape: not the singular beat that was previously heard to represent the woman's heartbeat at the hanging ceremony, but an unsettling rhythm that serves to portray the confused and chaotic actions of the characters onscreen. Jay is confused as to whom he is fighting, and the wild brandishing of knives provides a stressful, tense atmosphere – in seeing Jay's body in danger onscreen, we can equate his own endangered corporeality to the fragility or precariousness (as Winters notes) of our *own* bodies, maybe even flinching as the knife edges towards his skin. Here, we are encouraged to take on the fear that Jay feels as he is physically attacked, and to understand the wild, frenzied movements *through* the chaotic drumbeat. As Jay finally defeats his opponent, stabbing the figure numerous times in the back, the drumbeat ceases, once again drawing a connection to the drumbeat and the corporeality of characters onscreen; we can immediately understand that the hunched figure's heart has stopped because of the ceasing of the drum. However, whilst reinstating this connection between drumbeat and corporeality, this scene also illustrates how the drumbeat can dictate the emotions felt by the audience, and particularly the level of horror and fear in the folk horror narrative.

By aligning the drumbeat with moments of fear, then, we can see one of the ways in which folk horror films effectively produce a *feeling* that is crucial to the affect of the genre: a phenomenological disposition that encourages uneasiness and terror. Achieved subtly through the sonic appearance of a drumbeat, moreover, folk horror films can successfully dictate our emotions as spectators and fulfil the genre's own goal of evoking fear. For example, in *Blood on Satan's Claw*, one scene shows Ralph rolling up his trousers to reveal a furry patch of 'devil's skin' on his leg; however, he is soon interrupted by a sinister presence at the door. As he stares intently at the doorway, terrified of what lies on the other side, a steady, hollow drumbeat begins to play as Ralph then cowers in the corner of the room in fear. Here, the drumbeat is used to convey Ralph's emotional state of fear, and synchronises perfectly with the rising and falling of his chest: the drum represents his heartbeat. Terrified of what might enter the room, Ralph continues to take deep intakes of breath that coincide with the drumbeat, aligning us sensorially to his body and encouraging us as viewers to take on his feeling of fear. With each beat, the drum gets louder, representing a greater thud of Ralph's own pulse, and you can almost *feel* the blood thumping around his heart, which is contracting in fear and reflected sonically onscreen. Through the drumbeat in this scene, we can immediately empathise with Ralph's physical situation and corporeally understand his level of fear – through the amplified beat of the hollow drum, coinciding with Ralph's frantic breathing and terrified expression, this scene invites our own heartbeat to quicken as we empathise with his situation, resulting in phenomenological alignment and encouraging viewers to *feel* the fear of a folk horror film.

Similarly, in *Psychomania* (1973), a similar affect is created. Following Tom (Nicky Henson) and his violent gang of motorcyclist friends, a drumbeat is effectively used to indicate a fearful vision experienced by the protagonist. As he explores the mysterious room in which his father died, Tom arrives at a mirror where he proceeds to have an unsettling vision accompanied by the beating of a drum. First seeing a frog (which is later revealed to be a god worshipped by the folk community), Tom then sees the 'Seven Witches' – an arrangement of standing stones in his local area. As his vision continues to show an eerie figure riding a motorcycle around the stones, the film alternates between presenting the vision and a close-up of Tom's face as he squirms in discomfort. The hollow drumbeat that was faintly present at the start of the vision then begins to grow in volume and gathers speed as Tom raises his hands to his ears in fear. With Tom clenching his eyes shut and breathing heavily, the quickened beat of the drum indicates first that the protagonist is fearful of something within the vision, and second that we as viewers should understand and adopt this fear; we are naturally drawn to consider our own heartbeat and thus share the concern expressed by the character in a state of fear (Winters 2008: 13).

Cry of the Banshee (1970) also produces a similar phenomenological affect through its use of drums, and employs a drumbeat to indicate the fearful situations in which the characters are placed. The film focuses on Lord Edward Whitman (Vincent Price), who, upon attempting to rid his town of witches, discovers a demonic coven and their sinister leader, Oona (Elisabeth Bergner). In one scene, where Oona and her community of followers are practising a ritual in the woods, Lord Whitman and his associates attempt to capture the group – using a large net, two men on horseback entrap Oona's tribe and a drumbeat suddenly builds in speed and volume through the film's soundtrack, sonically embedding the panic that is unfolding onscreen. This reflection of fear through a drumbeat is again echoed later in the film, where Oona performs a ritual with her followers and uses a voodoo doll to control Maureen (Hilary Dwyer), Lord Whitman's wife. As her name rings through the grand house, mirroring Oona's chanting at the ritual, Maureen wakes from sleep and begins cautiously walking through the halls. The beat of a drum begins to be heard and steadily builds in force and volume as Maureen arrives at the room in which her possessed lover Roderick (Patrick Mower) is held captive. After a brief interlude of silence, where Maureen realises that Roderick has disappeared, a frantic drumbeat suddenly erupts into the soundscape; Maureen is attacked by Roderick, and her sudden panic and fear are reflected through the beat. With the film alternating between the attack and Oona's ritual, moreover, the drumbeat not only signifies the ritualistic folk community and the physical heartbeat of Maureen's character as she is attacked, but it also serves to build a strengthened level of fear within the narrative. As Maureen slowly steps through her house at night, with minimal light to illuminate her surroundings, the drum serves to heighten the *horror* of the film itself – the dark house, frightened protagonist and potential for danger at any point. Here, the drum *prepares* audiences to watch a horror film and, through its steady building of tension, fulfils the intended goal of the film's genre. Similarly, through the combination of a drumbeat and the physical voodoo doll used in Oona's ritual, another layer of fear is added to the narrative. Whilst reductive in its use, playing upon sensational stereotypes of the Afro-Caribbean religion of Voudon, the use of a voodoo doll in this scene draws upon a subtle fear surrounding mythology and ritual – two important narrative elements of folk horror. Accompanied by a beating drum, which is often a guaranteed sonic element in rituals of this kind, the voodoo doll adds a sinister potential to the folk community's actions. Whilst we are aware that such a practice should not have any tangible effects (its use should not logically inflict harm on others), the tribe's sincere belief in the doll's powers is enough to evoke suspicion and fear in viewers, particularly when that belief (often conveyed through chanting and movement) is strengthened by the steady, intimidating beat of a drum. This use of drums in *Cry of the Banshee* is owed to Wilfred Josephs's original soundtrack; however, this was replaced upon the film's release with a staggeringly different score by Les Baxter. The change was made for the film's heavily edited American release, where particular scenes of violence and nudity were deleted, and as a result, the distinct use of drums was erased from the film's score. Whilst the original version has since been re-released (all DVD releases of the film feature the original cut with Wilfred Josephs's intended score), the edited American version certainly lacks a phenomenological pull – even the director Gordon Hessler noted that Wilfred Josephs's original score 'held the picture up' and made it 'more mysterious' (Reis 2002), acknowledging the integrity of the score's depth and power. To remove the drums from *Cry of the Banshee* is to remove an essential part of its sensory affect, and through the restoration of Joseph's original score we can understand and appreciate the significant ways in which the drum is effectively used to build panic and fear within the film.

Conclusion

Through a focus on phenomenological analysis throughout this chapter, the ways in which sensory theory enhances our understanding of folk horror as a genre are clear. By avoiding 'motif-spotting' (Koven 2008: 3) when trying to understand a genre, as Mikel J. Koven identifies, we can begin to understand how folk horror is affectively *felt*, and examine the techniques that are employed to strengthen phenomenological alignment. One significant example of a technique used to reflect the affectual aims of folk horror, moreover, is the use of a drumbeat. It is evident from focusing on *Kill List*, whilst also illustrating this recurring technique through secondary examples, that the drum in British folk horror cinema is not merely another layer of the soundtrack blended into the wider soundscape. Whether diegetic or non-diegetic, played by the folk community onscreen or recognisably present through the film's soundtrack, a distinct folk horror drumbeat (complete with an isolated rhythm and deep resonance) has a wealth of meaning and affect.

First, by uniting the folk community (a crucial element to a folk horror narrative) and strengthening their culminative power as a synchronised group, the drumbeat serves to alienate both the protagonist and us as viewers from the tribe onscreen; the beat belongs to *their* ritual and conjures a rhythm specific to *them* as a collective, thus isolating everyone else. On the other hand, a drumbeat is also used within folk horror to signify the physical corporeality of the folk community and protagonists onscreen. By acting as a sonic identifier for a human heartbeat, the drum indicates the mortality and emotions of characters onscreen and, in turn, encourages viewers to use their *own* corporeal knowledge to understand and engage sensorially with the events that unfold in the narrative. As Winters notes, viewers (upon hearing a heartbeat in a film) are 'naturally drawn' to consider their own heartbeat and 'therefore share the concern expressed by the character' (Winters 2008: 13), illustrating the third and final way in which a drumbeat achieves a sensory affect: to represent and encourage a strengthened level of horror and fear. Through this 'natural' reference to our own corporeality when interacting with bodies onscreen, we arguably take on a greater level of discomfort and fear as our bodies physically align to the characters within the folk horror narrative; we use our own bodies to understand those onscreen. Consequently, when folk horror then uses a drumbeat to emphasise endangered corporeality, moments of intense horror, and disjointed or frenzied movement, we can affectively *feel* this within our own bodies and experience fear as a result – the ultimate goal of the genre. The drumbeat is not the only way in which a sensory affect can be achieved through the genre, however, and we can understand the unsettling 'ambiance and aesthetic' (Paciorek 2018: 15) that makes up a folk horror film through various filmic elements, such as landscape and *mise-en-scène*. Whilst my own research focuses on unpicking this sensory affect, there is significant space for additional contributions in the fields of folk horror and phenomenological theory, and it is my hope that this chapter shows the strengthened potential of this combined area of scholarship.

Music serves a crucial purpose within each genre of horror film, and whether it is the melodramatic orchestral score of a Hammer film or the progressive rock soundtrack in a *giallo* film, each piece of music creates a desired atmosphere of dread and fear. Even specific sounds within horror are crucial in creating a certain effect, with 'repetitious drones, clashing dissonances, and stingers (those assaultive blasts that coincide with shock or revelation) [affecting] us at a primal level' (Lerner 2010: ix). Folk horror is no different. Rejecting the twee strumming of acoustic guitars or soft, choral harmonies that some may consider upon hearing the term 'folk music', folk horror pushes further, using a wealth of jarring sounds to disrupt the idyll. Presenting uncomfortable frequencies; guttural chanting; and, most importantly, a panic-inducing drumbeat, folk horror takes a misconception of 'folk', with preconceived notions of idyllic pastoralism and gentleness, and violently distorts these expectations. Through the drum, one of the oldest instruments used by humankind, folk horror takes an atavistic object representative of folkloric tradition and uses it to reject any fraction of comfort found within our past. Through its soundscape, folk horror becomes physical and involving, and induces a fear that is rooted in discomfort; like the protagonist onscreen, we are not welcome or safe in the folk horror world, and this will always be disclosed through the beat of the drum.

References

Groves, Matilda (2017), 'Past Anxieties: Defining the Folk Horror Narrative', #FolkloreThursday, folklorethursday.com/halloween/past-anxieties-defining-folk-horror-narrative/ (accessed 29 June 2022).
Henderson, Kate (2014), 'Shamanic Drumming', *TomTomMagazine*, tomtommag.com/2014/02/shamanic-drumming/ (accessed 29 June 2022).
Keetley, Dawn (2020), 'Introduction: Defining Folk Horror', *Revenant 5* (March), 1–32.
Koven, Mikel J. (2008), *Film, Folklore and Urban Legends*. Lanham, MD: Scarecrow Press.
Lerner, Neil (2010), 'Preface: Listening to Fear/Listening with Fear', in Neil Lerner (ed.), *Music in the Horror Film: Listening to Fear*. London: Routledge, pp. viii–xii.
Paciorek, Andy (2018) 'Folk Horror: From the Forests, Fields and Furrows. An Introduction' in Andy Paciorek, Grey Malkin, Richard Hing and Katherine Peach (eds), *Folk Horror Revival: Field Studies*, 2nd edn. Durham: Wyrd Harvest Press, pp. 12–20.

Reis, George (2002), 'An Interview with Gordon Hessler', *DVD Drive-In*, www.dvddrive-in.com/hessler.htm (accessed 29 June 2022).

Reyes, Xavier Aldana (2016), *Horror Film and Affect: Towards a Corporeal Mode of Viewership*. London: Routledge.

Scovell, Andy (2017), *Folk Horror: Hours Dreadful and Things Strange*. Leighton Buzzard: Auteur.

Sobchack, Vivian (2004), *Carnal Thoughts: Embodiment and Moving Image Culture*. Oakland: University of California Press.

Winters, Ben (2008), 'Corporeality, Musical Heartbeats, and Cinematic Emotion', *Music, Sound, and the Moving Image* 2:1 (Spring), 3–25.

11

'Nature came before man': human as subject and object within the folk horror anti-landscape

David Evans-Powell

Adam Scovell's folk horror chain – still the pre-eminent theory in terms of defining and characterising folk horror as a screen tradition – places significant emphasis on the diegetic landscape. Landscape is the first link in the chain, 'where elements within its topography have adverse effects on the social and moral identity of its inhabitants' (Scovell 2017: 17). Scovell's chain creates a direct and intrinsic relationship between the landscape and the community that dwells there, with the topography having a specific and tangible impact upon the society, culture, creed and behaviour of the inhabitants.

Many screen traditions place emphasis upon the landscape. Heritage and historical drama frequently utilise genteel and picturesque topographies, which become inescapably intertwined within the wider commodification of British history within the film industry. The social-realist tradition too emphasises the industrial landscapes of British northern and Midlander cities, as backdrops to working-class narratives.

Folk horror is attentive to the landscape in a different way. In contrast to the picturesque environs of heritage drama, or the grittier environments of social realism, it is intimately concerned with the landscape as a worked, and working, space: 'a world we are living in' rather than 'a scene we are looking at' (Wylie 2007: 1). It is a tradition that explores the fundamental relationship between topography and community, challenging established notions of the form, function and ownership of the landscape and its supposed subordination to the needs of its inhabitants. The landscape is characterised as having an agency, sentience or autonomy that, in other generic traditions, are either underemphasised or largely absent.

This chapter will explore these contested notions of the demarcation, ownership and control of the landscape through a focused analysis of *Blood on Satan's Claw* (1971) and comparative discussion of other, more contemporary folk horror films, including *Dogged* (2017), *The Fallow Field*

(2009) and *The Unkindness of Ravens* (2016) – films that have received comparatively little in the way of critical appraisal. In doing so, it will illustrate the tension between landscape and anti-landscape and examine how these tensions can be read as representative of other cultural tensions, such as those between nature and civilisation, the classical and the romantic, and the masculine and the feminine.

Folk horror and the classical landscape

Given director Piers Haggard's upbringing on a farm, it is unsurprising that *Blood on Satan's Claw* is intimately concerned with the rural landscape as a worked, habitable space, one where there is a tangible 'haptic materiality' (Newland 2016: 167) to the earth as a pliable, physical material. Haggard has commented several times about his interest in representing 'the power of the darkness of the countryside' (Haggard 2019), something he would have been well acquainted with given his childhood.

The cinematography of the pre-credits sequence emphasises the materiality and physicality of the earth, with the sound of the plough grinding into the soil, the muted palette and naturalistic lighting, and the positioning of 'the camera in the furrow [signifying] what's coming up from down below' (Haggard 2019).

This attention to working and managing the land is present throughout the film. Haggard's representation of the countryside is characterised by notions of ownership, form and function. The film is set in the early eighteenth century at a point shortly before the advent of the industrial and agrarian revolutions, so this focus feels entirely appropriate given that, even as late as 1900, one in ten workers in Britain was still engaged in agricultural work (Payne 1994: 6).

The landscape in the film illustrates some of these gradual impositions of human control over the form and function of the countryside, through the animal pens outside the Banham farmhouse, the linearly ploughed field worked by Ralph (Barry Andrews), the footpath where Ralph and the judge (Patrick Wymark) encounter the Revd Fallowfield (Anthony Ainley), and the hedgerows that border the footpath. Older pre-agricultural societies made no distinction between landscapes; it was the development of cultivation and the domestication of animals that led to the subsequent categorisation of land into the cultivated and uncultivated. The prevailing opinion until the eighteenth century was that cultivated land was far preferable to uncultivated land because it demonstrated order, intelligence and structure (Newland 2016: 168). This sat at the very centre of medieval and early modern thought.

Paul Newland has read the contrast between the open fields and the demarcated pens outside the Banham house within the historical context of enclosure: the practice of seizing smallholdings and consolidating them into larger farms that moved land from common to private ownership (2016: 168). Enclosure was a common, although often controversial, practice in England from the early sixteenth century until into the nineteenth century. It fundamentally changed not only English society by transferring more direct control over larger tracts of land to a smaller number of affluent landowners, but also the English landscape: enclosure took land that had been held in common for centuries and contained and demarcated it into private smallholdings (Hoskins 2005: 166). These forms of control and demarcation – straight lines of hedgerows and hawthorn bushes – would become a frequent sight across the English landscape by the early eighteenth century and are evident in *Satan's Claw*, from the hawthorn used to crown Cathy (Wendy Padbury) to the hedgerows in which the Revd Fallowfield is found hunting for snakes.

Unsurprisingly – given how comprehensively the British landscape has been shaped according to agricultural, transport, conservation and habitation needs – these marks of function and ownership are commonplace across folk horror film texts. The farm in *The Fallow Field*, like the farmland and the manor house in *Blood on Satan's Claw*, is characterised by footpaths, gates, fences and tracks: indicators of the intimate connection between the public and the private, and the closeness between the two. *The Unkindness of Ravens* extensively details protagonist Andrew's (Jamie Scott Gordon) journey into the Highlands, down dirt paths, beside long fences and through gates, until he reaches his destination: a remote cottage in the Highlands. The attention to these outpost examples of civilisation's reach into the wilderness serves to emphasise both how remote these locales are from urban centres, and how – even in these distant parts – civilisation's reach can be felt.

Conferring function through agriculture, or ownership through boundaries, characterises the countryside as an environment subordinated to human use and defined only by how it is exploited as a resource. This is an illustration of the classical attitude to the landscape in which 'the creation of livable [*sic*] spaces and usable spaces is a mark of civilisation. Human use confers meaning on space' (Short 1991: 6). A characteristic of civilisation is the transformation of physical space for human need; landscape is given meaning and sense by being adapted to human habitation and cultivation.

The topography in the folk horror tradition explores the tensions and frictions between the classical and its oppositional 'anti-landscape'. Before considering this other form, it is helpful to contextualise the topography in

Satan's Claw by examining the classical mapping of the landscape in more contemporary British folk horror films.

The Fallow Field sees protagonist Matt (Steve Garry) move from his house in the suburbs to a farm in the countryside – the two topographical areas subordinated to being liveable and usable spaces for the benefit of urban society. The island community in *Dogged* is established as a typical British rural community. The social and cultural hubs – church and pub – are present, alongside tearooms and a mix of traditional and more contemporary houses. Whereas *Blood on Satan's Claw* is historically set – and illustrates the rural landscape to be at a distance from the closest urban centres – *The Fallow Field* and *Dogged* are set in modern times and illustrate the immediacy and apparent pervasiveness of urban tastes and culture. The mechanisation of the farm in *The Fallow Field*, and its apparent location at the hinterland of suburban Britain rather than in the depths of the countryside, suggests the closeness of the rural to the urban landscape. The gentrification of the community on Farthing Island in *Dogged* – the large, modern houses, the younger generation going to university, the presence of tea shops and boutiques – indicates the pervasiveness of urban sophisticate taste and a permeability between the rural and the urban, with the rural becoming an extension of the urban. *The Unkindness of Ravens*, meanwhile, represents the rural landscape as a therapeutic and artistic topography, a place subordinated to the urban space as a refuge and haven from the unforgiving rigours of city life. The idea of the rural space subordinated to the urban one as a place of retreat and convalescence is also evoked by *Eden Lake* (2008) – in which Jenny (Kelly Reilly) and Steve (Michael Fassbender) are urban types on a camping holiday by a wooded lake – and in *The Fallow Field*, where Matt, a suburbanite afflicted by blackouts and a sense of purposelessness, finds himself returning to the countryside, suggestive of the rural landscape as a restorative to urban ennui (albeit a recuperative function that ultimately goes unfulfilled, given the traumatic and disturbing experiences that befall the protagonists in these environments within these films).

The classical attitude extends beyond the spatial and into the temporal, as it also sees human activity as a progressive linear trajectory of improvement. As such, the shaping of the landscape to suit human needs is a positive act. *Blood on Satan's Claw* illustrates this through its eighteenth-century setting. This period saw the flowering of the Enlightenment, when philosophy moved away from divine revelation and towards a more anthropocentric worldview that celebrated the human ability to comprehend nature through reason. Enlightenment thought is frequently espoused by the judge, whether sneering at the villagers' superstitions or decrying the doctor's (Howard Goorney) beliefs in witchcraft. His acceptance of the fiend only comes through reasoned examination. The classical approach, and Enlightenment reasoning, together suggest an inevitable and positive move from chaos to order, from abandonment to control, and from the untamed to the managed.

Folk horror and the romantic anti-landscape

However, *Satan's Claw* sees this classically constructed and managed landscape under threat. The pre-credits sequence teases at these anxieties. The shot of Cathy calling to Ralph from across the fields demonstrates how vast the countryside is and how diminished they appear to be within it. This sense of 'comprehensive dispossession and vacancy' is the first indicator that man is not master of nature (Hutchings 2004: 29). Given the sheer scale of the landscape, those marks of land management – the ploughed furrows and animal pens – appear small and insignificant. Consequently, civilisation itself – as the owner of the cultivated space – is reduced in authority and potency. The effect of this distancing and reducing is 'a shift in perception [of the landscape] from the idyllic to the ominous' (Johnston 2017). Earlier, the camera was positioned in the furrow looking up at Ralph, 'as if the earth is glaring up at him' (Scovell 2017: 19). The cinematography codes the countryside as a vast but watchful environment, and one that is at best dispassionate and at worst hostile towards its human occupants.

The rural landscape becomes what Peter Hutchings has termed an 'anti-landscape', a 'landscape that provocatively throws into question the very idea of the human ... as the owner of landscape, as a figure in that landscape, or as an observer of it' (Hutchings 2004: 29). Hutchings asserts that

Figure 11.1 *Blood on Satan's Claw*, 1971

the otherness of the anti-landscape becomes emphasised to the point that it displaces the agency of people and civilisation, 'with the human either completely disappearing or becoming subject to uncontrollable impulses or compulsions, or regressing to something that is less than human' (2004: 29). This is an apt description of *Satan's Claw*, in which human agency is diminished within a vast natural topography, the village children are drawn away to enact brutal rituals in the forest wilderness and individuals are compelled to sacrifice their selves to resurrect an atavistic horror.

The forest wilderness is a space that is demarcated as separate from the cultivated space, sitting at a point beyond the impositions of civilisation. This separation allows the fiend and its followers to use the woodland as they wish, and to effect different structures, demarcations and notions of ownership. The film implies that the forest was not always such a forsaken topography. The presence of the ruins suggests that the forest was once part of the occupied and managed space. The film does not elaborate further, and as such their presence is ambiguous and open to interpretation. They could suggest a fundamental change to the demarcation of the forest, as a space once managed and defined through human use but long since abandoned. Or they could indicate an alternative social and topographical structure, one that demarcated the landscape according to their fiendish worship. In this latter case, the fiend's reoccupation of the space would represent a return to a previous ownership and a restoration of its historic function.

The cult's adoption of the ruins as a sacred space is suggestive of the traditions of nature worship in Graeco-Roman antiquity that considered the physical landscape to be occupied by *genii locorum*, guardian spirits that were worshipped for the protection they offered. The majority were associated with natural features such as mountains, trees, springs and caves, and the veneration of these spirits saw, by extension, the veneration of the place protected by the spirit. *Satan's Claw* demonstrates both the demarcation of the wilderness into sacred sites, and this numinous sense of the landscape mapped as a series of sacred spaces.

The desacralisation of these spaces following Christianisation saw a reorientation of civilisation's outlook in the medieval period onto the church, located at the urban centre, surrounded by the occupied and cultivated landscapes, with the abandoned wilderness now at the margins. Over time the wilderness, no longer a sacred space, ceases to be familiar and instead becomes associated with mystery and threat, with the former spiritual guardians now perceived as malign, haunting presences. As such, the former sites of pagan worship become regarded as places of danger, as the homes of monsters, or the sites for executions and violent death (Legard 2015: 368–370). We see this pattern of movement from the sacred periphery to the sacred centre very clearly in *Satan's Claw*, with Fallowfield's church usurping the sacred function while the ruins become the locus for dangerous rituals and the home of the fiend.

Until the eighteenth century, the uncultivated wilderness was feared as a place beyond human reach. It was thought to have the power to 'uncivilise' people and draw them away from society. Those who spent too long in the wilderness ran the risk of becoming part of it; isolated within these large and remote landscapes, individuals could regress to savage, uncivilised behaviours (Short 1991: 9). This premodern fear of the wilderness is brought to life in *Satan's Claw* as we see characters led away from the village to join the cult in the forest.

The anti-landscape, which resists human encroachment, ownership and subordination, is a characteristic common across the folk horror tradition, as is the notion that humans owe their ownership or mastery over the land to the benevolence of the landscape, rather than to any supposed authority or ingenuity on the part of civilisation. Repeatedly, folk horror texts emphasise the vastness of the wilderness and the sheer insignificance of human presence there. *The Fallow Field* begins with Matt waking up on the ground amid a vast, empty, pastoral landscape. *The Unkindness of Ravens* opens with a starkly beautiful shot of a Highland woodland swathed in mist. *Dogged* starts with a shot of a wide field with pylons in the far distance: an illustration of the proximity between the urban and rural spaces.

The dispossession of man as owner of the landscape is made apparent in other ways. In *The Fallow Field*, we see man become subordinated to the demands of the landscape. Farmer Calham (Michael Dacre) cultivates a field, in which nothing has ever been successfully grown, by killing and burying people there, only for them to be resurrected days later. While Calham appears to be owner and manager of the field – and the field has been put to work for the purposes of cultivation and sustenance – this is instead a subversion of the usual ownership and function of farmland. Rather than having authority over the land, Calham instead describes his repeated murder and burial of people within the field – and their subsequent resurrection – as a compulsion: it is the purpose of the field and he must serve that purpose. In *Dogged*, the male villagers of Farthing Island form a secret cult dedicated to purifying the island through blood sacrifices. They are led by the island's priest (Toby Wynn-Davies), who states that 'nature came before man, and we will return to nature'. While the film is light on the details of the cult's beliefs, there is an implicit connection made – as in *The Fallow Field* – between the demands of the landscape and the offering of human sacrifices. In these instances, the classical relationship between person and landscape is inverted, with civilisation subordinated to the desires and demands of the wilderness. Not only is humankind placed in a subordinate position, but it is also sacrificed to enable the land's sustenance, the landscape effectively utilising humans for its own vitality, rather than the other way round. *The Unkindness of Ravens* refers to human dispossession by suggesting equivalence between the Highland landscape and a war zone. Protagonist Andrew is a former soldier, haunted by the traumas he witnessed while serving abroad (in a conflict implied to be somewhere in the Middle East). Images of ravens picking at the carcasses of deer, rabbits and birds are interspersed throughout the film with flashback sequences where Andrew re-experiences being caught in the horror and confusion of explosions and firefights. The juxtaposition of images of death and violence across these two topographies suggests that both are landscapes in which humans are not secure and are not in control, vulnerable to unseen threats and a denuded, hostile landscape.

The depiction of the landscape as something awesome and fearful sits in the Romantic tradition, which perceives the wilderness as having a 'purity which human contact tends to sully and degrade' (Short 1991: 9). The space untouched by civilisation is to be revered in a manner reminiscent of the pagan nature worship of antiquity, as it represents a historic, idyllic past. The Romantic perception has gained traction in the modern period, as the wilderness has been transformed over time from a vast and encroaching landscape to an environment under threat from human encroachment. Rather than representing a fearful absence of civilised authority, the wilderness is celebrated precisely because of this absence of civilised authority. *Dogged* explores this notion that civilisation and wilderness are inimical to each other with the priest's insistence on blood sacrifices to the island to correct impurities in behaviour, impurities for which wider civilisation beyond Farthing Island is implied to be responsible. Protagonist Sam (Sam Saunders) returns home from university to attend a funeral on the island. He is described by the priest as being 'from this place but ... not one of us'; Sam's relocation to wider civilisation on the mainland, and his entry into the educational establishment, has rendered him impure, and anathema to the island. *Dogged* holds to a Romantic notion of the landscape in which the Farthing Island villagers guard against encroachment by values and behaviours they perceive as impure influences from the mainland.

Where the village and the fields are defined by the landscape being mapped according to the classical tradition, the forest wilderness is organised according to the Romantic tradition. Nature becomes a space of veneration once again. We observe this in *Satan's Claw* when Cathy is crowned with hawthorn, led in procession to the ruins, and then ritually raped and murdered to help the fiend restore its body. Margaret's (Michele Dotrice) reading of the 'Book of Behemoth' during this sequence – invoking the fiend to 'rise now from the forests, from the furrows' – casts it as a revenant *genius loci*, resacralising the wilderness and sustaining the social hierarchy of the cult

(Evans-Powell 2021: 36). The fiend's return, and a restoration of the wilderness as a numinous space, suggests a backward-looking and regressive attitude, at odds with the progressive outlook that has fashioned and driven the cultivated space. As such it refutes the tenets of the Enlightenment, its elevation of man's capacity for reason and narrative of inevitable improvement. Instead, it implies that these notions upon which modern civilisation has been founded are fundamentally unsound.

Movement between landscape and anti-landscape

However, the relationship between classical landscape and Romantic anti-landscape is more complex. Rather than the two being separate and distinct, there is a considerable degree of permeability between them. In *Blood on Satan's Claw*, this osmosis between landscape and anti-landscape is catalysed by the fiend's unearthing. While coded as a revenant spirit of the wilderness, the fiend does not emerge from the forest, but instead is ploughed up from the field. Its appearance from the cultivated earth challenges the notion of humanity as the owner and manager of the rural landscape and implicates the cultivated earth itself as an agent in the fiend's return, suggesting a sentience and hostility towards its human managers (Macfarlane 2015).

The fiend steps outside the demarcation of the land between landscape and anti-landscape. Where Ralph, Cathy and the other villagers are diminished by the scale and ubiquity of the rural landscape – their autonomy to operate within it restricted by notions of land use and occupation – the fiend appears to move freely, a freedom it grants to its followers who show no fear in occupying the forest or, in the case of Angel Blake (Linda Hayden), appearing naked within the church. The fiend transgresses notions of ownership and function, operating across cultivated land, the wilderness and the farmhouse without care or consideration for social hierarchy or use of space. Civilisation, and how it constructs meaning for itself through ownership, function and demarcation, is mocked by the fiend's ability to move anywhere and inflict trauma. As a result, the certainty that civilisation has over its ownership and mastery of the cultivated space is exposed as flawed and hubristic. The fiend's actions transform the landscape into an anti-landscape, 'a realm that snags, bites and troubles', marked by repulsive objects, sites of abandonment and savage behaviours (Macfarlan 2015).

Farthing Island in *Dogged* similarly represents this ambiguity between landscape and anti-landscape, in that it is a tidal island, rather than a true island, and as such is part of the mainland at low tide. This uncertainty as to the topography's true state – a separate space or a contiguous part of the mainland – exemplifies the tensions and permeability between the civilised landscape of the mainland and the wilderness anti-landscape of the island. It is a place both familiar through its church, pub and high street shops, and unfamiliar in the lurking threat from the cult and its blood sacrifices.

There are other examples of the permeability and fluidity between the landscape and anti-landscape in *Dogged*. The local authorities represent a microcosm of the civilised establishment on the mainland: the priest and his church, the local doctor. We see these archetypes too in *Blood on Satan's Claw*, a localised image of a national socio-political structure. However, these figures are not safeguarding the authorities they represent, but instead are covertly maintaining the status quo of the anti-landscape. By contrast, those more sympathetic figures in the film – Jim the woodsman (Tony Parkin) and Sparrow the hippy (Nadia Lamin) – are viewed with scorn and excluded from the community. The hippies make a distinction between the islanders (a term they use to describe all island inhabitants) and the villagers (who are implicitly associated with the cult). This distinction creates a complex series of contested ownerships over the island, a topography that is both part of the mainland and separated from it, inhabited by a community that is a microcosm of the mainland establishment from which it has become alienated, and occupied by another community who have dropped out from the mainland civilisation but are also excluded by the island community. It is fascinating that, like the fiend in *Blood on Satan's Claw*, several characters in *Dogged* transgress the demarcations between wilderness and cultivated/occupied space. The woodsman is an itinerant who moves freely between the wild countryside and both the public and private spaces in the village (appearing secretly in peoples' gardens, as well as living in the woodland). The hippies have been excluded from the village, and therefore must make their home within the wilderness. The cultists move between public and private space, and between cultivated and uncultivated spaces, without regard for land ownership or function, in their pursuit of Sam.

Farthing Island appears separated between the cultivated, civilised space of the village and the uncultivated wilderness of the wider island, where the hippies and the woodsman reside. Despite this separation, the priest and the cult appear to move between the two freely. The priest presides over two separate spiritual focal points on the island, each within separate zones of ownership: the church in the village, and the standing stones in the wilderness, the sacred locus for the cult. Tidal islands have become popular in British folk horror within the past decade in representing this ambiguous, liminal and troubled permeability between wilderness and civilisation, featuring as they do in *Amen Island* (aka *Unhappy Birthday*, 2011), and the 2020 television series *The Third Day*.

Figure 11.2   *Dogged*, 2017

The tidal island spaces find analogy in the landscape in *Blood on Satan's Claw*, where the church occupies the sacred space of the village, and the ruins form the numinous heart for the activities of Angel and her group. However, in *Satan's Claw*, while there is a permeability between the cultivated and uncultivated spaces, there still exists a division between the establishments of the village and the cult, which inimical and opposing hierarchies of authority established for each. In *Dogged*, there is a far greater degree of fluidity between hierarchy, ownership, function and demarcation. The priest functions as an authority for two overlapping and ostensibly oppositional spiritual hierarchies, one of which is a clandestine authority hidden within the public framework of the other. The public establishment of church and village is the visible, legitimate representative of the island – a microcosm of the mainland establishments beyond, despite being in localised competition – which defines who is perceived as an islander by including or excluding individuals from the community. However, this visible and civilised image of the Farthing Island community is mirrored by a hidden, reversed version that claims dominion over the wilderness. The priest claims spiritual ownership over the whole island and all its communities through a series of intersecting boundaries and overlapping expressions of ownership, describing himself as the father of the island. However, where the fiend in *Blood on Satan's Claw* can move freely between the private, public, cultivated and wild spaces, the movement of the priest and the cult in *Dogged* is restricted in terms of their personae: they appear as themselves in the village; however they wear animal masks when behaving as cult members and engaging in ritualistic activities. These masks are a visible sign of their citizenship of the wilderness. While there may be considerable permeability between the cultivated and uncultivated space, they remain separate spaces requiring differing observances for ownership to be recognised.

The Fallow Field, too, explores the contravention of established boundaries of form and function. Calham describes the soil of the resurrection field as 'cemetery soil', rather than as a medium for agriculture. This represents the abject contamination of a space designated for food production and the sustenance of civilisation: the topography has become a site for death and burial, rather than cultivation and growth. However, the field is not a repository for the dead, but is rather a site for unnatural resurrection, making a mockery of its substitution as a graveyard. It has become a hybrid space of multiple and mutually exclusive functions of life, death and afterlife. It has also subverted its designated function as a topography for the sustenance of civilisation, and instead determines its own function as a mimicry of the life it was subordinated to serve.

Abject tensions between landscape and anti-landscape

In *Blood on Satan's Claw*, the fiend's emergence from the earth, a space traditionally gendered as female – in opposition to the patriarchal sociopolitical structures of the civilised spaces of cultivation and habitation – marks it as symbolic of the ancient and abject feminine. The relationship the fiend has with its followers – demarcating parts of their bodies with fur – is analogous to what Barbara Creed and others have identified as the mother's instrumental role in mapping the infant body during childhood, zoning it into clean and unclean areas (Creed 2007: 40). Where the mother zones the infant body to identify and remove the uncleanliness, the fiend does the opposite: its actions are to create areas of unclean fur and remove the areas of cleanliness. There is a clear parallel in the film between the demarcations of landscape and anti-landscape and the zoning of the bodies of the children between clean and unclean. The fiend transforms the cultivated spaces of civilisation back into the uncultivated wilderness of nature, across the topographies of both the landscape and the body. It uncivilises, driving human occupation – and its subordination of the topography – into retreat. The result of this is that the landscape moves to a form and function not only entirely outside anything useful or recognisable to civilisation, but fundamentally inimical to it. The primitive, atavistic and symbolically matriarchal become intrinsically associated with the wilderness, as the urban, modern, cultivated and symbolically patriarchal become associated with civilisation.

The fiend's awakening, from beneath the very land we cultivate, demonstrates the fallacy of our mastery over nature, the inherent fragility of civilisation and the lurking of our abject selves at our horizons. As Creed states in relation to *The Exorcist* (1973), but with relevance to *Satan's Claw* and other folk horror texts, the abject 'can never be successfully obliterated but lies in wait at the threshold of the subject's identity, threatening it with possible breakdown' (2007: 40). As with our bodies, our control of our landscape rests on our ability to subordinate it to our needs through constructs of ownership and function. And, as with our bodies, there are watchful threats waiting in the wilderness to resist civilisation and overturn its authority.

The resumption of the ownership of the feminine primitive wilderness over the masculine cultivated space is represented in other ways too. In *The Wicker Man* (1973), *Kill List* (2011) and *Dogged*, we see people dressed in animal masks at points where they are enacting ritualistic violence. The villagers of Summerisle and Farthing Island symbolically take on the roles of beasts in their reconnection with, veneration of and subordination to nature, becoming part of the wilderness itself. In *The Wicker Man*, the islanders similarly adopt animal masks when surreptitiously observing Sergeant Howie (Edward Woodward), the police officer from the mainland, while he is in his seaplane; in doing this they are arguably adopting a defensive guise, becoming part of the island wilderness into which they are seeking to integrate him, while protecting it from his interloping values.

The tension between patriarchal civilisation and matriarchal wilderness – and their competing ownerships and formation of space and function within the landscape – is a recurrent theme throughout British folk horror cinema. In *The Unkindness of Ravens*, Andrew is an amateur photographer and is encouraged by his counsellor to use his photography as a way of managing his trauma while he is at the Highland retreat. In doing so, Andrew is repeatedly confronted by images of atavistic horror, from episodes that cause him to re-experience his harrowing wartime experiences to his frequent sightings of ravens ripping at carcasses. This could be interpreted as Andrew's male gaze – a gaze he has brought from the urban, modern space – resisted by the matriarchal wilderness. Andrew uses his photography to attempt to capture those qualties he feels should be inherent in the landscape: it is tranquil, serene, restorative and inanimately attractive. However, the landscape itself appears to resist these efforts to be subordinated to Andrew's pereceptive needs. Instead, the topography offers up denuded, hostile or savage aspects of itself, challenging attempts to fit it into an imposed civilised ideal.

In *Dogged*, the opposition between the matriarchal wilderness and patriarchal civilisation is both more stark and more complex. The nature-worshipping cult exclusively comprises men. The men – heads covered by animal masks – smear their naked skin with blood, an abject reference to notions of masculinity associated with hunting and slaughter. The female villagers are explicitly excluded from the membership, rituals and spaces of the cult; towards the end of the film, the priest states that women have no place on the part of the island where the sacred standing stones are located. Women are separated from the sacred traditions of wilderness worship on Farthing Island and are instead confined to the civilised spaces. This speaks of a reversal of the usual symbolic associations between the rational masculine and the irrational feminine, with men occupying the numinous topography of the wilderness. However, excluding women from the uncultivated space, and confining them to the cultivated space, does not empower them by association with the modern, urban and civilised. Instead, it appears to diminish them as captives within the traditionally male space. *Dogged* presents us with an attempt to subordinate all space to patriarchal authority, whether through a microcosm of wider civilisation or by reforming the wilderness from a female, to a male, owned and utilised space. It is telling that the film ends with the women stoning the cult members within the stone circle, either killing them or inflicting life-limiting injuries, with Sam's mother stating 'we islanders handle our own problems'. This appears to indicate a victory for the civilised feminine over the irrational masculine and a crystallisation of this reversed dynamic. However, the final sequence of the film sees Sam's mother acknowledging the need to sacrifice her son, suggesting a victory for the wilderness and the traditional resumption of it as a symbolically matriarchal space.

The Fallow Field too plays with the subordination of feminine nature to masculine civilisation in the reversal of the farmer Calham's traditional role from establishing and managing the form and function of the earth to serving needs and functions that have no benefit to the sustenance and health of civilisation.

The resistance and restoration of the feminine wilderness sees a consequent resumption of those abject materials and behaviours cast out by the masculine status quo. This demonstrates the fragility of the patriarchal status quo, its laws and its structures. The awakening of atavistic threats from beneath the very land we walk upon and cultivate for our sustenance and survival tells us that our abject selves remain hidden at our horizons. In *Blood on Satan's Claw*, the abject fixation on the body and its matter is located within the feminine cult: a clear association between the feminine, the physical body and assaults upon it, and substances that come from it. For full acceptance into the sphere of patriarchal order, all forms of 'unacceptable, improper or unclean' speech, action or behaviour must be repressed or rejected (Creed 2007: 37). The abject state is associated with the archaic, the same ambiguous antiquity whence the fiend originates, and represents a point at which an understanding of physical boundaries coalesces. The corporeality of the cult members, and their sense of individuality and agency, is degraded, in that they are used to reproducing the form of the demon physically. As with the cultists in *The Wicker Man*, *Dogged* and *Kill List*, there is a permeability between civilisation and wilderness, between man and beast, represented in physical transformation and ritualistic dress and behaviour.

Conclusion

Landscape in folk horror cinema is more complex and nuanced than simply the setting for the restoration or clandestine continuation of atavistic, folkloristic practices hidden in plain sight in the British countryside. It provides topographies that explore notions of form, function, ownership and heritage. It repeatedly draws attention to the inherent hubris of civilisation in its assumption of unchallenged ownership over the environment and its unfettered freedom to subordinate it to self-serving functions. It suggests an unforeseen agency, sentience and autonomy within the wilderness that resist and snag at attempts to be subordinated to imposed, outside demands. Critically, it highlights the artificiality of the polarity between wilderness and civilisation, a division emphasised by human society to demarcate the environment according to utilitarian need. Instead, it presents us with a fluid, shifting boundary between the rational and irrational, the masculine and feminine, the cultivated and uncultivated, the secure and the unsecure. In this way civilisation is eroded, its essential self-belief and confidence undermined as those boundaries used to separate and define it from the untamed wild areas beyond are demonstrated to be untrustworthy.

References

Creed, Barbara (2007), *The Monstrous Feminine: Film, Feminine, Psychoanalysis*, 6th edn. London: Routledge.
Evans-Powell, David (2021), *The Blood on Satan's Claw*. Liverpool: Liverpool University Press.
Haggard, Piers (2019), 'Touching the Devil: The Making of *The Blood on Satan's Claw*', *The Blood on Satan's Claw* Blu-ray. Screenbound Productions.
Hoskins, W. G. (2005), *The Making of the English Landscape*. London: Hodder and Stoughton.

Hutchings, Peter (2004), 'Uncanny Landscapes in British Film and Television', *Visual Culture in Britain* 5:2, 27–40.
Johnston, Derek (2017), 'The Sublime Horror of the English Countryside', *Humanities Commons*, hcommons.org/deposits/item/hc:23929/ (accessed 30 April 2023).
Legard, Phil (2015), 'The Haunted Fields of England: Diabolical Landscapes and the *Genii locorum*', in Katherine Beem and Andy Paciorek (eds), *Folk Horror Revival: Field Studies*. Durham: Wyrd Harvest Press, pp. 365–379.
Macfarlane, Robert (2015), 'The Eeriness of the English Countryside', *Guardian*, 10 April, www.theguardian.com/books/2015/apr/10/eeriness-english-countryside-robert-macfarlane (accessed 30 April 2023).
Newland, Paul (2016), 'Folk Horror and the Contemporary Cult of British Rural Landscape: The Case of *Blood on Satan's Claw*', in Paul Newland (ed.), *British Rural Landscapes on Film*. Manchester: Manchester University Press, pp. 162–179.
Payne, Christiana (1994), *Toil and Plenty: Images of the Agricultural Landscape in England 1780–1890*. New Haven: Yale Centre for British Art/Yale University Press.
Scovell, Adam (2017), *Folk Horror: Hours Dreadful and Things Strange*. Leighton Buzzard: Auteur.
Short, John R. (1991), *Imagined Country: Society, Culture and Environment*. London: Routledge.
Wylie, John (2007), *Landscape*. London: Routledge.

12

Hieroglyphics: Arthur Machen on screen

Mark Goodall

> The nearest woods are now stricken with holy terror.
> (Jacques Réda, *The Ruins of Paris* (1996))

If folk horror can be defined as exploring the 'potential darkness of rural landscapes' (Hurley 2019), then the work of Arthur Machen (1863–1947) stands as an ideal representation of this theme. Machen explored the enchanted landscapes of his rural Welsh upbringing while at the same time transposing the terror of ancient traditional cultures onto the modern cityscape. Few adaptations of Machen's writings appear on film, but this chapter will explore those that do exist, along with the film *Holy Terrors: Six Weird Tales by Arthur Machen* (2017) co-produced and directed by the current author. I will discuss some of the key elements of folk horror and map those onto Machen's writings in order to reveal what the genre can offer future potential supernatural cinematic works.

Arthur Machen and folk horror

> In Machen's universe, horrific events aren't the result of human perversity; they are sewn inextricably into the fabric of nature. (Bradfield 2021)

Though Machen worked as a journalist, cataloguer, translator and actor, he is most famous today for his collection of novels and short stories concerning the relationship between the natural and supernatural realms. The secret mysteries of the British landscape and its profound effect on human characters seeps to some extent into almost all of Machen's storytelling. In *The Hill of Dreams* (1907), for example, written in the style of a *Künstlerroman* and one of Machen's most famous novels, a young aspiring author, Lucian, undergoes a profound occult experience in that ancient and mysterious Welsh countryside around Caerleon that Machen knew so well. In the story, Lucian's subjective experience continually comes up against the changes in both the hidden and the tangible natural world, and the form of external things affects him like a drug. He exists in a waking sleep where 'landscape is a sentient and menacing force to be struggled with' (Fisher 2010: xi). This idea connects with another television play linked with the folk horror genre, Alan Clarke's *Penda's Fen* (1974), where the 'erosion' of an individual's belief system occurs through a series of disturbing encounters with the landscape, a 'common component of many works often discussed under the banner of folk horror' (Scovell 2019: 85). Machen's episodic novel *The Three Imposters* (1895) includes the story *Novel of the White Powder*, in which a young lawyer is gradually corrupted (emotionally and physically) by a mysterious drug created out of the occult rituals of the ancient rural landscape, and other Machen texts explore similar terrain. Machen's stories tend towards the folk horror domain, where there exists a 'simultaneous grounding in the real world rural and the mythologizing effect it also rates, where fantastical surreal and horrific events can spring forth' (Scovell 2017: 81)

Machen's particular talent lies in developing a powerful atmosphere drawn from landscape – dark woods, imposing hills and ruined structures. This is expressed vividly in the 1949 sonnet entitled 'On Reading Arthur Machen' by one of Machen's staunchest admirers, the literary critic Frank Belknap Long (1949):

> There is a glory in the autumn wood;
> The ancient lanes of England wind and climb
> Past wizard oaks and gorse and tangled thyme
> To where a fort of mighty empire stood:
> There is a glamour in the autumn sky;
> The reddened clouds are writhing in the glow
> Of some great fire, and there are glints below
> Of tawny yellow where the embers die.
> I wait, for he will show me, clear and cold,
> High-raised in splendor, sharp against the North,
> The Roman eagles, and through mists of gold
> The marching legions as they issue forth:
> I wait, for I would share with him again
> The ancient wisdom, and the ancient pain.

The southern Welsh landscape is used as a backdrop for Machen's stories, as in 'The Great God Pan' (1894), or as a main feature of a narrative, almost a living presence, as in 'The Shining Pyramid' (1923). As Lovecraft observes, in paying tribute to Machen, his central preoccupation is that of the unseen uncanny and the form it takes: 'beneath the mounds and rocks of the wild Welsh hills dwell a squat primitive race whose vestiges give rise to our common folk legends of fairies, elves and the "little people"', whose actions disturb normal human existence (Lovecraft 1973: 92). Even the Machen stories set in urban locations (for which he has been identified, for example by Coverley (2006), as pioneer of psychogeography) are imbued with the supernatural spirits of the rural landscape, where the mystical intrudes upon the quotidian. A nice example of this is the story 'N', set in Stoke Newington, where a metropolitan vista glimpsed through a house window is in a moment transformed into a 'panorama of unearthly, of astounding beauty' (Machen 1975: 131) not unlike the lush, surreal terrain described in Edgar Allan Poe's *The Domain of Arnheim* (1847).

Despite the suggestive cinematic flourishes found in Machen's writings there are few adaptations of his work on film, but we can still consider how these, and his work as a whole, connect with what we now understand as the philosophy and aesthetics of a visual 'folk horror'. Thus far we have understood folk horror as largely a rural genre, the action taking place in country fields, pastures, churches and small remote villages where urban figures become exposed to some weird alternative reality. However, it is also a term that defies easy categorisation, in which the genre 'seems to be so many things inside and outside of reality' (Scovell 2017: 184). At the same time folk horror has been offered up as 'a way of opening up discussions on subtly interconnected work and how we now interact with such work' (6). Aside from the fact that filmmakers have utilised the British landscape as a 'heritage' marketing device to sell their films to foreign markets (Hutchings 2004), landscape plays an important role in any notion of 'folk horror', or, as Hutchings argues, as a form of 'anti-landscape', a 'landscape suffused with a sense of profound and sometimes apocalyptic anxiety ... a landscape of a comprehensive dispossession and vacancy' (2004: 29). On film, this landscape can be represented as 'abandoned' or 'savage and pagan'. Writing at the monumental high point of industrialisation and urbanisation, Machen was aware that the push to replace the natural ancient world with the rational and scientific would lead to a violent clash, the eruption of suppressed spirit myths into the modern.[1]

It is worth noting that while Machen's stories do contain 'horror' elements they are more often categorised under the term 'supernatural'. Mark Gatiss's definition of folk horror in his *A History of Horror* TV series as a body of work sharing a 'common obsession with the British landscape, its folklore and superstitions' is, I think, a good description of Machen's principle drive. Further, in retrospect, we can see that Machen's work demonstrates a deep and profound engagement with Scovell's three points of categorisation for folk horror, in that he (1) uses folklore to imbue his work with a sense of the arcane for eerie, uncanny or horrific purposes (for example 'The Shining Pyramid'); (2) presents a clash between such arcana and their presence within close proximity to some form of modernism ('The Novel of the White Powder'); and (3) has created his own folklore through various forms of popular conscious memory (the legend of 'The Bowman' (1914)) (Scovell 2019: 7).[2]

Machen's conception of *ecstasy* as a 'desire for the unknown' expressed (in art) through the manifestation of an 'other consciousness' of humankind, a 'shadowy, unknown or half-known Companion who walks beside each one of us all our days' (Machen 1960: 12), relates to certain aspects of horror (in this passage he cites Poe as an example of this tendency).[3] As the surrealist and impressionist filmmakers discovered, the film camera has a powerful hypnotic capacity to 'penetrate beneath the surface of the apparently normal and secure' (Butler 1967: 10) and to reveal this 'shadowy unknown' in a haunting and unforgettable manner. The camera's capacity for 'drawing the spectator into itself by use of the close-up' (Butler 1967: 10) is an aspect that I tried to draw on in my adaption of Machen's stories. Horror's capacity to reanimate ancient beliefs and old religions, as evident in folk horror especially, finds expression in Machen's writings and philosophy.

Holy Terrors: a twenty-first-century adaptation

The questions concerning the adaptation of a literary work into a work of moving pictures are numerous and problematic. In this section I seek to explore some of these as applied to my own setting of six of Arthur Machen's short stories as a portmanteau feature film: *Holy Terrors: Six Weird Tales by Arthur Machen*, co-directed and produced with Julian Butler and released by Obsolete in April 2017. I will also discuss how the film relates to certain aspects of folk horror (those already identified and some suggested new additions), both in its conception and realisation, even though, in common with the original trio of films subsequently marked as such by Scovell (2017), it was not consciously produced as a folk horror film.

Aside from the prospect of 'filming' Arthur Machen as an exercise in creative expression, I was conscious, as noted above, of the fact that there are few cinematic adaptations of his writings. In fact, the only audio-visual adaptation of a Machen story to hand is a version of his story 'The Shining Pyramid', made in 1979 and starring Edward Petherbridge and Anton Rodgers. This TV film, originally shown in two parts, was made by HTV Wales for its *Border Country* series created by poet Emyr Humphreys. The film was directed by Gareth Davies. The adaptation is intriguing in relation to folk horror, as it sets out to explore the common Machen theme as discussed previously: namely, the curious relationship between the modern and ancient worlds, signified by Vaughan (Petherbridge), a poetic writer, and Dyson (Rodgers), a Harley Street GP. The film opens with Dyson's car traversing the River Severn crossing as ominous and eerie music plays. This echoes the transitory sequence in some adaptations of Bram Stoker's *Dracula*, especially F. W. Murnau's *Nosferatu* (1922), when Hutter crosses a bridge and the boundary between the real world, and the nightmare is marked by the intertitle 'And when he crossed the bridge, the phantoms came to meet him.' The dichotomy between the ancient and modern is clearly symbolised by the journey from 'civilised' London to the 'barbaric' Welsh border land. The film is a loose adaptation of Machen's original story, with new characters added and others altered completely (the missing girl Annie, for example, is transformed here into a witch). The adaptation reflects the recent contemporaneous countercultural preoccupations with the occult, with the character of Vaughan repeatedly spouting esoteric beliefs (Jung's notion of the 'collective unconscious' and various eastern mystical ideas) to emphasise the narrative's tension between rationalism and spiritualism. Vaughan urges Dyson to 'see through the veils of sense' in order to understand the effect the ancient landscape is having, and the question of whether this is 'sorcery or sanctity' appears throughout. The film captures the atmosphere of Machen's Welsh territory, utilising a sense of a 'Welsh weird', where the Roman amphitheatre of Caerleon which Machen was fascinated by is (still today) a 'brooding presence at twilight' (Russell 2019: vii). Caerleon becomes 'Caermaen' in some of Machen's stories, most notably as the background for *The Hill of Dreams*. Other Welsh locations that feature in the story are the valley of Soar in Gwent and the medieval bridge at Newbridge-on-Usk (also Gwent), described in 'The Shining Pyramid', which is seen in a landscape montage at the end. The final shot is of the Glen Usk house, while the narrator (Vaughan) intones: 'On such a day I saw that lovely valley and the river winding in mystic esses and the forest bending down to it. And I saw the house between the forest and the river and out of them I struggled to discover the soul of a strange country and exchange it for my own.' This final paraphrasing of Machen lyrically expresses the psychological effect of such a location on the sensitive mind of a human individual.

At first glance, one difference between *Holy Terrors* and 'The Shining Pyramid' is that visually the latter stays resolutely in the 'real world', whereas the former mostly stays in the 'weird' world of the unknown. This is largely a result of the difference between a television adaption and a cinematic one. Television productions at this time (especially low-budget ones) often drew on theatrical devices to relay the narrative. This accounts for the somewhat hammy nature of the acting and the straightforward script-based direction. As noted though, Davies's film makes effective use of location, and with *Holy Terrors* we took note of this 'landscape-character', making sure that the location and setting were key components of the film (although our settings are not as clearly identifiable to an audience), Machen's narratives being as much about place as they are about people.

The creators of *Holy Terrors* were keenly aware that Machen's bibliophilic followers would be suspicious about a film adaptation of the stories. Most cinematic adaptations of literary works ruin the power of the text by alteration, simplification, literalisation and misinterpretation, the main corruption being to actualise in visual form something that is elusive, imaginary and poetic. The *ekphrasis* in the original text becomes, through the medium of moving pictures, a crass realisation of these subtle poetics. Nevertheless, we were aiming to capture some of the 'ecstasy' of the Machen stories as relating to his ideas about the supernatural in art. This concept derives from Machen's own thinking about the power of expression. As he notes in his essay on 'fine literature', 'Hieroglyphics', regarding 'ecstasy':

> Substitute, if you like, rapture, beauty, adoration, wonder, awe, mystery, sense of the unknown, desire for the unknown. All and each will convey what I mean; for some particular case one term may be more appropriate than another, but in every case there will be that withdrawal from the common life and the common consciousness which justifies my choice of 'ecstasy' as the best symbol of my meaning. (Machen 1960: 21)

Machen applied this term to texts and identified 'ecstasy' as writing that 'leaves the street and the high road to wander the eternal hills' (48). It is an art form that proceeds from the placement of the human organism in the midst of the natural world laced with an existential 'mood of lonely reverie' (176). He also, in passing, noted the artifice of photography, stating that 'the camera and the soul of man are two different things' (65). Yet I am arguing here that the thrust behind the meaning can be applied to other art forms, or hybrid forms of expression, such as those adaptations made for the *Holy Terrors* film.[4] Machen was scathing of the attempt in art to use embellishments in place of true artistry – 'Let the artifice be sufficiently artificial and it will be art' (70) – a process we could use to condemn many TV and film adaptations of literary works, with their emphasis on sensation and immediacy. Rather than a surfeit of exposition and quickly dated special effects, it is the small detail, 'the Idea that lies buried beneath the plot' (79), that retains a deeper (if somewhat latent) power.[5]

In terms of the art of cinema itself, the approach we took to realising Machen's stories was inspired in part by the writings of the French surrealist playwright and filmmaker Antonin Artaud (1896–1948). Artaud's concept of the 'Theatre of Cruelty' was an influential form of theatre, a means by which an artist assaults the senses of the audience, opening them up to feeling the unexpressed emotions of the subconscious. With *Holy Terrors* we tried to offer our viewers a palpable sense of the occult and the unknown, which, if not an outright 'assault' of the kind Artaud and fellow avant-garde practitioners intended, was still designed to be the overwhelming sensation (rather than sentimentalisation or easy comprehension).

However, it was Artaud's brief but important essay called 'Sorcery and the Cinema', written around 1928 when cinema was a new art form, that we found most striking. In the essay, Artaud argues that cinema contains 'a whole element of contingency and mystery' that can't be found in other art forms; film offers a 'secret movement of images': this we can interpret as the way in which film has the potential to invoke or express elements of the occult. Artaud is particularly interested in the way that cinema isolates and fetishises objects and 'endows them with a second life' (Artaud 2000: 103). We decided it was crucial that our representation of Machen's stories bring such techniques to bear on our rendition of the elements of the stories. This not only relates to objects such as leaves, trees, buildings and domestic items, but also to the representation of the human face, especially the eyes. Many of the scenes in the film try to express the emotion of the characters and offer, through the way that the landscape of face is filmed, a glimpse into their souls (we often did this instead of showing actual events and actions from the stories: see the climatic ending of 'The Happy Children', for example).

Artaud was also fascinated by the distortions of the film camera lens, and this creative practical aspect of filmmaking is also evident in *Holy Terrors*. Examples of can be found in the story of 'The Cosy Room' when the looming, twisted shapes of the viaduct echo the anguish of the murderer and his black conscience, and 'The Ritual' when the hideous faces of the children are contorted out of all proportion. At the same time the *photogénie* of the film image could be brought to bear on the elements of Machen's stories to create wonder and mystery. *Photogénie* was a process beloved of the surrealist artists and, according to Robert B. Ray, is defined as the way that the camera renders ordinary objects 'luminous and spellbinding' (Ray 2001: 4). We replicate this in *Holy Terrors*: the white powder in the story of the same name, the woods in summertime, a landlady's craggy face …

Artaud believed that the true potential of film was that it could evade 'stupid order and habitual clarity' and fully realise the supernatural, arguing that 'If the cinema isn't made to express dreams or everything that in waking life has something in common with dreams, then it has no point' (Artaud 2000: 104). The 'chance' elements favoured by surrealist filmmakers echo Machen words: 'the finest things are not designed' (Machen 1960: 126).

So much for the conceptual dimension to the conceiving of *Holy Terrors*. We can now move on to the making of the film itself as an example of a 'folk horror' film.

Form

> In his essay on the uncanny, *Das Unheimliche*, Freud said that the uncanny is the only feeling which is more powerfully experienced in art than in life. If the genre required any justification, I should think this alone would serve as its credentials. (Stanley Kubrick in Ciment 2001)

The first consideration was how to present Machen's stories as a complete finished film. Here, we were reminded of those portmanteau horror films of the 1970s, films such as *Asylum* (1972), *Tales from the Crypt* (1972) and *The Vault of Horror* (1973). While this compilation style of film has its limitations, with Machen we believed it would work, as it would retain the 'literary' form of the selected short stories (and at the same time echo the Penguin collection *Holy Terrors*, published in 1946 shortly before Machen's death). I would argue in any case that Machen's work was that of the artistic 'film age', not the 'movie' age (when the commercialisation of cinema became perfected by the American studios known colloquially as 'Hollywood'). Machen's writing seems closer to the mysterious early cinema experiments of the French impressionist and surrealist pioneers (such as Artaud) and the German expressionist films that emerged around the same time that Hollywood developed.

One of the most memorable films from this tradition that I personally had in mind when adapting the Machen stories was *The Fall of the House of Usher* (1928), adapted from Edgar Allan Poe's story by Jean Epstein (co-written with Luis Buñuel), where a terrain profoundly affects the human players caught in its power. It is probably the 1960 Roger Corman adaptation of the Poe tale that is most famous, which, with its garish colour schemes and sets and over-the-top acting by Vincent Price, is rightly acclaimed as a masterpiece of modern gothic horror. Yet my feeling was that Machen's stories required a different approach, and the Epstein film plays more around the latent and magical aspects of the dream world that Machen (and Poe) loved to evoke. Epstein used 'slow-motion in narrative not as a symbol of a state of mind or physiological state but for a profounder metaphysical or poetic purpose' (Montagu 1964: 42). In *Theory of Film* Siegfried Kracauer suggests that Epstein's technique 'makes an effort to suggest the presence of supernatural influences through visuals which are straight records of material phenomena' (Kracauer 1978: 91). There are scenes in Epstein's film that are some of the most beautiful and evocative ever made (the scene where Roderick Usher sings 'The Haunted Palace', or where Madeline reappears from the tomb, for example), and we wanted to capture some of this in our film. The 'beauty' of horror, not always realised but evident since the earliest films of the genre (Dreyer's extraordinary *Vampyr* (1932), for example) was something we tried to retain in the framing and lighting of characters and settings, with a nod towards the 'transcendental style' defined by Paul Schrader (Schrader 1972).

Freud's concept of *das Unheimliche* ('uncanny' or 'strangely familiar') was also significant – a mood captured in, for example, the early expressionist films of F. W. Murnau and the films of Jacques Tourneur, whose *Night of the Demon* (1957) is identified as one of the first folk horror films. We thus set out deliberately to make the stories in *Holy Terrors* 'strange'. Russian formalist critic Viktor Shklovsky called this 'making strange' *ostranenie*, the evocation of the puzzling and the weird. In cinema, *ostranenie* occurs when the indexical reality of the film photographic image is challenged, upturned and reworked by the inclusion of elements that disturb the perspective of film realism. Obviously, this occurs at different levels within different film genres, but in the realm of the supernatural film great use can be made of 'making strange' the everyday. It has been known for years that the 'unseen is often more frightening than the seen' (Butler 1967: 13).

It was not only in the imagery of *Holy Terrors* that we tried to express this. In the adaptation of 'The Cosy Room', for example, the confusion around precisely what has happened or not in the main character's narrative is left ambiguous (as I believe it is in the original 1929 story). It is possible that the only concrete assertion to be made about the story is that it is a tale about (religious) guilt, how landscape closes in on a character in a way that can be real or imaginary and how the senses of a human being can be overwhelmed by the tormented workings of internal mind. The images that flow past during the film are indeed puzzling and strange – fragments of anguish and fear and delusion – but so is the outcome at the end of the story, and we retained this by abstruse use of the setting and the actor's performance. It is fair to say that Machen preferred to retain this ambiguity in his work, letting the reader establish the 'facts' about the subject of the narrative, rather than supplying a ready and satisfying conclusion to the story.[6] All we know is that the landscape surrounding the protagonist, in true Machen style, tragically alters their consciousness.

We also sought to imitate certain aspects of pyschogeographical and hauntological states. Psychogeography is now a widely used term, writers such as Will Self and Iain Sinclair routinely adapting it in their work. It derives from the (often inebriated) practices of radical French groups the Situationist International and the Lettrist International who sought to escape the dreariness of modern capitalism by following their autonomous dreams, drifting across the city and writing down the results. Psychogeography is defined as 'the study of the precise laws and specific effects of the geographical environment, consciously organized or not, on the emotions and behaviour of individuals' (Debord 2007: 8). The *dérive*, meanwhile, is another revolutionary strategy defined as 'a mode of experimental behaviour linked to the conditions of urban society: a technique of rapid passage through varied ambiances' (Knabb 2007: 51). We also had in mind the fabulous Lettrist text 'Formulary for a New Urbanism' by Ivan Chtcheglov. Chtcheglov writes:

> You can't take three steps without encountering ghosts bearing all the prestige of their legends. We move within a *closed* landscape whose landmarks constantly draw us toward the past. Certain *shifting* angles, certain *receding* perspectives, allow us to glimpse original conceptions of space, but this vision remains fragmentary. It must be sought in the magical locales of fairy tales and surrealist writings: castles, endless walls, little forgotten bars, mammoth caverns, casino mirrors. (Chtcheglov, 1953)

This inspired us to make manifest, through sound and image, the psychic affect of space on the characters in the *Holy Terrors* tales.

Machen is claimed by some critics as a harbinger of these concepts, with his emphasis on the liberatory sense created by a rejection of rational certainty (the driver for capital) and a profound engagement with the occult manifestations of certain landscapes and sites. While psychogeography is generally understood to be an urban phenomenon, its effect can take place also at a rural level, as we see in 'Midsummer' during Leonard's meditation on his found retreat (the precise location of which we remain unsure of) in comparison with the London he has left. It is also evident in 'The Cosy Room', although the psychogeographical outcome of this story, while possibly a release, is largely malevolent. 'Hauntology', meanwhile – a phrase coined by the French philosopher Jacques Derrida – relates to 'undecidability', and has been applied by cultural critics to any state where experiences, narratives and phenomenon can't be fully 'explained'. Derrida used the term politically to critique the supposed 'death of communism', and yet it can also be useful in comprehending the psychic state where one is not sure about the 'truth' or otherwise of a moment, situation or experience. Machen's characters often exist in this in-between world, and not always successfully. Hauntology has been identified in relation to folk horror as being both 'the resurgence, with hindsight, of interest in occultism' and the 'presence of an urban setting' in rural film genres (Scovell 2017: 123). The character in 'The Cosy Room' experiences the intense psychological pressures, moral and physical, of both urban and rural territories.

Sound and image

In film theory and criticism it is often the image that is privileged over the audio dimension. This is a pity, as it is frequently the sound dimension of a film that is most crucial. We certainly took this into consideration in the post-production of *Holy Terrors*. The soundscape of the film was designed to be like another character, another dimension to the drama. In 'The Cosy Room', the music (composed by David Chatton Barker) is the only sound we actually hear; there is no dialogue, nor any sound effect used (other than those suggested and evoked by the music). As with the 'Shining Pyramid' TV episode, the music had to express both the uncanny, mystical nature of the locations and the inner psyche of the protagonists. The briefly psychedelic sequence at the end of 'The Shining Pyramid' is echoed in 'Midsummer' (and the opening of 'The Happy Children') where the landscape of the ancient woods and the mysteries they evoke overwhelm the characters. The other crucial dimension to the soundscape is the narration, spoken by two actors, Joyce Branagh and Jon Preece. We took great care to find the correct tone and inflection to the voices. If the story is to be completely narrated (without any dialogue) then the voice must be captivating and express the language, the 'literariness' of the author (Machen).

The images in *Holy Terrors* pass slowly and deliberately. Artaud noted that cinema in its raw state is akin to the 'atmosphere of the trance' (Artaud 2000: 104), and we sought to capture this dream-like state. The film was shot at a higher frame rate, so that when viewed back everything is illusory. There is much to criticise about the digital camera, but we were able to utilise the clarity and sharpness of the image to suggest the external reality of the drama, while the slow pace and the filters rendered the entire narrative dream-like and woozy. 'The Shining Pyramid' now seems slightly dated with its 'theatrical' presentation of the drama and the acting style (Gareth Davies was an actor as well as a director), but in *Holy Terrors* we endeavoured to tone down the acting and reduce the principle characters to ciphers for Machen's text (which we hardly altered at all). In opposition to creating an external drama that viewers simply 'watch' we were conscious of Artaud's claim that 'Cinema seems to me to be made, above all else, to express things of the mind, the inner life of consciousness, not so much through the play of images as through something more imponderable that restores them to us with their matter intact, without intermediate forms, without representations' (Artaud 2000: 104).

The final story in *Holy Terrors*, 'Midsummer', is evocative of the eerie atmosphere created by the 1967 novel *Picnic at Hanging Rock* by Joan Lindsay. A film by Peter Weir, another progenitor of folk horror, was subsequently made of the novel, and there are some traces of this work in 'Midsummer'. First, the idea of strange occurrences, not within the gloom of night or the shadows, but in broad and intense daylight, was fascinating to us and seemed appropriate for this particular Machen story. Second, the idea of a study of female innocence imbued with a hint of mystery, sexuality and the occult was a powerful aspect of the novel and the film, albeit one that is potentially problematic from a contemporary perspective.

In Machen's written work the same theme is evident. In *The Hill of Dreams*, for example, Lucian's muse Annie is described as 'the symbol of all mystic womanhood' (Machen 2010: 193). The scene at the end of 'Midsummer' where the narrator (Leonard) appears to experience visions of an occult ritual involving the 'girls of the village' seemed to echo elements of the potent sexuality of landscape in *Picnic at Hanging Rock* and other folk horror narratives, including the TV version of 'The Shining Pyramid' and our own film *Holy Terrors* (see Figure 12.1a–b).[7]

In an epigram at the start of the novel, Joan Lindsay quotes lines from Edgar Allan Poe's poem 'Dream within a Dream': 'All that we see or seem / Is but a dream within a dream / Is all that we see or seem / But a dream within a dream?' (Poe 1850). However, in Weir's film version Poe's words are altered to become 'What we see, and what we seem, are but a dream, a dream within a dream.' This sense of bewilderment is key to the best works

Figure 12.1a–b Leonard's point of view of 'the girls of the village' in the woods in *Holy Terrors*, 2017

of the mysterious and the supernatural, and lies at the heart of folk horror cinema. Meanwhile in our adaptation of story of 'The Ritual' we sought to highlight the spirit of the Bacchanalian ceremony found often in the folk horror film. As Machen noted referring to this, 'If a writer can create the image of eternal human ecstasy, we are agreed that in such a case the writer is an artist' (Machen 1960: 168).

Inevitably, adapting an exceptional body of literary work into something as transient as a feature film is challenging. It is clear that the work of Arthur Machen is related to ideas about what constitutes folk horror as it 'connects the past and present to create a clash of belief systems and people' (Scovell 2017: 183). Film adaptations of Machen's stories can therefore make a contribution to 'a type of social map that tracks unconscious ley lines between a huge range of different forms of media' (Scovell 2017: 183). In *Holy Terrors* we ultimately sought to step away from trying to represent Machen's majestic textual imagery with the panoply of film tricks: complex special effects and grandiose props and settings (although this was also a budgetary consideration). Instead, we adopted the approach taken by the early pioneers of film impressionism, where the viewer's imaginative mind, like that of a reader, supplies all the fear, enchantment and ecstasy that are required for an experience that is unusual and profound. In doing this we can say that *Holy Terrors* can be appraised as a contribution to the (albeit shifting and contested) genre of folk horror.

Notes

1 This theme continues today with works such as Lars von Trier's *The Kingdom* (1994).
2 This is Machen's most famous story, in which the ghostly spirits of the bowmen of Agincourt return to help the English army defeat the Germans during the First World War.
3 The concept also connects with Paul Schrader's notion of the 'Wholly Other' in cinema, a phenomenon going beyond the normal human experience (Schrader 1972) that is akin to the religious themes, however perverted, of many folk horror films.
4 My interpretation is that Machen felt, in the early twentieth century, that the photographic image, with its 'automatic' reference to reality, shows too much to be truly 'ecstatic'; this is something we grappled with in our adaptation of his writings by adopting the surrealist *détournement* of the automatic nature of the film camera.
5 The example Machen is discussing here is *Dr Jekyll and Mr Hyde*. Ray (2000) also discusses this in relation to film adaptation.

6 Something critics of Machen complain about, of course. In a discussion some years ago on Machen's work with Harry Kümel, the director told me that in his view Machen 'couldn't do endings'.
7 A fascinating reading of the occult aspects of the novel can be found in *The Murders at Hanging Rock* by Yvonne Rousseau (1988).

References

Artaud, Antonin (2000), 'Sorcery and Cinema', in Paul Hammond (ed. and trans.), *The Shadow and Its Shadow: Surrealist Writings on the Cinema*. San Francisco: City Lights Books.
Bradfield, Scott (2021), 'The Ecstasies of Arthur Machen', *Los Angeles Review of Books*, 24 July, lareviewofbooks.org/article/the-ecstasies-of-arthur-machen/ (accessed 30 April 2023).
Butler, Ivan (1967), *The Horror Film*. London: Zwemmer.
Chtcheglov, Ivan (1953), 'Formulary for a New Urbanism', Bureau of Public Secrets, www.bopsecrets.org/SI/Chtcheglov.htm (accessed 30 April 2023).
Ciment, Michael (2001), *Kubrick*. London: Faber.
Coverley, Merlin (2006), *Psychogeography*. Harpenden: Pocket Essentials.
Debord, Guy (2007), 'Introduction to a Critique of Urban Geography', trans. Ken Knabb, in *The Situationist International Anthology* (Berkeley: Bureau of Public Secrets, 1981), pp. 23–27.
Fisher, Catherine (2010), 'Foreword', in Arthur Machen, *The Hill of Dreams*. Parthian: Library of Wales, pp. ix–xiii.
Hurley, Andrew Michael (2019), 'Devils and Debauchery: Why We Love to Be Scared by Folk Horror', *Guardian*, 28 October, www.theguardian.com/books/2019/oct/28/devils-and-debauchery-why-we-love-to-be-scared-by-folk-horror (accessed 30 April 2023).
Hutchings, Peter (2004), 'Uncanny Landscapes in British Film and Television', *Visual Culture in Britain* 5:2, 27–40.
Knabb, Ken (2007), 'Definitions' (*Internationale Situationniste #1* (Paris, June 1958)), *Bureau of Public Secrets*, www.bopsecrets.org/SI/1.definitions.htm (accessed 4 May 2022).
Kracauer, Siegfried (1978), *Theory of Film*. Oxford: Oxford University Press.
Long, Frank Belknap (1949), 'On Reading Arthur Machen: A Sonnet'. Pengrove: Dog and Duck Press.
Lovecraft, H. P. (1973), *Supernatural Horror in Literature*. Mineola, NY: Dover Publications.
Machen, Arthur (1960), *Hieroglyphics: A Note upon Ecstasy in Literature*. London: Unicorn Press.
Machen, Arthur (1975), 'N', in *Tales of Horror and the Supernatural*. St Albans: Panther, pp. 117–142.
Machen, Arthur (2010), *The Hill of Dreams*. Cardigan: Parthian Books.
Montagu, Ivor (1964), *Film World*. Harmondsworth: Penguin.
Poe, Edgar Allan (1850), 'A Dream within a Dream', in *The Works of the Late Edgar Allan Poe*, ed. R. W. Griswold. New York: J. S. Redfield, available at www.poetryfoundation.org/poems/52829/a-dream-within-a-dream (accessed 10 May 2023).

Ray, Robert B. (2000), 'Mystery Trains', *Sight and Sound*, November.
Ray, Robert B. (2001), 'How a Film Theory Got Lost', in *How a Film Theory Got Lost and Other Mysteries in Cultural Studies*. Bloomington: Indiana University Press, pp. 1–14.
Réda, Jacques (1996), *The Ruins of Paris*. London: Reaktion Books.
Rousseau, Yvonne (1988), *The Murders at Hanging Rock*. Melbourne: Sun Books.
Russell, R. B. (2019), *Occult Territory: An Arthur Machen Gazetteer*. Leyburn: Tartarus Press.
Schrader, Paul (1972), *Transcendental Style in Film: Ozu, Bresson Dreyer*. Boston, MA: Da Capo Press.
Scovell, Adam (2017), *Folk Horror: Hours Dreadful and Things Strange*. Leighton Buzzard: Auteur.
Scovell, Adam (2019), 'And in the Soil, There Be Mirrors: *Penda's Fen* and Folk Horror', in Matthew Harle and James Machin (eds), *Of Mud & Flame: The 'Penda's Fen' Sourcebook*. London: Strange Attractor, pp. 83–90.

13

Albion unearthed: social, political and cultural influences on British folk horror, urban wyrd and backwoods cinema

Andy Paciorek

I recall once being told that 'Design is objective. Art is subjective', and whilst I believe that holds fast with regard to design, which by its very nature entails the creation of something that will serve a specific task or solve a particular problem, I have always thought that art occupies a greyer area. I feel this is particularly true in the narrative arts, especially the art of filmmaking. There is most frequently the clear objective of telling a story, albeit one wrapped in a particular style. Furthermore, movie directors and their creative teams employ all manner of techniques and additional factors, from music to pace to colour schemes and beyond, to evoke a certain mood or feelings within the viewer. There are of course auteurs such as the American film director David Lynch, who is well known both for cryptic storytelling in movies such as *Mulholland Drive* (2001) and the television show/film *Twin Peaks* (1990–1991, 1992, 2017) and for being tight-lipped on the meaning of his films, stating 'I don't ever explain it. Because it's not a word thing. It would reduce it, make it smaller.' But he also notes: 'I need to know for myself what things mean and what's going on. Sometimes I get ideas, and I don't know exactly what they mean. So, I think about it, and try to figure it out, so I have an answer for myself' (Carroll 2018). Many other filmmakers have a clear story to tell in a forthright manner, but that may not be the whole picture, so to speak. Beneath the apparent drama unfolding there may be another tale symbolically veiled. This secondary narrative or message may be hidden for deliberate reasons, such as for the sake of protection of the creator, to avoid political censors or for other reasons; however, in other cases the presence of a subtext may not have been consciously intended by writer or director but may be a manifestation of the influence of the times or conditions in which the film was made and viewed.

One notable famous case of a strong secondary message, which is relevant topic-wise to this study of folk horror, was first brought not to screen but to stage in 1953 by the American playwright Arthur Miller. Miller's play *The Crucible* is based upon the Salem witch trials, a tragic true-life event that befell the area around Salem in Massachusetts between 1692 and 1693. A mixture of mass psychogenic illness, religious fundamentalism, petty rivalry, gossip and the socio-psychological effects of isolation in colonial frontiers resulted in a number of townsfolk and villagers facing trial and prosecution for the crime of witchcraft. At least twenty-five people died because of these trials and judgments, most of them unsurprisingly women, as 'Puritans viewed the female body as weaker than the male body, meaning it was believed that the Devil could more easily invade a female body and possess her soul in doing so than it could a male body' (Arva 2017). The Salem witch trials themselves present information regarding gender politics in America both in the seventeenth century and moving forward to the present day. Its grim portrait of the belief in and reaction against the suspected crime of witchcraft has earned Miller's play and the film adaptations *Hexenjagd*, or *Les Sorcières de Salem* (1957) and *The Crucible* (1996) their place in the folk horror canon. However, *The Crucible* was also a deliberate allegory of McCarthyism. Named after Senator Joseph McCarthy (1908–1957), McCarthyism in its essence existed before his time in office, and lingered after his death. The paranoia, fervour and fear that developed as a consequence of McCarthyism's endeavours were reminiscent of the actions and social atmosphere of the time to the historical 'witch-hunts'. As a result of his personal experience of McCarthyism, Miller wrote *The Crucible* in response, stating in 1996 (when involved with the screenplay of the film adaptation of that year):

> *The Crucible* was an act of desperation. Much of my desperation branched out, I suppose, from a typical Depression-era trauma ... the blow struck on the mind by the rise of European Fascism and the brutal anti-Semitism it had brought to power. But by 1950, when I began to think of writing about the hunt for Reds in America, I was motivated in some great part by the paralysis that had set in among many liberals who, despite their discomfort with the inquisitors' violations of civil rights, were fearful, and with good reason, of being identified as covert Communists if they should protest too strongly. (Miller 1996)

Another film that directly utilises the witch panic era as an allegory for the political situation in which it was born is Otakar Vávra's 1970 Czech movie *Kladivo na čarodějnice* (*Witchhammer*). The film experts Kat Ellinger and Peter Hames both note the proximity and association between this movie detailing the historical trials and injustices of the scourge on accused witches in Moravia in the 1670s with the Soviet invasion of Czechoslovakia in 1968 and the subsequent communist show trials that followed (see Hames 2010; Ellinger 2018).

Though perhaps not as specifically politically motivated, several other folk horror films are indeed the fruit of the times they were conceived in. In seeking the subtext of a film there is always the potential of bias in any critical film theorisation and the risk of reading too much into the narrative; nonetheless, British folk horror, the associated subgenre of 'backwoods' and the urban wyrd mode all offer up interesting suppositions about the spirit of the times they were born into. Urban wyrd is a term originated by the writer and filmmaker Adam Scovell (2021) and, following discussion between him and myself, explored further in the books *Folk Horror Revival: Urban Wyrd 1: Spirits of Time* (Paciorek and Silver 2019a) and *Folk Horror Revival: Urban Wyrd: Spirits of Place* (Paciorek and Silver 2019b). Briefly, urban wyrd is not simply 'folk horror in a city', and is not actually a genre but a loose mode. Allied particularly to the concepts of psychogeography, hauntology and the uncanny, and relating to the Old English word *wyrd* meaning fate, the urban wyrd gives agency to the built-up environment, liminal areas and technology that affect a person psychologically (even if unrealised save perhaps for a strange sense of uneasiness) – and when applied also to fiction/folkloric storytelling the urban environment or the technology of the time set can strongly dictate the narrative or perhaps even be seen as a character in its own right.

Before we delve into cinematic examples, it is worth considering the revolution in both British cinema and television in the 1960s. In the late 1950s and 1960s filmmaking and programming became more accessible to working-class creatives who wanted to tell their own stories, and those of people they identified with, in their own way. Thus was born the element of British New Wave cinema known as kitchen sink realism; a mode that continues strongly in current times in varied forms in much of the UK's film and TV output. The moniker 'kitchen sink' arose in 1954 when art critic David Sylvester commented that the artwork of John Bratby and other social realism painters contained 'everything except the kitchen sink, no, the kitchen sink too' (Sylvester 1954). It was not meant to be complimentary, but it was apt and was adopted to refer also to films, photography, theatre and TV shows that depicted life experienced by many working-class or unemployed Britons in all its grim glory: poor living conditions, little income, harsh experiences – real life. Whilst some of the situations and dwelling spaces to be found in films such as *A Taste of Honey* (1961), *Alfie* (1966) and *Kes* (1969) may be considered horrible, horrific even, they are a long way from horror movies as such. Horror films do not necessarily depict real life as we know it, but may offer a form of escapism, albeit an oft-uncomfortable escape. It may be argued, however, that the best 'horror' (that which scares the most) is successful because it places the viewer in a position and setting where they can identify with the people and places involved in the drama – where they could truly imagine such things happening to them no matter how initially fantastic the premise may be. Though much of the first wave of British folk horror was still quite distant from kitchen sink in style (something that would change over time, as we will discuss later), being more like *The Crucible* than *Coronation Street*, a television play that could be considered a precursor to *The Wicker Man* hinted at it.

Of the three 'big' British folk horror movies of the first wave, only one, *The Wicker Man* (1973), was set in contemporary times. The other two, *Witchfinder General* (1968) and *Blood on Satan's Claw* (1971) were set in the seventeenth and eighteenth centuries respectively. Matthew Hopkins, the titular Witchfinder General, was an actual historical figure, who, along with his associate John Stearne, was responsible for the condemnation, trial and execution of more people in England in the period 1644–1647 than any other such authority in over 100 years prior. Hopkins's career was short but lucrative, yet he was not to enjoy a long opulent retirement, for he died from suspected tuberculosis in 1647, aged no more than twenty-eight years at most. In Michael Reeve's 1968 film Hopkins is portrayed by the much older Vincent Price, appearing in one of his most sombre and powerful roles. Neither the film nor the novel by Ronald Bassett (1966) upon which it is based remains entirely loyal to historical accuracy, although some social and political factors remain. It is set against the backdrop of the English Civil War, when the times were ripe for the direst consequences of othering, and the fear of witchcraft was also prevalent. This was a situation that the likes of Hopkins and Stearne were keen and ready to exploit. Whilst there were elements of religious zealotry, the handsome financial rewards that could be claimed by witchfinders could lead to questions about the true nature of their motives. Furthermore, since torture was an integral tool to the profession, confessions and accusations of further suspects were prevalent, but as Reeves's film portrays, there could also have been sadistic motivation present within those active in the witchfinding trade.

Within the context of the late 1960s, religious sectarianism was far from being a thing of the past. Its presence was and is still felt most strongly in Northern Ireland but it also exists to a lesser degree in Scottish and English locales such as Glasgow and Liverpool. As with the English Civil War, the religious differences between the different Christian camps were not the sole factor of adversity, with the divisions even filtering down to the world of sport, whereby conflict between supporters of different football teams that historically were either Protestant or Catholic club may occur (see Richardson 2016). Furthermore, a section of the 1960s hippy movement followed esoteric curiosity into what was dubbed the 'Occult Revival' (see Callow 2008). A resurgence of interest in witchcraft and other non-mainstream beliefs, be it Wicca, the Church of Satan, Thelema, UFO cults, the Process Church and so forth, was fair game for tabloid fodder, which could instil fear, paranoia and prejudice within conservative-minded readers. A reflection of the fear and hatred felt by some towards the left-field faiths can be seen by the witch panic prevalent in the film. Another aspect of the film, and indeed in the study of the witch trials, is the treatment and representation of women. Though not all of those historically condemned as witches were female, in most countries it was indeed the case that the majority of victims were women.

As mentioned, many hippies got into the 'Occult Revival', but far from dropping out entirely many were also involved in politics, some through support of the civil rights movement and opposition to the war in Vietnam and nuclear arms, while many acted by negating capitalist society and materialist norms by setting up their own agricultural self-sufficiency 'back to the land' communes. There was also a strong feminist stance among many of the flower children. This manifested across a number of issues, mostly in reaction to the 1950s portrayal of women. No longer would young women fall into the mould of being 'perfect housewives' dressing to please their men. A stance demanding both freedom and equality was taken, with symbolic actions such as burning bras, eschewing cosmetics and the shaving of body hair if women wished, along with fighting for the rights to contraception, abortion and divorce, as well as campaigns against domestic violence. The right to 'free love' was also expressed, whereby women could choose to be promiscuous or celibate or somewhere in the middle if they so wanted, promiscuity being a lifestyle choice that is often glorified in men but stigmatised in women. It was about the right for a female to choose what to do with her own life and her own body free from oppression and control by men. The interests in Wicca and witchcraft also provided an empowerment choice, as Goddess worship and the role of priestesses was a break from the mainstream patriarchal religions.

Blood on Satan's Claw would reflect this spirit of the 1960s in its tale of seventeenth-century devil worship, but not necessarily the positive message of the times, for by 1971 elements of the hippy dream had dramatically turned to nightmare (particularly in America). The film follows a simple enough agrarian village in England turned upside down by the unearthing of strange animal remains that fall into the hands of a group of teenagers, whose earthly leader is a girl named Angel Blake. Here we see the power of both youth and womanhood as strived for by factions of the hippy movement. Angel attempts to seduce the local minister but he spurns her advances only to be accused by her of rape. At this point the villagers believe Angel's testimony, for in their minds she is still an innocent child. Reflected here is the anxiety that some parents feel when they see their children become involved in youth movements, the psychedelic years being a time notorious for the ethos of 'sex, drugs and rock 'n' roll'. Although Linda Hayden, the actress playing Angel Blake, was eighteen at the time of the film's release (a legally adult age in the UK) her character was still of schooling age, so the precociousness and the full-frontal nudity depicted in the scene where she attempts to corrupt a man of the cloth exhibits a developing attitude towards the depiction of nudity and sex in British horror cinema around that time. It is also telling that the film came about in the era when 'baby groupies' gained notoriety. 'Baby groupies' was the name given to teenage girls (and some even younger) who would frequent clubs, indulge in drink and drugs, and have sex with famous and not-so-famous rock and pop stars. *Blood on Satan's Claw*, however, was to broach even darker territory than Angel's attempted seduction of a priest.

Teenage brother and sister Mark and Cathy are less inclined to religious revolution than the other youths, but Mark's attraction to Angel is to prove his downfall as he is lured to his murder at the hands of the village children. Under the auspices of Angel Blake, Cathy is subjected to rape by one of the village youths before being killed by Angel. The rape scene is the most controversial element of *Blood on Satan's Claw*, taking up a considerable amount of screen time (especially bearing in mind that Mark's murder occurred off-screen) and filmed voyeuristically forcing the viewer to be almost party to the crime. Whilst the children and a couple of elderly acolytes lasciviously watch the sexual assault upon a teenage girl, uncomfortable moments pass on the screen. Understandably considered too uncomfortable and unacceptable by some viewers, the rape scene is incredibly powerful, as it leaves no doubt as to the depth of corruption that has infested the children. More discomfiting, however, is that the cinematic descent into evil had been influenced by several true-life events of the era. In 1968 the Scotswood area of Newcastle upon Tyne, a locale that would then have provided an apt setting for a kitchen sink realism movie, became the scene of a real-life horror. A few months apart, a four-year-old boy, Martin Brown, and three-year-old Brian Howe were lured away from their homes and murdered. The killer, Mary Bell, was herself a ten-year-old child. The murders shocked the area to the core and still hold resonance today. How could a child do something so violent, so horrific, to other children?

The second crime that bore a strong influence upon *Blood on Satan's Claw* was rather different, occurring as it did not in the working-class terraces of north-east England but in the opulent mansions of Hollywood. Under the influence of the criminal turned charismatic LSD-messiah Charles Manson, a number of his devotees, including several very young women, committed murder apparently upon his orders. The most famous victim of the 'Family' commune turned cult was Sharon Tate, the actress and wife of controversial film director Roman Polanski. Tate was heavily pregnant at the time she was stabbed to death. Here we see how the film was grimly inspired by the cases of terrible corruption within the youth and the powerful influence of the cult mentality, but the Manson case was symbolically more than the details of the case alone. Within the zeitgeist it was seen symbolically as signifying the corruption of the hippy dream. Alongside the Rolling Stones concert at the Altamont Free Festival in 1969, when the Hells Angels employed as security turned on members of the crowd and murdered eighteen-year-old Meredith Hunter (not the only death recorded at the concert), and the deaths at a young age of rock icons Jimi Hendrix, Brian Jones and Janis Joplin, it was one of the toxic weeds that choked the garden of flower power. *Blood on Satan's Claw* may serve as an allegory for the fight for women's rights, but it also nods to the conservative fear of movements in which such changes may occur. Furthermore, there are class elements within the film; the poor villagers are seen as those most at risk of corruption and harm, and the more highly educated and wealthier characters – the doctor, the priest and especially the judge – are seen as the forces of order, godliness and control. At the finale the status quo they represent appears to have triumphed over the evil (although there may be some ambiguity there). Yet the filmmakers, the director Haggard and screenwriter Robert Wynne-Simmons, were children of the counterculture themselves. Within their tale there is the warning of fruits turning with the season – how a worm within an apple could spread rot to the whole barrel – and though the establishment seemingly triumphs, the portrayal of the sanctimonious judge does not paint him to be much of a likeable hero (Evans-Powell 2021).

Though the third of the trinity, Robin Hardy's *The Wicker Man*, occurs in contemporary times, its setting and style are somewhat quirky. It is in essence a musical, but one unlike any that came before. The plot revolves around a Scottish mainland policeman, Sergeant Howie, visiting the island of Summerisle to investigate the disappearance of a young girl, Rowan Morrison. As practitioners of a pagan fertility cult, the Summerisle folk find themselves criticised and judged by the conservative Christian policeman on regular occasions. This can be seen to mirror the political climate of the UK at this time. The Government of Edward Heath's Conservative party elected in 1970 had followed Harold Wilson's Government, which had served throughout the years of the prolonged summer of love from 1964 to 1970 – a time when abortion became legal in the UK and women had fought for greater rights and balance, including sexual freedom.

The islanders' sexual freedom and other practices that disgust Howie are not simply lifestyle choices but are a matter of religious practice, albeit more liberal and fun than his own theological customs. But the problem is that the crops have failed and demand a further, more dire form of fertility cult ritual, that of sacrifice. The people of the island are happy to live under an economic-colonial lord whilst he can offer them the quality and way of life that they have grown accustomed to. According to their religious belief blood sacrifice is essential to placate the deities and ensure the bountiful crops that their lives depend on. But what, then, if the crops fail again? Howie himself puts that eventuality to Lord Summerisle: 'Don't you understand that if your crops fail this year, next year you're going to have to have another blood sacrifice? And next year, no one less than the king of Summerisle himself will do. If the crops fail, Summerisle, next year your people will kill you on May Day.'

Lord Summerisle proclaims that the crops will not fail, but there is a subtle glint of doubt, a hint of fear that passes across his face for just a moment. It is the case with all leaders, all empires, that no matter how long they have held power the possibility remains that in a very short time their leadership and empires can fall. If the people are no longer provided with what they want or need, change can and often does occur – in a democracy by the casting of an 'X' in a different box, in a totalitarian regime or monarchy when formerly loyal subjects become revolutionaries.

Cinematic folk horror in the UK largely slept for a while following *The Wicker Man* (although there were some strong television examples), but before we leap forward in time to its future incarnations, it is worth mentioning a 1971 British example of the associated subgenre of 'backwoods' film (sometimes referred to as hillbilly horror when associated with American films such as *Deliverance* (1972), *The Texas Chainsaw Massacre* (1974) or *Southern Comfort* (1981)), the film in question being Sam Peckinpah's *Straw Dogs* (1971). The plot revolves around an American academic, David, who moves to his British wife Amy's deceased father's farmhouse in a rural village close to the Cornish moors. The local men don't take too kindly to him, but what starts out as spiteful jest escalates to the killing of a pet cat and then to the controversial double-rape of Amy. The situation intensifies even more following the panicked killing of local teenager Janice by Henry Niles, a man with learning difficulties. David offers sanctuary to Niles in the farmhouse, intent on letting the proper authorities handle the matter, but the local men have different, bloodier intentions and lay siege to the farm. Although *Straw Dogs* does not contain a supernatural element it does tick some of the boxes common to folk horror, such as the isolated setting, differing moral codes and the matter of othering.

A more recent film that does not contain any paranormality but shares the same backwoods/folk horror modes is *Eden Lake* (2008). Here a middle-class couple visit a beauty spot for a camping trip but their enjoyment is marred by a group of rowdy local teenagers. Asking the youths to lower the noise, the man has a minor altercation with the gang, but that is a mere aperitif to the brutal meal that follows. Following the theft of their possessions by the teens, including a joy ride in their car, a more heated confrontation occurs in which the man accidentally kills the pet Rottweiler of one of the teenagers. The film then progresses down a harrowingly violent route.

Again, the socio-political 'othering' in this film can mostly be read in terms of class divisions, but may also be seen as highlighting generational differences. It came at a time when delinquency among teenagers and young adults in the UK was a matter of particular political and social concern. Horror films frequently play on real fears, and *Eden Lake* was among a number of films that were unofficially dubbed 'hoodie horror' (from the hooded garments these teenagers often wore). The political commentator Owen Jones took particular umbrage with the film in his book *Chavs: The Demonisation of the Working Class* (Jones 2011) seeing it as an attack on the nation's poorer people. As a working-class person from north-east England myself, I am not offended by the depictions of the 'feral youth' in Eden Lake because I am personally aware that sadly there is definitely an element in society like them roaming around, but it should go without saying that of course not ALL working-class people are like that. Many working-class people would take different routes when walking so as not to pass gangs like these, not because of a film demonising such gangs but because such groups existed to inspire the film, albeit generally not as murderous but no less unpleasant. A subset of the working class, or more often depicted not as industriously working but as an underclass – the 'chav gangs' – demonised themselves by their own actions and attitudes.

Other films, such as *Dead Man's Shoes* (2004) and *Possum* (2018), are set in a twenty-first-century variation of kitchen sink realism with decaying council estates, slum housing and social problems. But both also include a supernatural element of sorts, and may be considered to belong to the 'urban wyrd' mode. The urban wyrd is not simply folk horror set in a town or city; its presence is more complex than that, but sometimes there are distinct similarities between the styles. This is perhaps most evident in Ben Wheatley's 2011 film *Kill List*. As with *Dead Man's Shoes*, *Kill List* also draws on 'Brit grit', a form of gritty realistic crime cinema, television and literature that the UK does well. Both also draw on the fate of British military men once they have left the service. Conflicts in the Balkans, Iraq and Afghanistan have taken many lives and changed many more. Ex-servicemen have sometimes struggled tremendously to readapt to civilian life following their departure from war zones. Posttraumatic stress disorder and other factors have led to deteriorating personal relationships; difficulty in finding other work; and, in the case of the Middle East conflicts, physical ailments related to the still mysterious Gulf War Syndrome (as represented in Lawrie Brewster's 2016 film *The Unkindness of Ravens*). Some veterans have fallen into drink- and drug-addiction and some are homeless as a consequence of their experiences. The political relevance of this is that the British Government through successive leaderships has been seen to have badly failed these former soldiers. In *Dead Man's Shoes* we see a hardened ex-serviceman hunt down drug gang members on a Derbyshire housing estate, to avenge their cruel treatment of his brother with learning disabilities.

Kill List, despite its genre-bending inclusion, too, of elements of urban wyrd, Brit grit and kitchen sink realism, is also seen as one of the founding films of the new wave of folk horror (see Jolly 2018 and Paciorek 2018). It follows Jay and Gal, two ex-army men who had served on a secret mission in Ukraine, as they accept a job to work as assassins. They receive orders to eliminate three men. The first is dubbed 'The Priest', who thanks Jay for killing him. The second is named 'The Librarian' and, as well as having a library of brutal torture videos of a nature not specifically revealed, also seems to work with or for people who have kept files on Jay and Gal. Jay (whose life and psyche are more strained than Gal's) inflicts grievous, excruciating pain and death upon this target. They decide, after taking a large quantity of cash from the safe of 'The Librarian', to forfeit the rest of their mission. They are informed, however, that they must complete their assignment upon pain of their families' deaths, and so embark on their final hit, 'The MP', who lives in a mansion in the countryside. Here things get really weird. *Kill List* is a very cryptic film with Arthurian references (Jolly 2018) and ambiguous scenes. We are not informed who exactly they are hired by but it is clearly a group with wealth at its disposal and an ambition to restructure the nation – but into what, we do not know. The organisation is clearly ritualistic, but 'The Client', who hires Gal and Jay, seems to be upper-middle or upper class, and has the air of an establishment figure. There is certainly a political undercurrent to *Kill List*, but the precise details as to the nature of that are wreathed in mystery. The film's director, Ben Wheatley, has become one of the most prominent creators of the folk horror revival, also making the serial killer dark comedy *Sightseers* (2012), the cryptic English Civil War psychodrama *A Field in England* (2013) and the adaptation of J. G. Ballard's urban wyrd commentary on class aspirations *High Rise* (2015). Bringing us right up to date is his latest pandemic-era film *In The Earth* (2021); in its tale of worship of an elemental entity and research into mycorrhizal symbiosis in this time of environmental crises and existential threats, it returns us to the late-1960s eco-political concerns of the hippy movement, which, as we saw, were reflected in the rustic commune of *Blood on Satan's Claw* and the agricultural fertility rites of *The Wicker Man*.

In recent times, largely following the 'Brexit' referendum in 2016 to decide whether the UK should leave the European Union, there has been a considerable escalation of division among politicians and among members of the public alike – initially as to whether they were 'Leavers' or 'Remainers', but from there further discord and division arose. Race relations, religious intolerance, xenophobia, gender politics, homophobia and transphobia have all come to the fore. More recently still there has been conflict between those following official health guidelines for COVID-19 and the 'anti-vaxxers'/ 'anti-maskers'. On social media, so-called 'culture wars' rage between those deemed 'woke' (alert and considerate to social injustices) and the 'anti-woke'. Such divisions and turmoil are stoked by far-right agitation groups, professional 'grifters', and both amateur and professional conspiracy theorists. Furthermore, it is evident that politicians more frequently employ a deny-distract-deflect-divide policy, whereby they can point a finger of blame for failings elsewhere whilst avoiding greater scrutiny of their own deeds and misdeeds by having the populace argue amongst themselves. In such a climate of isolating into fixed groups and othering, it is little wonder that folk horror has again seen a resurgence in film, literature, music and art.

But in this time of pestilence, economic chaos, looming wars, weak and/or corrupt leadership and catastrophic climate change, just what exactly are we going to do 'if the crops fail'?

Acknowledgements

With thanks to Richard Hing and Grey Malkin for proof-reading this chapter.

References

Arva, Lauren (2017), *The Involvement of Puritanism in the Salem, Massachusetts Witch Trials*, ontheedgeofeverything.com/2017/06/11/the-involvement-of-puritanism-in-the-salem-massachusetts-witch-trials/ (accessed 22 September 2021).
Bassett, Ronald (1966), *Witchfinder General*. London: Pan Books.
Callow, John (2008), *Embracing the Darkness: A Cultural History of Witchcraft*. London: I.B. Tauris.
Carroll, Rory (2018), 'David Lynch: "You gotta be selfish. It's a terrible thing"', *Guardian*, www.theguardian.com/film/2018/jun/23/david-lynch-gotta-be-selfish-twin-peaks (accessed 22 September 2021).
Ellinger, Kat (2018), 'Darkness, Beauty, Fear and Wonder: Exploring the Grotesque and Fantastical World of Czech Folk Horror', in Andy Paciorek, Grey Malkin, Richard Hing and Katherine Peach (eds), *Folk Horror Revival: Field Studies*, 2nd edn. Durham: Wyrd Harvest Press, pp. 435–447.
Evans-Powell, David (2021), *Devil's Advocates: The Blood on Satan's Claw*. Liverpool: Auteur/Liverpool University Press.
Hames, Peter (2010), *Czech and Slovak Cinema: Theme and Tradition*. Edinburgh: Edinburgh University Press.
Jolly, Aaron (2018), 'Kill Lists: The Occult, Paganism & Sacrifice in Cinema as an Analogy for Political upheaval in the 1970s and 2010s', in Andy Paciorek, Grey Malkin, Richard Hing and Katherine Peach (eds), *Folk Horror Revival: Field Studies*, 2nd edn. Durham: Wyrd Harvest Press, pp. 291–304.

Jones, Owen (2011), *Chavs: The Demonisation of the Working Classes*. London: Verso.

Miller, Arthur (1996), 'Why I Wrote *The Crucible*: An Artist's Answer to Politics', *New Yorker*, 21 and 28 October, 158–64.

Paciorek, Andy (2018), 'An Arthurian Antichrist: Alternate Readings of *Kill List*', in Andy Paciorek, Grey Malkin, Richard Hing and Katherine Peach (eds), *Folk Horror Revival: Field Studies*, 2nd edn. Durham: Wyrd Harvest Press, pp. 422–434.

Paciorek, Andy and Stuart Silver (eds) (2019a), *Folk Horror Revival: Urban Wyrd 1. Spirits of Time*. Durham: Wyrd Harvest Press.

Paciorek, Andy and Stuart Silver (eds) (2019b), *Folk Horror Revival: Urban Wyrd 2. Spirits of Place*. Durham: Wyrd Harvest Press.

Richardson, Norman (2016), *Division, Diversity and Vision – Challenges for Religion in Education: A Case-Study from Northern Ireland Q & A*, UCL MediaCentral, mediacentral.ucl.ac.uk/Play/ (accessed 25 August 2021).

Sylvester, David (1954), 'The Kitchen Sink', *Encounter* (December), 61–63, www.unz.com/print/Encounter-1954dec-00061/ (accessed 19 August 2021).

14

'Isn't folk horror *all* horror?': a wyrd genre

Diane A. Rodgers

The notion of folk horror as a distinct subgenre has developed in leaps and bounds in the post-2000 period, with the most oft-cited paradigm examples being distinctly from British 1970s cinema. A revival of interest in films from this era occurred alongside the release of a number of titles after 2000 that echo qualities of those from this earlier period. In 2017 Ben Wheatley, director of *Kill List* (2011), *A Field in England* (2013) and *In the Earth* (2021) (films considered seminal in the modern folk horror canon) wondered in my 2018 interview with him: 'Isn't folk horror *all* horror?'. He goes on to muse upon folkloric tales of vampires and (quite rightly) wonders 'isn't the werewolf's tale a folk horror tale … usually a village dealing with someone who transforms? That's all folk tale stuff. So, in a way, most horror is folk'.[1] The roots of horror are indeed often firmly based in folk tales, myth and legend: unofficially recorded histories, campfire tales and urban legend. However, although I and others have argued elsewhere (Rodgers 2019, Cowdell 2019) that the use of folklore is absolutely integral to many horror narratives, conversely, not all horror is folk horror in terms of the genre we know it as today. Folk horror, in fact, can be viewed as quite separate from and atypical of more conventional examples of cinema horror to the extent that I suggest that rather than being a subgenre of horror, folk horror is a truly 'wyrd' genre in its own right. It is useful, therefore, first to establish what typically conventional horror *is*, in order to outline more clearly what folk horror *is not*.

Classic horror

There are records of folk tales and legends about undead beings consuming the blood or flesh of the living dating back to ancient civilisations, with depictions of vampires 'found on ancient Babylonian and Assyrian pottery going back thousands of years before Christ' (McNally and Florescu 1994: 117). Similarly, werewolf legends or tales of lycanthropy (the mythological ability of a human to undergo transformation into an animal, or animal-like state) date at least as far back as the 'Romans and Greeks [who] were cursed by the man-wolf[;] Vikings revered him, medieval peasants feared him and witches tried to control him' (Beresford 2013: 7). Contemporary perceptions of such folkloric creatures, however, tend to be shaped by the media, predominantly those representations in film and television. Although there were earlier significant onscreen incarnations (such as Murnau's *Nosferatu* (1922), for example), it was arguably the classic horror films of Universal Studios in the 1930s that established what became the most enduring iconography associated with these legendary monsters. *Dracula*, in 1931, became synonymous with Bela Lugosi's becaped aristocrat with a hypnotic close-up stare, whilst *The Wolf Man* (1941) was embodied by Lon Chaney Jr, whose memorable onscreen transformation helped firmly establish him in the classic title role. Both actors would reprise these roles in a number of sequels in the successful Universal Monsters series, helping reinforce the public perception of, and familiarity with, these iconic characters.

It was not simply the characters that were made iconic, though, during this period, as these films also marked what is referred to as the classical or traditional period for the horror genre (with earlier films such as *The Cabinet of Doctor Caligari* (1920) and *Nosferatu* being part of what is known as the genre's 'primitive' stage of growth). The 1930s films, therefore, clearly established a set of onscreen characteristics that helped to cement a number of distinct conventions for the horror genre. Some of the most instantly recognisable rules or generic conventions in relation to classic horror tend to relate to stylistic choices in terms of lighting (such as low-key lighting or back-lit characters to create distinct and frightening shadows), the use of dramatic music to underline impending disaster, or sound to elicit physical 'jumpscare' reactions from an audience. Even the visual presentation of 'monsters' themselves became a type of recognisable uniform convention, from Universal's iconic monsters through to slasher villains such as Freddy Krueger in *A Nightmare on Elm Street* (1984), made distinct by his striped jumper, worn fedora and razor-claw glove, and *Candyman* (1992, remade in 2021), with sinister pirate-like hook replacing a hand. Though these more recent examples have clear origins in folk myths, satanic panics and urban legend – Krueger as a modern take on the manifestation of nightmares and sleep paralysis (an area written extensively upon by folklorist David Hufford (1982, 1995)), and the 'hookman' urban legend (which began circulation in 1950s America) about a killer with one hand replaced with a hook (Brunvand 2003) – the films in which such characters appear are not seen as *folk horror*.

'Isn't folk horror all horror?': a wyrd genre

In defining genre, we tend to look for recurring patterns, whether these be in terms of themes, styles, paradigms or motifs. Steve Neale describes genre as a process that, though 'dominated by repetition' (such as in the conventions outlined above) is also 'marked fundamentally by difference, variation, and change', suggesting that elements of a genre 'are always *in* play rather than being simply *re*played' (2000: 165). This approach is echoed by my own application of the term 'wyrd' to expand our understanding of folk horror, which encompasses:

> folk horror, hauntology, and gothic sub-genres of media texts that have folkloric content and an eerie effect ... Wyrd (the Anglo-Saxon original of 'weird') describes that which is strange, mysterious, or even frightening, and connects the common eerie element across the aforementioned genres ... while suggesting a sense of the ancient, the folkloric, and the unexplained ... [linking] with more intangible hauntological notions of eeriness and horror. (Rodgers 2019: 135)

Folk horror

The term, though having been traced back at least as far as 1936,[2] is popularly attributed to director Piers Haggard, who, in 2003, used it to describe his film *Blood on Satan's Claw* (1971), which is now canonised as one of the 'unholy trinity' of folk horror films alongside *Witchfinder General* (1968) and *The Wicker Man* (1973). Haggard's use of the phrase was less about naming and defining a particular folk horror subgenre than distinguishing

Figure 14.1   Piers Haggard directing *Blood on Satan's Claw*, 1971

his work from what he saw as more typically conventional, clichéd or exploitative horror:

> the definition was initially defensive ... when I made [*Blood on Satan's Claw*] the dominant mode of horror was absolutely the ... Hammer tradition ... [but *Satan's Claw*] didn't ... tick the obvious boxes ... I just said in conversation 'well of course this isn't really sort of a *horror* horror film, this is ... sort of a *folk* horror really' trying to tap into the things which I thought were moving and interesting and which had emotional, historical cultural depth and resonance.[3]

Adam Scovell has sketched useful thematic outlines for folk horror as a genre, proposing that folk horror can be considered as a mode that utilises 'forms of popular conscious memory', channelling aesthetic or thematic folklore 'for eerie, uncanny or horrific purposes' (2017: 7). However, as *Hookland* author David Southwell remarks, folklore in folk horror is not 'mere tinsel for a story' but instead functions 'as integral infrastructure' (Southwell 2019): folklore is clearly a thread woven throughout horror in the broadest context. I have made a case elsewhere about bringing folklore to the fore of folk horror, so here I wish to take up the notion of folk horror as a *mode* (in the sense of a manner or style in which something is expressed) and apply it to onscreen aesthetics and generic convention. Where folk horror has been explored to date, it is not generally in direct comparison with more broadly typical examples of what Piers Haggard refers to as '*horror* horror' and generic conventions such as those discussed above. Andy Paciorek has been instrumental in defining the folk horror genre as specifically centred around 'British movies of the late 1960s and '70s that have a rural, earthy association to ancient European pagan and witchcraft traditions or folklore ... as well as some creepy British children's television shows of the era' (2015: 9). Additionally, 'this loose-knit genre is not always filmic and not *necessarily* horrifying ... The eerie dissonance of folk horror can be observed extending beyond boundaries of genre and medium ... to include science fiction, fantasy, television plays, television series, and even public information films' (Rodgers 2019: 134). Therefore, it is useful to consider a variety of examples from both film and television (particularly from this 'classic' period of 1970s folk horror) through this lens of generic convention, to help bring more sharply into focus what folk horror *is*, but also what it *is not*, in terms of that which separates it from horror in general.

Folk horror vs 'horror horror'

The examples of classic mainstream and slasher horror (what Piers Haggard describes as '*horror* horror') discussed above have central monstrous figures who, in some cases, lead the story as well as posing the main threat within the narrative. Though they may lurk in the shadows at times, they are nonetheless recognisably iconic and easily defined in distinctly physical terms (for example sporting a hockey mask, a striped jumper or a hook-hand). In many examples of folk horror, it is rare that a monster or threat is so distinctly knowable, if there is even a well-defined threat at all. For example, in the Iranian folk horror film *Zalava* (2021) we witness fear, torment and physical affliction suffered by a community on screen, all attributed to the presence of a demon in the village. An exorcist carries out complex rituals using a glass jar to carefully trap the demon inside, and later, at various points, we see the jar treated irresponsibly, dropped accidentally and even opened disrespectfully. The actual existence of any demonic presence is never confirmed nor denied for the audience beyond unfortunate events and mysterious coincidences (to the extent that we are encouraged to wonder if there was anything present at all). In *Zalava*, eerie phenomena are *suggested* on screen in a manner that Robert Macfarlane has described elsewhere as 'glimpsed but never confronted' (2015): as variously unsettling, in a context that could plausibly be no threat at all, or simply a figment of the villagers' collective imagination. The possibility that there was never a physical threat present at all is left open.

The threat here is created by suggestion and inference, less distinct and 'knowable' than in classic horror: the fear in folk horror comes from absence rather than presence. We are not afraid, in these cases, of a Freddy- or Jason-like character jumping out from the shadows, and thus there is a different kind of tension or anticipation for the audience. The atmosphere created is less about waiting for an expected jumpscare and is more of a general unsettling eeriness; Mark Fisher, in his writing on hauntology, suggests this is created by this notion of absence, discussing it in relation to the terms 'weird' and 'eerie' (2016). He notes that both terms relate to that which is strange and frightening, but argues that 'it would be wrong to say that the weird and the eerie are necessarily terrifying' (8). 'Eeriness', in Fisher's terms, is a sensation that 'occurs either when there is something present where there should be nothing, or there is nothing present when there should be something' (61). In classic examples of folk horror, there is usually a general sense of brooding fear throughout a text, and rarely a string of spectacular onscreen deaths. When something sinister does occur in the genre, it is more likely to happen off screen. For example, when a ritual sacrifice murder takes place near the conclusion of *Robin Redbreast* (1970), it is merely suggested off screen by a brief scream, and in *A Field in England*, whatever mysterious thing happens to Whitehead (Reece Shearsmith) to cause prolonged shrieking and one of the most unsettling grimaces in cinema history, it happens entirely out of sight in a tent. There are, of course, exceptions, when there *is* a visual reveal or spectacle in folk horror, such as in the infamous ending of *The Wicker Man*, but here the horror comes from understanding the psychological impact of the moment (in the context of the story or for a particular character), which can be more disturbing on a fundamental level for an audience than entertaining splashes of gore.

The other major type of threat in folk horror comes in the shape of the 'skewed belief systems and morality' of a local populace, sometimes on account of its isolation, which may culminate in unpleasant events 'resulting … from this skewed social consciousness' (Scovell 2017: 17–18). That is, the threat comes from the folk themselves (rather than an external or necessarily supernatural force) and their actions based on their beliefs about religion, customs and rituals. This is most overt in *The Wicker Man* (1973) (a film covered at great length elsewhere, most effectively by Mikel J. Koven in his book *Film, Folklore and Urban Legends* (2008)) when the residents of Summerisle require a sacrifice, supposedly to restore fertility to the land. This narrative trope is used by so many texts considered to be (either classic or revival) folk horror (including television play *Robin Redbreast*, US series *The Dark Secret of Harvest Home* (1978), *Wake Wood* (2009), *Kill List* (2011), *The Ritual* (2017), *Apostle* (2018) and *Midsommar* (2019)) that it is safe to denote this as typically conventional of the genre.

In opposition to the settings and cinematography of mainstream classic horror, the *mise-en-scène* of folk horror is most associated with the onscreen use of landscape. As Mark Gatiss has noted in the BBC documentary series *A History of Horror* (2010), in classic folk horror this is most often manifested as 'a common obsession with the British landscape', and I would extend this not only to the British countryside, but also to its weather. For example, consider the bleak grey skies and hills of *The Wicker Man*, the

Figure 14.2 Angel Blake leading her *Satan's Claw* followers into temptation, 1971

autumnal trees and fields of *Witchfinder General* and the soft monochrome cinematography of *A Field in England*. Similarly evocative is Lawrence Gordon Clark's description of his experience filming elements of the *Ghost Story for Christmas* series (1971–1978): 'there was a thick mist so we got the more dramatic effect of the ... lamps burning through ... Autumn is a great time for filming in the English countryside. You get early sunsets, lovely mists and abundant cobwebs in the dew.'[4] The use of landscape and outdoor (often rural) settings in this way necessitates a tendency towards daytime filming, which contrasts the cover of night more often used as backdrop for classic horror such as *Dracula* (1931) and the music of his 'children of the night', or Freddy Krueger lurking in teenage dreamscapes. Rural folk horror settings also arguably provide a sense of realism, using naturalistic lighting – something Piers Haggard was conscious of using in opposition to what he saw as the stylisation of stifling sets and interiors favoured by Hammer.[5] Grey, overcast weather and Eastman Colour film stock 'pervasive in the 1960s and 1970s' with a 'reputation as cheap and easy replacement' for Technicolor (Heckman 2015: 46) meant that much folk horror of the 1970s had a low-contrast, desaturated look. Achieving this 1970s style is essential to some creators of the folk horror revival period, with films such as *Antrum* (2018), framed as a 'rediscovered' film from the 1970s, emulating a scratched print complete with bleached-out colour and an abundance of lens flare. Similarly, in television, the creators of the *Inside No. 9* episode 'The Devil of Christmas' (2016) used vintage 1970s cameras in order to achieve an 'authentic re-creation' of the atmosphere and look of 1970s television (writer-actor Steve Pemberton in Oglethorpe (2016)). This further concretes the 1970s as the definitive classic period for folk horror, whose lighting conventions differ greatly from the primary colours and high-contrast lighting conditions of the wider horror genre.

Classic horror soundtracks have a tendency to direct the audience's emotive response with the swelling of sad strings or a high-octane beat accompanying a frenzied chase sequence. In opposition to this, scores for folk horror films tend to be relatively minimal, or focus more on creating mood or atmosphere, such as the score for the Estonian film *November* (2017), which simply 'oozes dread at times' (Havlin 2019). Leaving audience response less obviously directed in this way allows for sinister interpretation of even the most benign onscreen moments, and for inexplicable events to seem all the more chilling, replicating a stunned silence and bleak outlook. Where folk horror soundtracks more pointedly use music, it often tends to be either in the form of traditional folk songs and music to evoke bygone eras or, particularly in post-2000 folk horror revival texts, as music that falls into the category of hauntology (Fisher 2012). The former is prevalent in the classic era of folk horror when the countercultural revolution of the late 1960s and early 1970s saw a modern reinvention and popularisation of folk music (Young 2000). The soundtrack of *The Wicker Man*, for example, famously incorporates a mixture of traditional songs (such as arrangements of traditional Scottish, Irish and English tunes) and songs that are reminiscent of ancient folk songs (such as the song the island children sing around the maypole). The use of folk song in such examples of folk horror is often to give the suggestion of a pre-Christian pagan culture and to hint at earlier, ancient times. Although *Blood on Satan's Claw* has an orchestral score fairly typical for horror films of this period (composed by Marc Wilkinson, whose credits also include scores for the 1968 film *If ...* and 1979's *The Quatermass Conclusion*), elements of the soundtrack were specifically crafted by director Piers Haggard 'to suggest a kind of coarse, degraded, bit of derivative, pseudo-plainsong'.[6] Similarly, an opening track near the start of *A Field In England* is percussion alone, emulating the beating of drums evocative of the period of the English Civil War.

Hauntological soundtracks, though retrospectively common in the classic 1970s period of folk horror, are most knowingly used in the post-2000 folk horror revival period, foregrounding 'technologies and explicit references to media texts ... from post-war Britain, particularly the 1960s and 1970s'. This type of output is most commonly typified by the Ghost Box record label, discussed in detail by Jamie Sexton, who states it is most specifically 'horror films and television which permeate the allusions made by the label', observing that their own website 'signals its main threads of inspiration' as coming from 'folklore, vintage electronics, library music, and haunted television soundtracks' (2012: 562–3, 566). The purpose of some of this music aims to recall the spooky nature of earlier media: most often cited are the title themes of 1970s and 1980s children's television programmes such as *The Owl Service* (1969–1970) and *Children of the Stones* (1977), which are seen as definitively creepy examples. Ben Wheatley posits the work of composer and sound designer Martin Pavey as integral to the hauntological effect of films in the modern film folk horror canon. Pavey's work is to be found not only in Wheatley's own films (such as *Kill List* and *A Field in England*) but also in several other paradigm examples of the folk horror revival including *The Borderlands* (2013), *Prevenge* (2016) and *Borley Rectory* (2017). Wheatley confidently states that if a film is 'scary ... you'll find Martin Pavey did the sound design on it ... Pavey did all the sound design for my stuff as well ... he's behind *lots* of stuff ... he's like the Conny Plank [innovative avant-garde West German sound engineer] of horror sound design' (pers. comm, 25 May 2018).[7]

Such approaches to score composition and the resulting hauntological soundtracks can themselves influence the reading of films as being at least folk-horror-adjacent in terms of the style and atmosphere they create, even when folk horror themes may be less obviously present in the narrative. Peter Strickland's *In Fabric* (2018), for example, about a haunted red dress, features a soundtrack by Cavern of Anti-Matter, a group comprising members of Stereolab, a band known for drawing upon nostalgic influences to create playful electronic mood pieces. The score of *In Fabric*'s 'unpredictable melodic patterns [which] suggest the creepy elegance of a Victorian music box' (Cardew 2020) combined with Martin Pavey's unsettling sound design has played a significant role in allowing audiences to understand the film 'as a mannered BBC folk horror plucked from pastoral countrysides and placed in cramped apartments and sinister department stores' ('Sugar' 2020). This mode, or haunted atmosphere, common throughout folk horror and wyrd media, is similarly evoked in the soundtrack of Strickland's *Berberian Sound Studio* (2012) composed by the band Broadcast, whose work brings to the film a 'sense of nostalgia and weirdness' (Daniels (n.d.)). Broadcast's music is often cited as a hauntological exemplar, drawing on 1970s influences with distinct folk horror flavours, combining 'the primitive electronics of the BBC Radiophonic Workshop, 1970s public information films, Czech surrealism, Moog organ, forgotten film soundtracks and kitsch ephemera' (Long 2011). *Berberian Sound Studio*'s psychological horror narrative revolves around the creation of a soundtrack for a 1970s Italian *giallo*, reminiscent of films such as *Suspiria* (1977), redolent with witchcraft, rituals and other forms of supernatural folklore. The hauntological, avant-garde nature of soundtracks such as these (along with other arthouse

Figure 14.3 *In Fabric* inviting us into the arms of folk horror with all 'the creepy elegance of a Victorian music box', 2018

aspects of the work), particularly in their stylistic references to British folk horror film and television of the 1960s and 1970s, allows such films to be placed apart from typically conventional examples of mainstream horror, aligning them more closely with a folk horror mode.

Conclusion

'Folk horror' was used by Piers Haggard as a term purposefully to set a certain strand of cinema apart from the broader brush strokes of Hammer and classic horror traditions, which, retrospectively, helps us align the genre more with an intellectual, arthouse style of cinema. Folk horror has come to be associated especially with a milieu of the 1970s and the British landscape (but is not restricted to Britain or rural areas) that coincided with the development of technology allowing outdoor filming more easily. Thus, folk horror is a mode linked with the style of European New Wave cinema, with distinctive aspects including the use of folklore, landscape and folk beliefs in remote communities, which suggests that films such as *Picnic at Hanging Rock* (1975) can be aligned with folk horror, whilst this is far less the case for *Gremlins* (1984). Wyrd films and television programmes are often presented with an arthouse sensibility, in that the audience must work at creating the meaning and emotional direction for themselves. Avant-garde approaches and more abstract narratives mean that at times folk horror has more in common with the work of David Lynch than that of John Carpenter: it is uncomfortable, troubling and unsettling, rather than being full-on visceral horror.

By placing paradigm examples of folk horror alongside those typical of mainstream, classic horror, it is clear that folk horror in onscreen convention alone is not typical of the broader horror genre and, in fact, has many generic conventions that are uniquely distinct. As it is not always 'horrifying', there is a further case for 'wyrd' as a genre, rather than folk horror merely being a subgenre. A comparable case might be that of romantic comedy, firmly established as a genre in its own right, to the extent that its staid conventions are examined in the documentary *Romantic Comedy* (2019), while parodies such as *They Came Together* (2014) and *Isn't It Romantic* (2019) spoof age-old genre tropes. Romantic comedy is thus not merely a hybrid or subgenre of comedy, but has entirely its own specific set of conventions as, it can be argued, does folk horror as separate from classic horror. Folk horror is, in fact, unconventional alongside 'horror horror' as, rather than being horrific, it has a tendency to be more weird, unsettling or vaguely eerie. There may be a scream or a cry heard, but it is unlikely these sounds will punctuate the entire texts, and the audience may never find out where the cry came from. The killer or threat is unlikely to be vanquished or escape in a folk horror narrative, if we even know who or what the threat is: it may be an entire community or it may even be ourselves.

Notes

1. Ben Wheatley, personal communication with the author, 25 May 2018.
2. By author Sarah K. Marr, who, using Twitter, found an entry in *The English Journal* and 'managed to trace its use back to 1936' (Skaldsummerisle 2018).
3. Piers Haggard, personal communication with the author, 5 June 2017.
4. Lawrence Gordon Clark, personal communication with the author, 11 June 2017.
5. Haggard, personal communication.
6. Haggard, personal communication.
7. Wheatley, personal communication.

References

Beresford, Matthew (2013), *The White Devil: The Werewolf in European Culture*. London: Reaktion Books.
Brunvand, Jan H. (2003), *The Vanishing Hitchhiker: American Urban Legends and Their Meanings*. New York: W. W. Norton.
Cardew, Ben (2020), '*In Fabric* OST: Cavern of Anti-Matter', *Pitchfork*, 5 June, pitchfork.com/reviews/albums/cavern-of-anti-matter-in-fabric-ost/ (accessed 4 May 2023).
Cowdell, Paul (2019), '"Practicing Witchcraft Myself during the Filming": Folk Horror, Folklore, and the Folkloresque', *Western Folklore* 78:4, 295–326.
Daniels, Alexandria (n.d.), 'A Study of Hauntology in Berberian Sound Studio', TalkFilmSociety.com, talkfilmsociety.com/articles/a-study-of-hauntology-in-berberian-sound-studio (accessed 4 May 2023).
Fisher, Mark (2012), 'What Is Hauntology?', *Film Quarterly* 66:1, 16–24.
Fisher, Mark (2016), *The Weird and the Eerie*. London: Repeater Books.
Havlin, Jamie (2019), '*November*: Film Review', *Louder than War*, 8 May, louderthanwar.com/november-film-review (accessed 4 May 2023).
Heckman, Heather (2015), 'WE'VE GOT BIGGER PROBLEMS: Preservation during Eastman Color's Innovation and Early Diffusion', *The Moving Image: The Journal of the Association of Moving Image Archivists* 15:1, 44–61.
Hufford, David (1982), *The Terror that Comes in the Night: An Experience-Centred Study of Supernatural Assault Traditions*. Philadelphia: University of Pennsylvania Press.
Hufford, David (1995), 'Beings without Bodies: An Experience-Centered Theory of the Belief in Spirits', in Barbara Walker (ed.), *Out of the Ordinary: Folklore and the Supernatural*. Boulder: University Press of Colorado, Utah State University Press, 11–45.
Koven, Mikel J. (2008), *Film, Folklore and Urban Legends*. Lanham, MD: Scarecrow Press.

Long, Pat (2011), 'Trish Keenan Obituary', *Guardian*, 18 January, www.theguardian.com/music/2011/jan/17/trish-keenan-obituary (accessed 29 April 2023).

Macfarlane, Robert (2015), 'The Eeriness of the English Countryside', *Guardian*, 10 April, www.theguardian.com/books/2015/apr/10/eeriness-english-countryside-robert-macfarlane (accessed 29 April 2023).

McNally, Raymond and Radu Florescu (1994), *In Search of Dracula*. Boston, MA: Houghton Mifflin.

Neale, Steve (2000), 'Questions of Genre', in Robert Stam and Toby Miller (eds), *Film and Theory*. New Jersey: Blackwell, pp. 157–178.

Oglethorpe, Tim (2016), 'Have a Spooky Christmas: Jessica Raine Gets the Fright of Her Life in *Inside No. 9*'s Homage to the Horror Shows of the 70s', *Mail Online*, 23 December, www.dailymail.co.uk/femail/article-4058182/Have-spooky-Christmas-Jessica-Raine-gets-fright-life-Inside-No-9-s-homage-horror-shows-70s.html.

Paciorek, Andy (ed.) (2015), *Folk Horror Revival: Field Studies*. Durham: Wyrd Harvest Press.

Rodgers, Diane (2019), 'Something Wyrd This Way Comes: Folklore and British Television', *Folklore* 130:2 (June), 133–152.

Scovell, Adam (2017), *Folk Horror: Hours Dreadful and Things Strange*. Leighton Buzzard: Auteur.

Sexton, Jamie (2012), 'Weird Britain in Exile: Ghost Box, Hauntology, and Alternative Heritage', *Popular Music and Society* 35:4, 561–584.

Skaldsummerisle (2018), 'A Guide for the Curious: An Interview with Sarah K. Marr', Folkhorrorrevival.com, folkhorrorrevival.com/2018/12/23/a-guide-for-the-curious-an-interview-with-sarah-k-marr/ (accessed 29 April 2023).

Southwell, David (2019), 'Receiving the Ghost Transmissions', paper presented at the 'Folklore on Screen' conference, 14 September, Sheffield Hallam University.

'Sugar' (2020), 'Creepy, Funny Homage' Best Buy, Customer Ratings and reviews, www.bestbuy.com/site/reviews/in-fabric-blu-ray-2018/34876272 (accessed 5 July 2022).

Young, Rob (2000), *Electric Eden: Unearthing Britain's Visionary Music*. London: Faber and Faber.

British folk horror filmography

Films cited in the text as folk horror

Amen Island (aka *Unhappy Birthday*). Mark Harriott, Mike Matthews, 2011, Peccadillo Pictures.
Anchoress. Chris Newby, 1993, Paul Breuls.
Apostle. Gareth Edwards, 2018. XYZ Films Severn Screen, One More One Productions.
A Banquet. Ruth Paxton, 2021. HanWay Films.
The Black Death. Christopher Smith, 2010, Egoli Tossell Film, HanWay Films, Ecosse Films, Zephyr Films.
Blood on Satan's Claw. Piers Haggard, 1971, Tigon.
The Borderlands. Elliot Goldner, 2013, Metrodome Distribution.
The Company of Wolves. Neil Jordan, 1984, Palace Pictures, ITC Entertainment.
Crow. Wyndham Price, 2016, Evolution Digital Films, Spinning Head Films.
Cry of the Banshee. Gordon Hessler, 1970, American International Pictures.
The Dark. John Fawcett, 2005, Constantin Film, Impact Pictures.
Darklands. Julian Richards, 1996, Metrodome Films.
The Devil Rides Out. Terence Fisher, 1968, Seven Art Productions.
Dogged. Richard Rowntree, 2017, Ash Mountain Films, Jibba Jabba, RedLight, Wignall Productions.
Doomwatch. Peter Sasdy, 1972, Tigon.
Enys Men. Mark Jenkin, 2022, Bosena, Protagonist Pictures.
The Fallow Field. Leigh Dovey, 2009, Figment TV Productions.
A Field in England. Ben Wheatley, 2013, Film4.
Following the Wicca Man. Jacqueline Kirkham, 2013.
Holy Terrors: Six Weird Tales by Arthur Machen. Mark Goodall, Julian Butler, 2017.
In the Earth. Ben Wheatley, 2021, Rook Films, Protagonist Pictures.
Kill List. Ben Wheatley, 2011 Root Films.
The Lair of the White Worm. Ken Russell, 1988, White Lair.
The League of Gentlemen's Apocalypse. Steve Bendelack, 2005, Film4, BBC Films, Tiger Aspect Pictures, Hell's Kitchen International.
Maya. K. Pervaiz, 2021, BadWolf Films.
Men. Alex Garland, 2022, DNA Films.
Night of the Demon. Jacques Tourneur, 1957, Sabre Films.
Outcast. Colm McCarthy, 2010, Vertigo Films.
The Plague of the Zombies. John Gilling, 1966, Hammer.

Psychomania (aka *The Death Wheelers*). Don Sharp, 1973, Benmar Productions.
Quatermass and the Pit. Roy Ward Baker, 1967, Seven Arts Productions, Hammer.
Requiem for a Village. David Gladwell, 1975, British Film Institute.
The Ritual. David Bruckner, 2017, The Imaginarium, eOne Films.
She Will. Charlotte Colbert, 2021, Popcorn Group, Pressman Films, Intermission Films.
The Shout. Jerzy Skolimowski, 1978, Recorded Picture Company.
Sightseers. Ben Wheatley, 2012, StudioCanal.
The Unkindness of Ravens. Lawrie Brewster, 2016, 3rd Monkey Productions.
The Wicker Man. Robin Hardy, 1973, British Lion Film.
The Wicker Tree. Robin Hardy, 2011, British Lion Film, Tressock Films.
The Witches. Cyril Frankel, 1966, Hammer.
Witchfinder General. Michael Reeves, 1968, Tigon.

Other films and television programmes cited in the text

28b Camden Street. David Gladwell, 1963.
Alfie. Lewis Gilbert, 1966, Sheldrake Films.
Alien. Ridley Scott, 1979, 20th Century Fox, Brandywine Productions.
And Now the Screaming Starts! (aka *Fengriffen*). Roy Ward Baker, 1973, Amicus.
Antrum, David Amito, Michael Laicini, 2018, Else Films.
Apocalypse Now. Francis Ford Coppola, 1979, Omni Zoetrope.
Asylum. Roy Ward Baker, 1972, Amicus.
Bagpuss. Peter Firmin, Oliver Postgate, 1974, Smallfilms, BBC2.
Battleship Potemkin/Bronenosets Potyomkin. Sergei Eisenstein, 1925, Mosfilm.
Berberian Sound Studio. Peter Strickland, 2012, UK Film Council, Film4, Warp X, ITV Yorkshire, UK.
Black Lake. K. Pervaiz, 2020, BadWolf Films.
Blood Runs Down. Zandashé Brown, 2018.
Borley Rectory. Ashley Thorpe, 2017, Carrion Films, Glass Eye Pix.
Brigadoon. Alan Jay Lerner, 1954, MGM.
Butterflies. Carla Lane, BBC, 1978–1983.
The Cabinet of Doctor Caligari/Das Cabinet des Dr Caligari. Robert Wiene, 1920, UFA GmbH.
Candyman. Bernard Rose, 1992, Propaganda Films, PolyGram Filmed Entertainment.
Casting the Runes. Lawrence Gordon Clark, ITV, 1979.
Children of the Stones. Peter Graham Scott, 1977, HTV West.
Confessions of a Window Cleaner. Val Guest, 1974, Columbia.
Coronation Street. 1960–, ITV.
The Crucible. Nicholas Hytner, 1996, 20th Century Fox.
Culloden. Peter Watkins, 1964, BBC.
Cult of the Cobra. Francis D. Lyon, 1955, UIP.
Curse of the Scarecrow. Louisa Warren, 2018, ChampDog Films.
The Daisy Chain. Aisling Walsh, 2008, ContentFilm International.
The Dark Secret of Harvest Home. Leo Penn, 1978, Universal Television.
Dead Man's Shoes. Shane Meadows, 2004, Warp Films, Big Arty Productions, EM Media, Film 4.
Deliverance. John Boorman, 1972, Warner Bros.
Devi. Kodi Ramakrishna, 1999, Sumanth Art Productions.

Doomwatch. Darol Blake *et al.*, 1970–1972, BBC.
Dracula. Tod Browning, 1931, Universal Pictures.
Dracula. Terence Fisher, 1958, Hammer.
Dracula. Jonny Campbell, Damon Thomas, Paul McGuigan, 2020, BBC.
Eden Lake. James Watkins, 2008, Rollercoaster Films, Aramid Entertainment Fund.
Entr'acte. René Clair, 1924, Rolf de Maré.
The Evil Dead. Sam Raimi, 1981, Renaissance Pictures.
The Exorcist. William Friedkin, 1973, Hoya Productions.
The Fall and Rise of Reginald Perrin. David Nobbs, 1976–1979, BBC.
The Fall of the House of Usher. Jean Epstein, 1928.
Friday the Thirteenth. Sean S. Cunningham, 1980, Georgetown Productions.
Get Out. Jordan Peele, 2017, Blumhouse Productions, QC Entertainment, Monkeypaw Produtions.
A Ghost Story for Christmas. Lawrence Gordon Clark, 1971–1979, BBC.
The Good Life. Bob Larbey, John Esmonde, 1975–1978, BBC.
The Gorgon. Terence Fisher, 1964, Hammer.
Green Snake. Tsui Hark, 1993, Tsui Hark, Ng See Yuen.
Gremlins. Joe Dante, 1984, Warner Bros, Amblin Entertainment.
Halloween. John Carpenter, 1979, Compass International Pictures, Falcon International Productions.
Happy Ever After. 1974–1978, BBC.
Hexenjagd/Les sorcières de Salem. Raymond Rouleau, 1957, Compagnie Industrielle Commerciale Cinématographique, Films Borderie, DEFA.
High Rise. Ben Wheatley, 2015, Recorded Picture Company.
The Hills Have Eyes. Wes Craven, 1977, Blood Relations.
Hisss. Jennifer Chambers Lynch, 2010, Venus Movies.
A History of Horror. Rachel Jardine, John Das, 2010, BBC.
The Horror of Dracula. Terrance Fischer, 1958. Hammer.
I Spit on Your Grave. Meir Zarchi, 1978, Barquel Creations.
I Walked with a Zombie. Jacques Tourneur, 1943, RKO.
If … Lindsay Anderson, 1968, Memorial Enterprises.
In Fabric. Peter Strickland, 2018, Rook Films, BBC Films, BFI, Headgear Films, Metrol Technology.
Inside No. 9. Reece Shearsmith, Steve Pemberton, 2014–, BBC.
Isn't It Romantic. Todd Strauss-Schulson, 2019, New Line Cinema, Bron Creative, Camp Sugar, Little Engine, Broken Road Productions.
Kes. Ken Loach, 1969, Woodfall Film Productions, Kestrel Films.
Killer's Moon. Alan Birkinshaw, 1978, Rothernorth Films.
King Kong. Merian C. Cooper, Ernest B. Schoedsack, 1933, Radio Pictures.
The Kingdom/Riget. Lars von Trier, 1994–1997, DR.
Let's Scare Jessica to Death. John Hancock, 1971, The Jessica Company.
Lisztomania. Ken Russell, 1975, Goodtimes Enterprises, Visual Programme Systems.
The Love Witch. Anna Biller, 2016, Oscilloscope Laboratories.
Madam White Snake. Yueh Feng, 1962, Shaw Brothers.
Midsommar. Ari Aster, 2019, Square Peg, B-Reel Films.
Miss Thompson Goes Shopping. David Gladwell, 1958, British Film Institute Experimental Film Fund.
The Monster Club. Roy Ward Baker, 1981, Chips Productions, Sword and Sorcery Productions.

Mulholland Drive. David Lynch, 2001, Les Films Alain Sarde, Asymmetrical Productions, Babbo, Le Studio Canal+, The Picture Factory.
The Music Lovers. Ken Russell, 1971, Russ-Arts, Russ-Films.
Nagin. Rajkumar Kohli, 1976, Shankar Movies.
Neither the Sea Nor the Sand. Fred Burnley, 1972, LMG.
A Nightmare on Elm Street. Wes Craven, 1984, New Line Cinema, Media Home Entertainment, Smart Egg Pictures.
Nosferatu: A Symphony of Horror/Nosferatu: Eine Symphonie des Grauens. F. W. Murnau, 1922, Prana Film.
November. Rainer Sarnet, 2017, Homeless Bob Production, Opus Film, PRPL.
O Lucky Man! Lindsay Anderson, 1973, Memorial Enterprises.
The Offence. Sidney Lumet, 1972, Tantallon.
Los Olvidados (aka *The Young and the Damned*). Luis Buñuel, 1950, Óscar Dancigers.
The Omen. Richard Donner, 1976, Mace Neufeld Productions.
The Other Lamb. Małgorzata Szumowska, 2019, Rumble Films.
The Owl Service. Peter Plummer, 1969, ITV.
Peeping Tom. Michael Powell, 1960, Michael Powell.
Penda's Fen. Alan Clarke, 1974, BBC.
Performance. Donald Cammell, Nicolas Roeg, 1970, Goodtimes Enterprises.
Picnic at Hanging Rock. Peter Weir, 1975, BEF Film Distributors, South Australian Film Corporation, Australian Film Commission, McElroy & McElroy, Picnic Productions.
Possum. Matthew Holness, 2018, BFI Film Fund, Dark Sky Films.
Prevenge. Alice Lowe, 2016, Western Edge Pictures, Gennaker Group, Ffilm Cymru Wales.
Psycho. Alfred Hitchcock, 1960, Shamley Productions.
Quatermass. Piers Haggard, 1979, Euston Films, Thames Television.
Queen Cobra: Snakes on a College Campus. Lewis Schoenbrun, 2007, David S. Sterling.
The Red Shift. John MacKenzie, 1978, BBC.
Relic. Natalie Erika James, 2020, Screen Australia.
The Reptile. John Gilling, 1966, Hammer.
Robin Redbreast. James MacTaggart, 1970, BBC.
Romantic Comedy. Elizabeth Sankey, 2019, Romantic Comedy Movie.
Rosemary's Baby. Roman Polanski, 1968, William Castle Enterprises.
The Secret of Lizard Woman. John Reynolds, 1995, Alan Sacks Productions, Greengrass Productions.
Seven. David Fincher, 1995, Arnold Kopelson Productions.
The Seventh Voyage of Sinbad. Nathan H. Juran, 1958, Morningside Productions.
The Shining Pyramid. Gareth Davies, 1977, HTV Wales.
The Snake Woman. Sidney J. Furie, 1961, Caralan Productions.
Southern Comfort. Walter Hill, 1981, Cinema Group Ventures, Phoenix.
Sssssss. Bernard L. Kowalski, 1973, Universal Pictures, The Zanuck/Brown Company.
The Stepford Wives. Bryan Forbes, 1975, Palomar Pictures.
Stigma. Lawrence Gordon Clark, 1977, BBC.
The Stone Tape. Peter Sasdy, 1972, BBC.
Straw Dogs. Sam Peckinpah, 1971, 20th Century Fox.

Strike/Stachka. Sergei Eisenstein, 1925, 1st Goskino Factory.
A Summer Discord. David Gladwell, 1955.
Suspiria. Dario Argento, 1977, Seda Spettacoli.
Tales from the Crypt. Freddie Francis, 1972, Amicus, Metromedia Producers Corporation.
A Taste of Honey. Tony Richardson, 1961, Woodfall Film Productions.
Terry and June. 1979–1987, BBC.
Texas Chainsaw Massacre. Tobe Hooper, 1974, Vortex.
They Came Together. David Wain, 2014, Showalter-Wain.
The Third Day. Felix Barrett, Dennis Kelly, 2020, Sky Studios, Plan B Entertainment, Punch Drunk.
Time Team. 1994–2014, Videotext Communications, Channel Four.
Twin Peaks. Mark Frost, David Lynch, 1990–1991, 2017, CBS/Showtime.
Twin Peaks: Fire Walk with Me, David Lynch, 1992, CIBY Pictures.
An Untitled Film (aka *The Killing*). David Gladwell, 1964.
Urban Ghost Story. Geneviève Jolliffe, 1998, Living Spirit Pictures.
Vampyr/Vampyr – Der Traum des Allan Gray. Carl Theodor Dreyer, 1932, Carl Theodor Dreyer-Filmproduktion, Tobis-Filmkunst.
The Vault of Horror. Roy Ward Baker, 1973, Amicus.
The Village. M. Night Shyamalan, 2004, Touchstone Pictures, Blinding Edge Pictures, Scott Rudin Productions.
Wake Wood. David Keating, 2009, Hammer.
Ways of Seeing. John Berger, 1972, BBC.
Welcome II the Terrordome. Ngozi Onwurah, 1995, Non-Aligned Communications.
Whistle and I'll Come to You. Jonathan Miller, BBC, 1968.
Winstanley. Kevin Brownlow, Andrew Mollo, 1975.
Witchhammer/Kladivo na čarodějnice. Otakar Vávra, 1970, Filmové studio Barrandov.
Wolf Creek. Greg McLean, 2005, Film Finance Corporation Australia, South Australian Film Corporation, 403 Productions, True Crime Channel, Mushroom Pictures.
The Wolf Man. George Waggner, 1941, Universal Pictures.
Woodlands Dark and Days Bewitched: A History of Folk Horror. Kier-La Janisse, 2021, Severin Films.
You Are Not My Mother. Kate Dolan, 2021, Fantastic Films.
Zalava. Arsalan Amiri, 2021, Touba Films.
Zéro de conduite. Jean Vigo, 1933, Argui-Films.

Index

Page numbers for notes are in the format 129n.1.

#MeToo 52
28b Camden Street (1963) 104

abject 8, 189, 192
Aboriginal Australia 7
Ackerman, Robert 36
Act of Uniformity, 1662 137
Acts of the Union, 1536 and 1542 137
Aeneid, The 29
Afghanistan 217
Africa 8, 29, 41
Agincourt, Battle of 206
agnosticism 31, 35
agrarian revolution 179
Ainley, Anthony 179, 180
Alexander, Anthony 107
Alfie (1966) 211
Alien (1979) 5
Altamont Free Festival (1969) 215
Altman, Rick 3, 5
Amazon USA 147, 151
Amen Island (aka *Unhappy Birthday*, 2011) 150, 187
America. *See* USA
American Federal Office of Rural Health Policy (FORHP) 59
American International Pictures (AIP) 2, 9
Americas 95
Amicus 2
Anchoress (1993) 7
ancient Britain 6
ancient Greece 19, 27, 29, 31, 37, 144, 222
ancient Rome 15, 16, 19, 26–28, 29, 31, 32, 36, 41, 58, 121, 134, 135, 142, 144, 195, 198, 222

And Now the Screaming Starts! (aka *Fengriffen*) (1973) 105
Anderson, Gail-Nina 117
Anderson, Ian 206
Anderson, Lindsay 104
Andersson, Roy 124
Andrews, Barry 169, 179
'Angel of History' (1940) 19
Anglesey 142
Anglicanism 32, 133, 137, 138, 142, 144
anti-landscape 8, 11, 13, 18, 106, 178–192, 196
Antrum (2018) 227
Apocalypse Now (1979) 45
Apostle (2018) 7, 16, 17, 78, 131–144, 226
Aquitane 36
Archaeology of Knowledge, The (1972) 57
Arizona 131
art cinema 123, 230
Artaud, Antonin 199, 200, 201, 204
ASDA 114
Asia Minor 27
Assyria 221
Asylum (1972) 201
atheism 31, 35
Aulus Hirtius 27
Australasia 95
Australia 13
avant-garde 229, 230
Aztec 129

Babylon 221
Bacchanalian 206

backwoods horror 10, 18, 40, 43, 211, 216
Bagpuss (1974) 1
Bahamas 92
Bailey-Bond, Prano 158
Balkans 217
Ballard, J. G. (James Graham) 218
Baloo My Boy 125
Bannen, Ian 87
Banquet, A (2021) 150
Barcelona 93
Barker, David Chatton 204
Barracuda Tanker Corporation 92
Barrett, Shona 105
Bassett, Ronald 212
Battleship Potemkin (1925) 109
Bauman, Richard 59, 60, 63
Bauman, Zygmunt 99
Bayman, Louis 131, 148, 149, 150
BBC 1, 2, 53, 87, 104, 122, 229
BBC Radiophonic Workshop 229
Beckett, Samuel 124
Belgium 26
Bell, David 112
Bell, Mary 214
Benjamin, Walter 19
Berberian Sound Studio (2012) 229
Berger, John 14, 104
Bergner, Elisabeth 173
Bhabha, Homi K. 118
Bible, the 141
Black Death, The (2010) 7, 16
Black Lake (2020) 155
Black Lives Matter 52
Black Mountains 137
Blanck Mass 130
'Blessing of Pan, The' (1927) 37
Blood on Satan's Claw (1971) 1, 2, 6, 7, 11, 14, 15, 17, 18, 20, 39, 40, 42, 48, 62, 67, 75, 81–82, 84, 87, 105, 111, 113, 122, 131, 134, 148, 169, 172, 178, 180–191, 212, 215, 218, 223, 224, 228
Blood Runs Down (2018) 150
Bloody Chamber, The (1979) 64
Bloody Women: Women Directors of Horror (2022) 147
body horror 9
Borderlands, The (2013) 228

Borley Rectory (2017) 228
Bowman, The (1914) 197
Boxer Uprising (the Yìhéquán Movement) 141
Boyes, Georgina 77
Boym, Svetlana 19
Brambell, Wilfrid 80
Branagh, Joyce 204
Brandeston 80
Brando, Marlon 45
Bratby, John 211
Break Up of Britain, The (1977) 13
Breton 134
Brewster, Lawrie 217
'Brexit' referendum (2016) 218
Brigadoon (1954) 13
Brith Gof (theatre company) 167
British Film Institute 105
British Film Institute Production Board 105
British Folk Revival 77
British Lion 2, 25, 33
British New Wave 105, 211, 214, 217, 218
British Petroleum 92
Brittany 92
'Broad Is the Road that Leads to Death' 139
Broadcast 229
Bronner, Simon J. 106
Brown, Allan 36
Brown, Dan 30
Brown, Martin 214
Brownlow, Kevin 124
Buchan, John 30, 32
Buddhism 61
Buñuel, Luis 105, 201
Bunyan, John 130
Burnt Offering: The Cult of the Wicker Man 63
Burton, Richard 136
Bush, Dick 122
Butler, Julian 197
Butterflies (1978–83) 108

Cabinet of Doctor Caligari, The (1920) 222
Caerleon 194, 198
Caesar, Julius 64
Cage, Nicholas 36

Cambridge 28, 80
Cameron, Alan 58, 59
Cammell, Donald 127
Canada 33, 131
Canby, Vincent 114
Candyman (1992, remade in 2021) 222
Capaldi, Peter 120
Cardiff 167
Cardwell, Sarah 115
Caribbean 131
Carpathian Mountains 15
Carpenter, John 230
Carroll, Beth 7, 17
Carter, Angela 64, 67
Casting the Runes (1979) 87
Catholicism 18, 42, 43, 80, 129, 130, 143, 212
Cavern of Anti-Matter 229
Celts 15, 16, 17, 19, 26–28, 32, 58, 63, 64, 70, 131–144, 167
'Cessation of Oracles, The' 19
Chaney, Lon, Jr. 222
Channel Islands 93
Chavs: The Demonisation of the Working Class (2011) 217
Chernobyl (2013) 130
Cherry, Brigid 47
Children of the Stones (1977) 228
China 141
Christianity 6, 7, 9, 12, 25, 28–35, 37, 39, 40–43, 45, 48–53, 58–59, 60–70, 83, 90, 121, 130, 136, 137–143, 144, 183, 212, 215, 228
Chtcheglov, Ivan 203
Church of Satan, The 212
Cilento, Diane 49
Civil War, English 2, 7, 76, 79, 81, 118, 123, 127, 128, 212, 218, 228
Cixous, Hélène 146, 147–148, 151, 152, 157
Claire, René 105
Clark, Lawrence Gordon 227
Clarke, Alan 195
Clearances 101
Clifton, Chas 52
Clover, Carol 10, 43, 45
Cocteau, Jean 105
comedy 218, 230

Communism 210
Company of Wolves, The (1984) 7, 17, 57, 64–70
Confessions of a Window Cleaner (1974) 108
Connery, Sean 114
Conny Plank 228
Conrad, Joseph 30
Conservative Party 9, 140, 215
Co-op 114
Cooper, Ian 80
Cooper, Timothy 92
Corman, Roger 9, 201
Cornwall 6, 33, 87, 91, 92, 93, 96, 97, 98, 99, 100, 102, 132, 134, 216
Coronation Street (1960–present) 212
Cotswolds 37
COVID-19 pandemic 158
Cowdell, Paul 3, 12, 76, 77, 81
Creed, Barbara 149, 189, 190
Creetown 35
Cromwell, Oliver 124
Crow (2016) 14
Crowley, Alastair 9
Crucible, The (1953) 209, 210, 212
Crucible, The (1996) 210
Crude Britannia 92
Cry of the Banshee (1970) 2, 113, 173, 174
Culloden (1964) 122, 124
Cult of the Cobra (1955) 129n.1
Cunliffe, Barry 134
Curse of the Lizard, The (2004) 129n.1
Curse of the Scarecrow (2018) 150
Curtis, Peter. *See* Lofts, Nora
'Cwm Garon' (1947) 37
Czechoslovakia 210, 229

Da Vinci Code, The (2003) 31
Dacre, Michael 184
Daily Telegraph 89
Daisy Chain, The (2008) 150
Dark Secret of Harvest Home, The (1978) 226
Dark, The (2007) 132
Darklands (1996) 8, 85, 167
Davies, Gareth 197, 204
Days of Destruction, Days of Revolt (2012) 90

de Coulanges, Fustel 36
Deacon, Bernard 98
Dead Man's Shoes (2004) 217
Debord, Guy 4
deindustrialisation 8
Deliverance (1972) 13, 40, 216
Demetrius of Tarsus 19
Department of Food, Environment and Rural Affairs (DEFRA) 59
Derbyshire 218
dérive 202
Derrida, Jacques 4, 110, 203
Devi (1999) 129n.1
Devil Rides Out, The (1968) 2, 167
Devil's Own, The (1960) 32
Devon 7, 92
Diggers 124
Divine King in England, The (1954) 31
Dogged (2017) 15, 178, 181, 184, 185, 187, 189, 190, 191, 192
Domain of Arnheim, The (1847) 196
Donnelly, K. J. (Kevin) 6, 7, 17, 131, 148, 149, 150
Donohoe, Amanda 120
Doomwatch (1972) 6, 16, 17, 87–101, 105
Dotrice, Michele 185
Doyle, Belle 49
Dr Jekyll and Mr Hyde (1886) 206
Dracula 5, 8, 17, 33, 39–53, 198
Dracula (1931) 222, 227
Dreyer, Carl Theodor 201
Druids 26–28, 33, 137–143, 144
du Maurier, Daphne 100
Dwyer, Hilary 173
Dyer, Richard 11

Earl of Essex 31
East Anglia 80
Eastern Europe 45
Eastmancolor 227
écriture féminine 146, 147, 148, 155, 157
Eden Lake (2008) 181, 216, 217
Edinburgh 8
Egypt 142
Einstürzende Neubauten 167
Eisenstein, Sergei 105, 109
Ekland, Britt 49

Eliot, T. S. 30
Ellangowan Hotel 35
Ellinger, Kat 210
Elliot, Gaz 152
Embery, Paul 20
empire 8, 13, 18, 19, 20, 28, 30, 44, 45, 63, 64, 78
Empire magazine 36
enclosures 15
England 7, 12, 17, 37, 43, 44, 77, 80, 83, 104–115, 119, 120, 127, 128, 131–144, 180, 195, 212, 213, 214, 217, 227, 228
English Channel 93, 97
English Journal, The 231
English popular art 12
Enlightenment 181, 182, 186
Entr'acte (1924) 111
Enys Men (2022) 7, 132
Episcopalianism 42, 43
Epstein, Jean 201
Essex 32
Estonia 227
Euhemerism 120
Europe 28, 29, 30, 41, 78, 94, 105, 111, 134, 210, 224, 230
European Commission 95
European Union (EU) 218
Evans, Dan 133
Evans, Gareth 134
Evans, George Ewart 111
Evans-Powell, David 7, 13, 18, 82
Evil Dead, The (1981) 5
Exorcist, The (1973) 190
Exton, Clive 87

Fairbrass, Craig 167
Fall and Rise of Reginald Perrin, The (1976–79) 108
Fall of the House of Usher, The (1928) 201
Fallow Field, The (2009) 7, 18, 150, 179, 180, 181, 184, 189, 191
Falvey, Eddie 151
Fangoria 81, 158
Fanshawe, David 105, 109
Fascism 210
Fassbender, Michael 181
Fellini, Federico 105

feudal 16
feudalism 118
Field in England, A (2013) 7, 8, 11, 17, 117, 118, 119, 150, 218, 221, 225, 227, 228
Film, Folklore and Urban Legends (2008) 226
Film4 126
FindersKeepers 37
Fine Fare 114
Fisher, Mark 4, 19, 100, 110, 129, 225
Folk Horror: Hours Dreadful and Things Strange (2017) 1
'Folk Horror Revival' (website and Facebook page) 1
Folk Horror Revival: Urban Wyrd (2019) 211
folklore 2, 12, 17, 28–31, 50, 58–70, 76, 77, 78, 100, 102, 118, 166, 176, 192, 196, 211, 221, 222, 223, 224, 228, 229, 230
Folk-Lore Society 12, 78
folksploitation 11
Following the Wicca Man (2013) 7, 17, 146, 150, 152–154, 157
Forster, E. M. 30
Fortey, Richard 119
Foster, Michael Dylan 77
Foucault, Michel 57, 70
Fowler, Catherine 114
France 26, 80, 199
Frankenstein 5, 8, 153
Franks 19
Franks, Jennie 206
Frazer, James 12, 16, 28–31, 36, 40, 42, 44, 45, 49, 50
Free Cinema 105, 112
French impressionism 197, 201
Freud, Sigmund 201, 202
Freudian 117
Friday the Thirteenth (1980) 40, 225

Gaelic 134
Gaius Asinius Pollio 27
Gallic 83
Galloway 35
Gardner, Gerald 48
Garry, Steve 181

Gatiss, Mark 2, 196, 226
Gaul 26–28, 36, 41, 144
German expressionism 15, 201
Germania 93
Germany 9, 26, 77
Germany, West 228
Get Out (2017) 5
Ghost Box (record label) 228
Ghost Story for Christmas, A (1971–1978) 87, 227
giallo film 9, 176, 229
Gladwell, David 104, 105, 108, 109, 111, 112, 113, 114
Glasgow 212
Glass, Rose 158
Gledhill, Christine 147
Gleeson, Judy 87
Glen Usk 198
gnostic 123
gnosticism 118, 126
Golden Bough, The (1922) 12, 17, 28–31, 33, 40, 45, 50, 63
Good Life, The (1975–78) 108
Goodall, Mark 18
Goorney, Howard 181
Gordon, Jamie Scott 180
Gorgon, The (1964) 121
gothic 2, 5, 6, 8, 15, 39, 45, 46, 47, 75, 81, 118, 121, 201
Graeco-Roman antiquity 183
Grant, Hugh 120
Graves, Robert 31
'Great God Pan, The' (1894) 195
Green, Anna 92
Gremlins (1984) 230
Grimm Brothers 69, 76
Groves, Matilda 165
Gulf War Syndrome 217
Gwent 198

Haggard, Piers 2, 14, 81, 179, 215, 223, 224, 227, 228, 230
Halloween (1979) 11
Hamburg 93
Hames, Peter 210
Hammer Film Productions Ltd. 2, 8, 9, 12, 33, 39, 45, 46, 47, 121, 122, 176, 224, 227, 230

Happy Ever After (1974–78) 108
Hardy, Robin 11, 17, 25, 35, 43, 45, 51, 57, 62, 63, 64, 87, 101, 215
Harmes, Marcus K. 2
Harris, Amy 7, 17
hauntology 4, 18, 19, 110, 129, 202, 203, 211, 223, 225, 227, 230
Hayden, Linda 169, 186, 213
Heart of Darkness 45
Heath, Edward 140, 215
Hedges, Chris 90
Helfield, Gillian 114
Heller-Nicholas, Alexandra 20
Hells Angels 215
Hendrix, Jimi 215
Heng, Geraldine 44
Henson, Nicky 114, 173
Her Hidden Children (2006) 52
Herder, Johann Gottfried 76
heritage cinema 114, 115, 118, 178, 196
Heritage of Horror, A (1973) 8
Hessler, Gordon 174
Hexenjagd or *Les Sorcières de Salem* (1957) 210
Hieroglyphics 199
Higgenbotham, Judith 51
High Rise (2015) 218
Highlands of Scotland 62
Higson, Andrew 118
Hill of Dreams, The (1907) 194, 198
hillbilly horror 10, 216
Hills Have Eyes, The (1977) 40
Hisss (2010) 129n.1
historicism 117, 118, 119
History of Horror, A (2010) 2, 196
Hodder and Stoughton 37
Hollywood 201, 214
Holy Terrors: Six Weird Tales by Arthur Machen (2017) 194–206
Home Counties 106
Hong Kong 129
hoodie horror 217
Hookland 224
Hopkins, Anthony 136
Hopkins, Matthew 212
Horror Obsessive 156, 158
Howe, Brian 214
HTV Wales 197

Humphreys, Emyr 197
Hunt, Leon 2, 9, 82
Hunter, Meredith 215
Hutchings, Peter 13, 106, 182
Hutton, Ronald 12, 16, 64

I Spit on Your Grave (1978) 40
I Walked with a Zombie (1943) 131
Icke, David 121
Icke's Struggle (2013) 130
If… (1968) 104, 228
In Fabric (2018) 229
In the Earth (2021) 7, 11, 218, 221
India 129
industrial revolution 179
Inside No.9 episode 'The Devil of Christmas' (2016) 227
Inside The Wicker Man: *How Not to Make a Cult Classic* (2013) 36n.2
International Atomic Energy Agency (IAEA) 93
Ipswich 108
Iran 225
Iraq 217
Ireland 20, 44, 80, 83, 130, 228
Irish Sea 93
Islam 61, 155
Island of the Ghouls. See *Doomwatch* (1972)
Isle of Man 132
Isle of Thanet 19
Isles of Scilly 91
Isn't It Romantic (2019) 230
Italy 9, 27, 92
ITV 87

Jacobite rebellion 2, 7, 82, 124
Jacobs, Joseph 69
James, M. R. 77, 87
Jennifer Saunders' Memory Lane (ITV, Wed 23 December 2020) 136
Jethro Tull 206
Johnston, Derek 2, 17, 20, 100
Jones, Brian 215
Jones, Owen 20, 217
Joplin, Janis 215
Jordan, Neil 17, 67
Josephs, Wilfred 174
Joyce, James 30

Judaism 45, 58, 61, 129
Julius Caesar 26–28, 36
Jung, Carl 198

Keegan-Phipps, Simon 85
Keetley, Dawn 1, 3, 6, 13, 17, 111, 117, 166
Kes (1969) 211
Kill List (2011) 9, 15, 18, 39, 54, 150, 151, 164, 167, 168, 169, 170–172, 175, 190, 192, 217, 218, 221, 226, 228
Killer's Moon (1978) 106
Kine Weekly 81
King Arthur 218
King James III 81
Kingdom, The (1994) 206n.1
Kirkham, Jacqueline 146, 147, 148, 150, 151, 152–154, 157
Kitchen Sink. *See* British New Wave
kitsch 229
Kladivo na čarodějnice (*Witchhammer*, 1970) 210
Klee, Paul 19
Kneale, Nigel 101
Koven, Mikel J. 2, 7, 12, 17, 50, 175, 226
Kracauer, Siegfried 201
krimi 9
Krzywinska, Tanya 149
Kubrick, Stanley 201
Kuleshov, Lev 109
Kümel, Harry 207

Labour Party 20
Lacoste, Monique 64, 67
Lair of the White Worm, The (1988) 6, 17, 117, 118, 119, 120–122, 123, 127, 128
Lamin, Nadia 187
Lampton Worm 120
Land Enclosures 180
Land's End 91, 92, 93
landscape painting 13, 15
Lane, John 37
Lang, Andrew 69
Lassally, Walter 105
Last Pagans of Rome, The (2011) 58
'Laugh of Medusa, The' (1976) 146

Lavenham 80
Lawrence, D. H. 30
League of Gentleman, The 2
League of Gentleman's Apocalypse, The (2005) 2
Lee, Christopher 33, 45, 46, 47, 51, 63, 64, 166
Lee, Vernon 147
Let's Scare Jessica to Death (1971) 1
Lettrist International 202
Lewis, C. S. 126
Lewis, Wyndham 30
Liberia 92
Light, Melanie 158
Lindsay, Joan 204, 205
Lisztomania (1975) 122
Little Red Riding Hood 64, 65, 66, 67
Liverpool 212
Lofts, Nora 32, 37
Lomax, Alan 12
London 8, 33, 37, 82, 87, 89, 101, 106, 131, 198
Long, Frank Belknap
Lord Dunsany 37
Los Olvidados (aka *The Young and the Damned*) (1950) 111
Love Witch, The (2016) 150
Lovecraft, H. P. (Howard Phillips) 195
Lowe, Alice 158
Löwy, Michael 19
Lugosi, Bela 222
Lyden, John 50
Lynch, David 209, 230

Macalister, Terry 92, 95
Macfarlane, Robert 225
Machen, Arthur 18, 32, 194–206, 207
Madam White Snake (1962) 129n.1
Magliocco, Sabina 52
Making of the English Working Class, The (1963) 12
Manson, Charles 214
Marr, Sarah K. 231
Marriott, James 92, 95
Marx, Enid 12
Marxism 109, 110
Maskell, Neil 165
Masks in Horror Cinema (2019) 20
Massachusetts 209

Matless, David 107
Maya (2021) 7, 17, 147, 155–157, 158
McCarthy, Joseph 210
McCarthyism 210
McLuhan, Marshall 17
melodrama 2, 8
Men (2022) 7
Metfield 105
Middle East 185, 217
Midsommar (2019) 226
Miller, Arthur 209, 210
Miss Thompson Goes Shopping (1958) 104
modernism 124
Mohrmann, Christine 58
Mollo, Andrew 124
Monster Club, The (1981) 13
monstrous feminine 8
Moog organ 229
Moravia 210
Morrisons 114
Mount's Bay 93
Mower, Patrick 174
Mulholland Drive (2001) 209
Mumford, Lewis 107
Murders at Hanging Rock, The (1980) 207
Murnau, F. W. (Friedrich Wilhelm) 202, 222
Murray, Margaret 12, 31, 36
Music Lovers, The (1971) 122

Nagin (1976) 129n.1
Nairn, Tom 13
Nazism 85
Neale, Steve 4, 5, 223
Neither the Sea Nor the Sand (1972) 105
New Blood in Contemporary Cinema: Women Directors and the Poetics of Horror (2020) 147
Newbridge-on-Usk 198
Newcastle upon Tyne 214
Newland, Paul 13, 15, 17, 57, 62, 83, 84, 100, 180
Night of the Demon (1957) 42, 202
Nightmare on Elm Street, A (1984) 222, 225

noir 2
North America 39
Northern Ireland 212
Nosferatu (1922) 15, 198, 222
'Novel of the Black Seal, The' (1895) 32
'Novel of the White Powder, The' (1895) 195, 196
November (2017) 227

O Lucky Man! (1973) 104
Oates, Simon 93
Obsolete 197
Occult Revival 212, 213
Offence, The (1972) 114
Omen, The (1976) 32
On Reading Arthur Machen (1949) 195
On the Black Hill (1988) 137
Orientalism 135
ostranenie 202
Other Lamb, The (2019) 150
Oto, Tatsujiro 156
Otter, Chris 95
Outcast (2010) 8, 150
Owl Service, The (1969-70) 54, 228
Oxford 96
Oxney 80

Pacific Ocean 29
Paciorek, Andy 1, 3, 18, 224
Padbury, Wendy 180
paganism 6, 8, 9, 15, 16, 17, 28–35, 37, 39–53, 57, 58–70, 83, 90, 114, 118, 132, 134, 136, 138, 139, 144, 183, 185, 196, 224, 228
Pakistan 155, 156, 158
Parkin, Tony 187
Paul, John 91
Pavey, Martin 228, 229
Payton, Philip 98
Peak District 119, 121
Peckinpah, Sam 216
Peeping Tom (1960) 11
Peirse, Alison 147
Pemberton, Steve 227
Penda's Fen (1974) 195
Penguin 201

Penzance 93
Performance (1970) 127
Perrault, Charles 69
Pervaiz, K. 147, 148, 150, 151, 152, 155–157, 158
Petherbridge, Edward 197
Phoenix 131
photogénie 200
Picnic at Hanging Rock (1967) 204
Picnic at Hanging Rock (1975) 205, 230
Pilgrim's Progress, The (1678) 130
Pinedo, Isobel 9
Pinner, David 33
Pinter, Harold 124
Pirie, David 8
Pitt, Ingrid 45, 49
Plague of the Zombies, The (1966) 105
Play for Today 79
Plutarch 19
Plymouth 93
Poe, Edgar Allan 196, 197, 201, 205
Polanski, Roman 214
Polkerris 93, 97, 99, 102
Pollard's Rock 92
Pope 43
Port Talbot 136, 137
Portland Horror Film Festival 147
Possum (2018) 217
postmodern horror 9
Pound, Ezra 30
Preece, Jon 204
Presbyterianism 29, 32, 43, 83
Prevenge (2016) 228
Prévert, Jacques 105
Price, Vincent 173, 201, 212
Process Church, The 212
Procopius 19
progressive rock 176
Protestant nonconformism 133, 137–143, 144
Protestantism 40, 43, 130, 212
psychedelia 125, 127, 128, 204
Psycho (1960) 131
psychogeography 4, 13, 196, 202, 203, 211
Psychomania (1973) 8, 9, 114, 173
Pudovkin, Vsevolod 105, 109
Puritanism 210

Putname 37
pyschogeography 202

Quatermass and the Pit (1967) 6
Quatermass Conclusion, The (1979) 228
Quatermass II (1957) 101
Queen Cobra: Snakes on a College Campus (2007) 129n.1

Radcliffe, Ann 147
Rashleigh Inn 97
Ray, Robert B. 200
realism 13, 178
rearview mirrorism 17
Red Shift, The (1978) 120
Reeves, Michael 80, 212
Reformation 140
Reilly, Kelly 181
Relic (2020) 150
Religion and the Decline of Magic: Studies in Popular Beliefs in Sixteenth and Seventeenth Century England (1971) 12
Renegade Film Festival (formerly Women in Horror Film Festival) 147, 158
Reptile, The (1966) 121
Requiem for a Village (1975) 17, 54, 104–115
Resnais, Alain 105
Revenant 1
Reyes, Xavier Aldana 168
Rhine 26
Ritual (1967) 33
Ritual, The (2017) 226
Robin Redbreast (1970) 79, 99, 123, 225, 226
Rodgers, Anton 197
Rodgers, Diane A. 7, 9, 18, 150
Roeg, Nicolas 127
Rolt, L. T. C. 37
Roman Catholicism 29
Romania 122
romantic comedy 230
Romantic Comedy (2019) 230
Romanticism 77, 117, 182–186
Rosemary's Baby (1968) 32
Rousseau, Yvonne 207

Royal Navy 91, 93, 96
Rufus, William 31
rural horror 5, 10, 17, 66, 106
Russell, Ken 120, 121, 122
Russia 202

Sacco, Joe 90
Salem Witch Trials 209, 210
Sammes, Aylett 28, 33
Samuel, Raphael 117, 128
Sasdy, Peter 87
Satanic Panic 39
Satanism 32, 34, 39, 41, 42, 43, 59
Saunders, Jennifer 136, 137
Saunders, Sam 185
Schatz, Thomas 4, 5
Schrader, Paul 202, 206
science fiction 6, 17, 87
Scotland 25, 28, 29, 32, 35, 83, 89, 93, 101, 132, 133, 180, 185, 212, 215, 228
Scovell, Adam 1, 3, 4, 13, 59, 60, 62, 64, 89, 90, 99, 101, 104, 106, 111, 132, 140, 150, 165, 178, 196, 211, 224
Secret of Lizard Woman, The (1995) 129n.1
Self, Will 202
Seven (1995) 5
Seven Stones Reef 92
Seventh Voyage of Sinbad, The (1958) 129n.1
Sexton, Jamie 228
Shaffer, Anthony 33, 35, 45, 63, 64
Sharp, Cecil 76, 77
She Will (2021) 7
Shearsmith, Reece 123, 225
Sheen, Michael 133, 136, 137
Shelley, Mary 147
Shepperton Studios 114
Shining Pyramid (1979) 204
Shining Pyramid, The (1923) 195, 196, 197, 198
Shining, The (1997 TV miniseries) 205
Shklovsky, Viktor 202
Short, John Rennie 107
Shout, The (1978) 7, 106
Shub, Esfir 109
Sightseers (2012) 150, 151, 218
Sinclair, Iain 202

Situationist International 202
Sitwell, Edith 30
Skin to Dance In, A (Tanya Kyzywinska, 2001) 149
slasher 7, 9, 11
Sleep No More (1947) 37
Smiley, Michael 123, 165
Smith, Vic 104, 108, 112
Snake Woman, The (1961) 121
Snell, Peter 33, 37, 46
Snowden, Kim 68, 69
Snowdon (Yr Wyddfa) 136
snuff movie 9
Soar 198
Sobchack, Vivian 169
'Sorcery and the Cinema' (1928) 200
South Asia 29
Southampton 140
Southern Comfort (1981) 216
Southwell, David 224
Soviet montage 104, 105, 109, 115
Soviet Union (USSR) 210
Spain 93
Spanish Inquisition 143
Spence, Lewis 142
Spencer, Stanley 105
Sssssss (1973) 129n.1
St. Agnes 98, 99
St. Austell Bay 97
Starburst (magazine) 157
Stearne, John 212
Stepford Wives (1975) 5
Stereolab 229
Stoke Newington 196
Stoke Park estate 108
Stoker, Bram 46, 47, 120, 198
Stone Tape, The (1972) 54, 87
Strabo 27–28
Straw Dogs (1971) 54, 105, 216
Strickland, Peter 229
Strike (1925) 109
Stukeley, William 142
sublime 13
Suetonius 36
Suffolk 104, 105
Summer Discord, A (1955) 104
surrealism 195, 196, 197, 199, 200, 201, 203, 206, 229
Suspiria (1977) 229

Sussex, Elizabeth 105, 113
Sutcliffe, Steven J. 42
Sylvester, David 211
Sylvester, Dorothy 137, 138
Synge, John 30

Tacitus 142
Tales from the Crypt (1972) 201
Taste of Honey, A (1961) 211
Tate, Sharon 214
Technicolor 227
Terry and June (1979–87) 108
Tesco 114
Test Department 167
Texas Chainsaw Massacre, The (1974) 13, 40, 216
Thailand 129
Thanatos 19
Theatre of Cruelty 199
Thelema 212
'Theses on the Philosophy of History' (1940) 19
They Came Together (2014) 230
Third Day, The (2020) 99, 187
Thomas, Keith 12
Thompson, E. P. 12, 128
Thoms, William John 12, 59
Three Imposters, The (1895) 37, 195
Thurgill, James 13, 59, 62, 78, 79, 106, 110
Tigon British Film Productions 2, 12, 87, 102
Time Team (1994–2014) 119
Toelken, Barre 60
topography 4, 13
Torrey Canyon 92, 93, 95
Tourneur, Jacques 202
Townsend, Lyndsay 15, 18
True Levellers 124
Turner, Victor 50
Tuttle, Joshua B. 132
Twin Peaks (1990–91, 1992 and 2017) 209
Twitter 231
Tylor, Edward Burnet 78

UFO cults 212
Ukraine 218
uncanny, the 202, 211

unclaimed point of view shot 11
Union Carbide (Belgium) Ltd. 93
Universal Studios 222
Unkindness of Ravens, The (2016) 7, 18, 132, 179, 180, 181, 184, 185, 190, 217
Untitled Film, An (aka *The Killing*) (1964) 105
Urban Ghost Story (1998) 150
urbanoia 10, 44, 47, 53
USA 9, 34, 35, 36, 44, 48, 51, 78, 87, 92, 93, 129, 174, 201, 209, 210, 213, 216, 222, 226

Vampyr (1932) 201
Vanishing Cornwall 100
Vault of Horror, The (1973) 201
Vávra, Otakar 210
Vertov, Dziga 109
Vietnam War 213
Vigo, Jean 105
Vikings 222
Village, The (2004) 78
Virgil 29
Vlad the Impaler 122
von Trier, Lars 206
voodoo 174
Voudon 174

Wake Wood (2009) 79, 226
Wales 7, 8, 14, 17, 37, 85, 92, 119, 131–144, 167, 194, 195, 198
Wallachia 122
Walton-on-Thames 114
Watkins, Peter 122, 124
Watts, Isaac 140
Ways of Seeing (1972) 14, 104
Weir, Peter 204, 205
Welcome II the Terrordome (1993) 53
Wembury 93
Westerns 43
Wheal Coates Mine 98
Wheatley, Ben 7, 11, 123, 126, 127, 129, 150, 151, 165, 217, 218, 221, 228
Wheatley, Dennis 32
Whistle and I'll Come to You (1968) 122
Whitaker, Cord J. 44

White Goddess, The 31
Whitehouse, Mary 9
Wicca 48, 49, 212, 213
Wicker Man, The (1973) 1, 2,
    6, 7, 11, 15, 16, 17,
    25–70, 76, 79, 82, 83–84,
    87, 90, 91, 99, 101, 105,
    106, 131, 140, 148, 149,
    152, 166, 167, 169, 190,
    192, 212, 216, 218, 223,
    225, 226, 228
Wicker Man, The (2007) 36
Wicker Tree, The (2011)
    11, 36
Wilkinson, Marc 228
Williams, J. H. 134
Williams, Moelwyn 137, 138
Williams, Raymond 14
Wilson, Harold 215
Wimpey Homes 109
Winstanley (1975) 124
Winter, Trish 84
Winters, Ben 164, 165, 170, 171,
    172, 175
witch trials 16
Witch Wood (1927) 32
Witch-Cult in Western Europe, The
    (1921) 12
Witches, The (1966) 2, 8, 37, 41, 42,
    54, 79
Witchfinder General (1968) 2, 6, 7,
    9, 17, 40, 47, 54, 75, 79–81,
    82, 84, 85, 87, 105, 123, 148,
    212, 223, 227

Witnesham 105
Wolf Creek (2005) 13
Wolf Man, The (1941) 40, 222
Women Make Horror
    (2020) 147
*Women, Monstrosity and Horror
    Film: Gynaehorror*
    (2016) 147
Wood, Robin 61, 112
*Woodlands Dark and Days Bewitched:
    A History of Folk Horror*
    (2021) 1, 150
Woodward, Edward 45, 89,
    166, 190
Woodward, Kate 137
World War One 127, 206
World War Two 19, 97, 99, 107
Wright, Melanie J. 42
Wymark, Patrick 179
Wynn-Davies, Toby 184
Wynne-Simmons, Robert 215
wyrd 18, 211, 217, 218, 221–231

Yeats, William Butler 30
You Are Not My Mother
    (2021) 150
Young, Rob 105, 111
YouTube 157
Yr Wyddfa. *See* Snowdon

Zalava (2021) 225
Zéro de Conduite (1933) 111
Zipes, Jack 69
Zwissler, Laurel 10, 17, 149

EU authorised representative for GPSR:
Easy Access System Europe, Mustamäe tee 50,
10621 Tallinn, Estonia
gpsr.requests@easproject.com

www.ingramcontent.com/pod-product-compliance
Lightning Source LLC
Chambersburg PA
CBHW051120160426
43195CB00014B/2272